BULLEID POWER

THE 'MERCHANT NAVY' CLASS

BULLEID POWER

THE 'MERCHANT NAVY' CLASS

A.J. FRY

ALAN SUTTON

First published in the United Kingdom in 1990 by
Alan Sutton Publishing Ltd · Phoenix Mill · Stroud · Gloucestershire

First published in the United States of America in 1991 by
Alan Sutton Publishing Inc · Wolfeboro Falls · NH 03896-0848

British Library Cataloguing in Publication Data

Fry, A.J. (Anthony John), 1942–
  Bulleid power : the Merchant Navy Class.
  1. Southern England. Railway services: Southern Railway Company.
  Steam locomotives
  I. Title
  625.26109422

ISBN 0–86299–751–8

Library of Congress Cataloging in Publication Data applied for

The author's royalties accruing from the sale of this book are being donated to the funds for the overhaul of the Bulleid 'West Country' class Pacific No. 34023 *Blackmore Vale* and the rebuilding of Bulleid 'Battle of Britain' class Pacific No. 34059 *Sir Archibald Sinclair*. Both these locomotives are based on the Bluebell Railway in Sussex.

Title page: No. 21C7 Aberdeen Commonwealth *departs from Dover Marine with a train for London on 13 October 1944, the first appearance of the class on the Eastern section other than for naming ceremonies – H.W. Attwell*

Front endpaper: No. 35024 East Asiatic Company *heads the up 'Devon Belle' near Honiton Tunnel in the early 1950s. Composed completely of Pullman cars, the train featured an observation car, which was turned at the end of each journey – Author's collection*

Rear endpaper: No. 35027 Port Line *returned to steam in 1988, and is seen on the evening of 13 June approaching Horsted Distant signal, with its first working on the Bluebell Railway – I.R. Wright*

Typeset in 10/12 Palatino.
Typesetting and origination by
Alan Sutton Publishing Limited.
Printed in Great Britain by
Dotesios Printers Limited.

To
Liz, Andrew and Peter

CONTENTS

FOREWORD

Ever since the building of the 'Merchant Navy' Pacifics by the Southern Railway in 1941, controversy has raged around them in one form or another. In a number of ways they were the running shed fitter's nightmare, while the boilersmiths and boilerwashers needed to acquire new skills and techniques related to steel boilers and fireboxes. Looking at them from a fireman's angle they were magnificent, with the Bulleid boiler being one of the most prolific steam raisers ever to grace British locomotive frames. As a fireman at Nine Elms during the 1940s, I never did have a moment's anxiety in producing steam. As a driver, the feeling of power behind the regulator had to be experienced to be believed, while the riding qualities were excellent, allied to extraordinarily free running. Apart from the exhaust flopping down, and obscuring the view ahead, especially in winter when the wind was on the wrong quarter, the locomotives were an engineman's delight. Controversial machines they may have been, but they would pull a train in no uncertain manner, and I deem it a privilege to have been associated with them during the whole of their working life.

Bert Hooker

PREFACE

This book has been written, not merely to expand the publications on the 'Merchant Navy' class of Bulleid Pacifics, but to fill a niche in the annals of the class. The genesis of the book came as a result of a hunt for photographs and information on a member of the 'West Country' class of Pacifics, to complete a model I was constructing. There appeared to be no ready source of information on the Bulleid Pacific classes, which showed them photographically both in original and rebuilt form, and which also gave details of the changes to their exterior format. *Bulleid Power: The 'Merchant Navy' Class* is an attempt to fill this gap, and the Pacifics will be completed with the companion volume on the 'West Country' and 'Battle of Britain' classes. It is hoped that the information and photographs will be of interest and benefit not only to the model makers, but also to the increasing number of enthusiasts of the class.

John Fry

ACKNOWLEDGEMENTS

In writing this book, my thanks are due to a large number of individuals who have given freely of their time to assist me. The photographic coverage owes much to the initial loan of material from Joe Kent and Walter Gilburt, and also to the numerous other photographers who have so kindly loaned prints and negatives. Many photographs have not been included, simply through lack of space, and possibly one reason for the prolonged gestation of the book is the many happy hours I have spent in the dark-room printing negatives for possible inclusion. All photographs have been acknowledged where the photographer is known, and any errors or omissions here are mine alone.

The text is the result of much painstaking research by a number of colleagues, and to Barry Fletcher I extend my thanks for the chapters on the tenders, external variations and liveries of the Pacifics. The driving and firing of the class has been recorded by Peter Christmas and Russ Coffin. Derek Winkworth contributed the history of the locomotives and has been an unfailing guide throughout the preparation of the book. I have been helped by a number of people in writing on the mechanical engineering of the Pacifics, and to Stephen Townroe, Harry Frith, Barry Cook and Les Warnett I record my thanks. Ted Benn has narrated his story of the Pacifics as an ex-Nine Elms fitter, a part of railway life that is too often forgotten or ignored. For the drawings of the locomotives and tenders, my thanks are due to the painstaking work of Richard Avery and Dennis Tillman. Mark Arscott has produced valuable data and drawings on the self-weighing tender. Kevin Robertson has provided fruitful sources of information and a frequent impetus to complete the book.

The library, and in particular the librarian, S.G. Morrison, of the Institute of Mechanical Engineers has provided its facilities freely. The Public Record Office and the library of the National Railway Museum have been additional sources of information on the history and records of the Pacifics. The book by the late Don Bradley, *Locomotives of the Southern Railway*, part 2, is probably without equal in the vast amount of information contained therein. It is essential reading for all who are interested in the Pacifics. The painting for the dust jacket is the work of Barry Freeman, a member of the Guild of Railway Artists, who has provided a true visualization of the Pacifics as many remember them in the days of the 1950s.

I must also thank my parents and relations in Wiltshire, without whom I might never have been introduced to travel behind the Pacifics.

Finally, to Liz, Andrew and Peter, thank you for encouraging the publication of the book, in spite of all the disruption it has caused!

John Fry
Worthing, Sussex
1990

DESIGN AND CONSTRUCTION

During the inter-war years the Southern Railway, under the leadership of Sir Herbert Walker, had a railway system undergoing electrification with steam traction receiving little new investment. Electric trains commenced on the Brighton and Worthing lines in 1933, with the third rail reaching Eastbourne, Hastings and Ore in 1935. The Chief Mechanical Engineer, appointed at the formation of the Southern Railway in 1923, was R.E.L. Maunsell. He modified the Urie 4–6–0 design of the N15 class, later named after characters and places of the Arthurian legends as the 'King Arthur' class. A total of fifty-four members of the class were then ordered, with construction divided between Eastleigh Works and the North British Locomotive Co. at Glasgow. Maunsell was also responsible for the design and building of the 'Lord Nelson' class and the smaller, but equally famous, 'Schools' class.

The N15 class took over traffic on the Western section, and after a programme of bridge strengthening and track overhaul on the Eastern section they hauled the boat trains, now loaded to 425 tons. Track occupation by frequent electric services in the London suburbs limited the overall speed of the boat trains, and even after leaving the suburbs the undulating nature of the route produced further demands on the locomotives and crew. Walker did not see the speeding up of passenger traffic on the short routes of up to 100 miles as commercially rewarding, and there was thus no great demand for a Pacific class of locomotive. The earlier attempts by Maunsell to provide adequate motive power in the form of a 4–6–2 design in 1933 and a 2–6–2 in 1934 were rejected by the civil engineer.

Maunsell's notification of retirement on the grounds of ill health was given to the Southern Railway board at its meeting on 27 May 1937. However, this was merely an official formality, since seventeen days earlier Oliver Vaughan Snell Bulleid, principal assistant to Nigel Gresley, the Chief Mechanical Engineer on the LNER, had been invited to apply for the position to be vacated by Maunsell. It was Maunsell who was the President of the Association of Railway Locomotive Engineers when Bulleid joined the Association in 1925.

Bulleid's appointment as Chief Mechanical Engineer to the Southern Railway was announced in the *Railway Gazette* on 4 June 1937; he accompanied the directors and Maunsell on a tour of inspection of the West of England on 9 June and, in his capacity as the new CME, arrived at Waterloo to start understudying Maunsell on 20 September 1937. The reason for appointing Bulleid rather than one of the assistants to Maunsell, has never been fully explained, but may relate to the fact that the obvious choice – that of Pearson, who acted as deputy to Maunsell – was also of retirement age. The other possible choice might have been Clayton, who was acting CME, but he was a sick man and eventually retired in 1938.

Bulleid was almost unknown on the Southern, apart from his investigation of the 2–6–4 'River' tank disaster with Gresley in 1927, when he first came into contact with the Chief Civil Engineer of the Southern, George Ellson. As part of this investigation he had the opportunity to ride on the footplate of No. E850 *Lord Nelson*, when the locomotive was running – without smoke deflectors – the Eastern section boat trains, and is

Oliver Vaughan Snell Bulleid (1882–1970), Chief Mechanical Engineer, Southern Railway and Southern Region of British Railways, 1937 to 1949

Author's collection

'Lord Nelson' class locomotive No. E850, *Lord Nelson* ex-works in shop grey and without smoke deflectors or nameplates at Eastleigh in August 1929

reported as saying that smoke and steam beat down badly – a comment which would come full circle; his own designs gave the same trouble on the Southern some fourteen years later. During his career on the LNER Bulleid had been closely associated with the development of the P2 2–8–2 design and the A4 Pacifics, and he had become fully conversant with the designs of André Chapelon. Indeed he had accompanied the P2 2–8–2 No. 2001 *Cock o' the North* when the locomotive was tested at the Vitry-sur-Seine testing plant in France. However, the railway that Bulleid took over was at the limit of its capability with regard to motive power, especially on the Dover and Folkestone boat trains. He saw he could modify the Maunsell designs, using as a basis the current developments on the LNER, with improved exhaust. Eventually a modified Lemaître exhaust arrangement, introduced on the Nord-Belge Railway and later on the French Nord locomotives was used. It consisted of five $2\frac{5}{8}$ in nozzles on a 12 in pitch circle, and in addition French designs, in the form of Chapelon-type free steam passages and new cylinders with 10 in piston valves, were proposed. All the 'Lord Nelson' class were fitted with the Lemaître blastpipe and large chimney, and all except Nos 851 and 863 were fitted with new cylinders. Some of the Urie 'King Arthur' class and half the 'Schools' class were also fitted with the Lemaître exhaust and, although improvements were noted, Bulleid's thoughts now turned to new designs.

The Chairman of the Southern, Mr Robert Holland-Martin, encouraged Bulleid to spend money on the neglected steam traction. Bulleid's design requirements were for an express passenger locomotive, later modified to a fast mixed traffic locomotive. The 2–8–2 and amended design for a 4–8–2 were turned down by the Chief Civil Engineer, George Ellson, although the initial proposal of a coupled wheel diameter of 6 ft 2 in was agreed. The late 1930s period was already clouded with the fear of war with Germany, and it was considered that the proposal to build express passenger locomotives would

P2 class locomotive No. 2001 *Cock o' the North* under trial in 1934 with an indicator shelter. The locomotive was fitted with Lentz rotary cam poppet valves

be more successful if these were termed mixed traffic engines. The Rolling Stock Committee of the Southern board agreed at its meeting in March 1938 to proceed with the construction of ten new main-line steam locomotives, of unspecified type, and this was confirmed by the Locomotive and Electrical Committee on 30 March 1938. It is probable that Bulleid's initial ideas were for a 4–6–2 Pacific design though further drawings show designs for a 2–8–2, dated 7 June 1938. Later that year a 4–8–2 drawing appeared, but this was too long for the existing turntables. The proposal for a 2–8–2, with a maximum axle loading of 19 tons, met Ellson's ideas and he agreed to the building of two locomotives of this type. Bulleid was not satisfied with this design and reverted to his initial thoughts of a Pacific.

The design work for the new engines was split between Brighton, Eastleigh and Ashford Works, with the major share being undertaken under the leadership of C.S. Cocks. Cocks was a Doncaster draughtsman, brought in by Bulleid after finding the Southern draughtsmen too cautious. The CME had been warned by the design team of the need to calculate the weight of every part of the locomotive, to avoid the total weight being over the diagram approved by the Chief Civil Engineer. If Bulleid had taken this advice, his first 4–6–2 would not have been drilled and cut down to save at least 5 tons overweight. Bulleid determined that the new class should not be hemmed in by poor boiler design and steaming. Having decided that the Southern workshops did not have the ability to build such boilers, with a pressure of 280 lb sq in and a hoped for superheat

Construction of the first series of boilers at the works of the North British Locomotive Co., Hyde Park, Glasgow. The boiler barrel has been partially riveted, and work is proceeding on the firebox. The position for the Nicholson thermic syphons can be seen on the lower section of the throatplate

Author's collection

temperature of 400°C, he ordered the first boilers for the new class from outside contractors in August 1939. The first ten were manufactured by the North British Locomotive Co.

It is for the design of the boilers that Bulleid's new class became famous, for the boilers were almost without equal in their steam-raising capacity. Much emphasis has been placed on the use of welding in the design of the boiler but, in fact, it was only the firebox that was of welded construction, the remainder of the boiler being of normal riveted fabrication. Bulleid was well versed in the fundamentals of welding; he had initially seen the technique used in 1918 at Richborough in Kent, and had been welding carriage underframes at Doncaster, although Gresley would not sanction wide use of welding in boiler construction. In 1949 Bulleid became the President of the Institute of Welding.

The choice of a steel rather than the conventional copper firebox was dictated by the need to save weight and money. Steel was cheaper than copper – which would ultimately be in short supply in the war – and the pressure and temperature to which the firebox would be subjected would lead to expansion and contraction problems with a copper firebox. Furthermore, the cost of maintenance could be reduced as repairs to the steel firebox could be undertaken by welding at the running depots. To provide additional support for the crown of the Belpaire-type of firebox with a grate area of

Boilers en route from the North British Locomotive Co.'s works at Glasgow, and loaded on to LNER Flatrol-U wagons. The date is probably 27 November 1940. The boiler nearest the camera has a regulator handle fitted to both the driver's and fireman's side, and the welding runs are seen on the sides of the firebox. This boiler, No. 1090, was fitted to No. 21C1, *Channel Packet*. The taper on the underside of these boilers was on the front ring
Author's collection

48.5 sq ft, Bulleid used Nicholson thermic syphons, supplied by Beyer Peacock Ltd, which helped to promote efficient water circulation within the boiler. The syphons were really a modern development of Drummond's water tubes of earlier years; their actual usefulness in promoting the success of the boiler was later questioned by the static Rugby experiments in the early 1950s, when the evaporation rate of the syphonless boiler was equated with the normal boiler with syphons. Further safety against a collapse of the crown sheet was provided by six fusible plugs, those used on the Pacifics having a soldered or drop-in pellet rather than a lead-filled core.

The construction techniques employed for the welding of the firebox are well described by Bulleid in his paper to the Institution of Mechanical Engineers in 1945 [*Proc Inst Mech Eng* (1945), *152*, 316] and further expanded by Burrows and Wallace in their paper to the Institution of Locomotive Engineers in 1958 [J *Inst Loco Eng* (1958), *48*, 242]. This latter paper summarizes the problems encountered up to 1957 and confirms Bulleid's use of steel as a firebox construction material. The design of the first ten boilers differed from those subsequently constructed, by having the front ring of the boiler tapered and the rear ring parallel, while the remainder had a parallel front and tapered rear ring. The reason for the change in design was to save weight both in steel and water content, since the heating surface area was the same for both types of boiler.

The steel fireboxes and syphons were the only parts that required repair during the life of the boiler. The fire heat is greatest above the fire at the elbow on the thermic syphons, where the collection of scale and other insoluble material impairs water circulation. Cracking of the syphons occurred here and at their junction with the throatplate, where the cracks appeared to originate from stay holes adjacent to the area pressed out for the syphon necks. Some of the cracks were caused by uneven cooling down of the firebox and boiler, and possible excessive stiffness of the throatplate. The practice of ejecting all hot ash from the fire, and of allowing the boiler a period of at least twelve hours to cool before washing out commenced, was instituted to reduce this problem. Cracks in the main structure of the syphon were repaired by cutting out the defective area and welding in a new section. Again, it was felt that controlled cooling down of the boilers, together with the use of Monel metal stays in the most stressed areas, would be an effective solution to reduce the fractured stays found in the area of the throat and wrapper plates. The lack of totally coordinated water treatment on the Southern Railway may well have been an additional cause of some of these defects. All the fireboxes in the first ten boilers were replaced within seven years. However, the syphons from these fireboxes were found to be in sufficiently good condition to be used in the replacement fireboxes. In the second series of boilers built at Eastleigh in 1944, even with improved syphon seating and adequate cooling down before washout, fireboxes were replaced during the period 1950–3, since these boilers were not subjected to a strict water treatment regime.

The first ten boilers constructed by the North British Locomotive Co., and those initially built at Eastleigh, had extensive x-ray examination of all the welds, a technique developed in conjunction with Babcock and Wilcox. This procedure, designed to ensure that the quality of the weld was to the required standard, was reduced to examination of 25 per cent of the weld length as Eastleigh's experience in welding grew.

The quotation for the ten boilers from the North British Locomotive Co., dated 19 August 1939, was £2,850 each. The order for acceptance was given on 4 October 1939, and from the company's records the gross cost was nearer £3,046 per boiler. The order for the second batch of ten boilers was placed with the same company on 13 May 1941, at an increase of £5, to £2,855 each! However, since the building of the second series of locomotives was not considered until early 1943 and no work had commenced on the

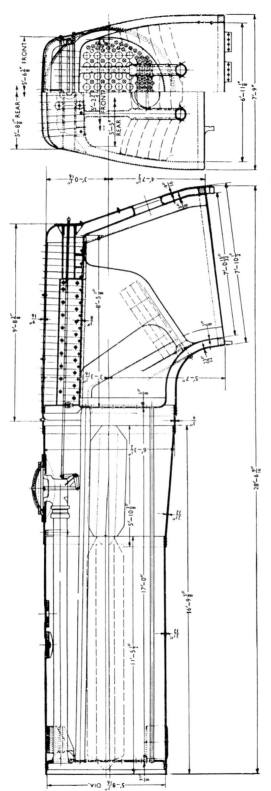

Sectional elevation and end cross-section of boilers fitted to the last twenty locomotives, and the five spare boilers. The taper was on the rear ring of these boilers

7

boilers at that time, Bulleid arranged for the works at Eastleigh to tender for these boilers, with an estimate of £3,700 per boiler, not far from the actual cost. The Southern Railway was notified of payment required for cancellation of the order of £374, and records of the North British Locomotive Co. show that the work on the boilers – essentially the estimating – was suspended on 15 April 1942. In the summer of 1940, Bulleid was pressing for new boiler fabricating equipment at Eastleigh, promising a saving of £1,000 per boiler over outside contractor's prices if the equipment were to be installed. No record is available of the cost of the new boiler equipment. The thermic syphons for the boilers were supplied by Beyer Peacock Ltd, at a cost of £304 per pair of syphons, although in the initial order for the second ten boilers the thermic syphons were omitted.

The use of thermic syphons in the fireboxes provided additional support for the brick arch and enabled the arch, built in three sections between the syphons, to be sited higher in the firebox, giving a greater free air space over the fire. Bulleid was beaten not only by Gresley in being the first to use thermic syphons on a British locomotive, but also twenty years earlier by Bowen Cooke of the LNWR. The LNER V4 2–6–2 No. 3402 was completed at Doncaster early in 1941, with a single Nicholson thermic syphon and a welded steel firebox. However, a single thermic syphon was fitted to a Claughton, No. 42, of the LNWR in 1921, although this boiler had a copper firebox. In the Bulleid Pacifics, the firebox was protected from direct admission of cold air by the use of an Ajax steam-operated firedoor, an American design manufactured by Whitelegg and Rogers Ltd. It could be opened by the fireman either manually or by depressing a foot-operated treadle, which admitted steam to the operating cylinder and then opened the doors. The mechanical opening of the firedoor, which was often not very precise, was not universally used by the firemen, and proved expensive to maintain.

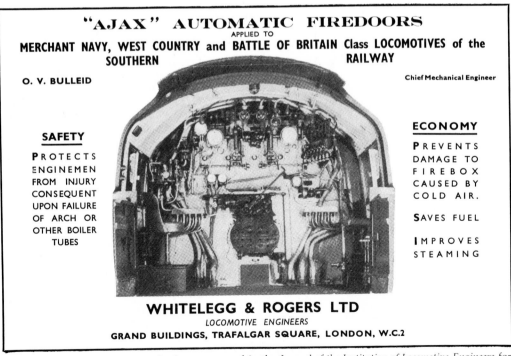

This advertisement for the Ajax firedoors appeared in the *Journal of the Institution of Locomotive Engineers* for November–December 1948

The smokebox departed from conventional practice in being fabricated from relatively thin plate and being of an irregular shape. Although 8 ft 1$\frac{3}{16}$ in long, much room was taken up by the steampipes for the outside admission piston valves, the inside cylinder and the superheater header. The steampipes were initially of cast construction, but because of cracking due to their rigidity in relation to frame movement, the design was changed to a flexible Aiton convoluted steel pipe. In the 'Lord Nelson' and 'Schools' classes the installation of the Lemaître blastpipe greatly improved the steaming of the engines so the design was continued in the 'Merchant Navy' class. Discharge of exhaust steam was accomplished through five nozzles, each 2$\frac{5}{8}$ in diameter, with the nozzles being positioned 1 ft 3$\frac{3}{8}$ in below the centre line of the boiler. The chimney itself was of the divergent/convergent pattern, fabricated from sheet steel with a choke diameter of 2 ft 1 in, the plain top of 2 ft 5 in diameter terminating almost flush with the casing of the locomotive.

The steam dome was situated towards the centre of the rear ring of the boiler, beneath which was located the annular seat or poppet valve-type regulator. The internal push-pull operating rod actuated the main valve via a crank, from which initial movement opened a small pressure-equalizing pilot valve, giving better control of the main valve. Three Ross pop safety valves were fitted on the front ring of the boiler. This position was dictated by the fear that turbulence occasioned by water circulation via the syphons might cause water and steam to be lifted from the boiler if fitted over the firebox. They were later resited between the dome and firebox, since it was water surging during braking that caused the expulsion of water and steam, rather than water turbulence. Steam from the superheater header was fed to the outside cylinders via two

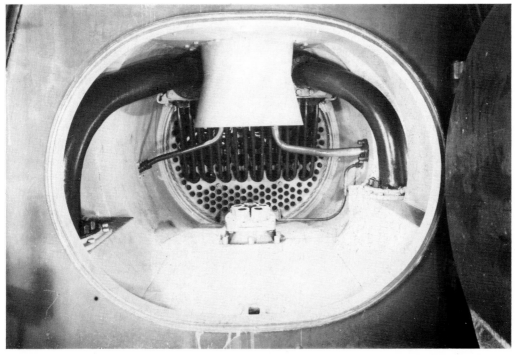

Inside the oval-shaped smokebox door, two of the main plain section steampipes are visible in the smokebox, with the blower pipe around the blastpipe. Behind the chimney is the front tube plate and superheater elements

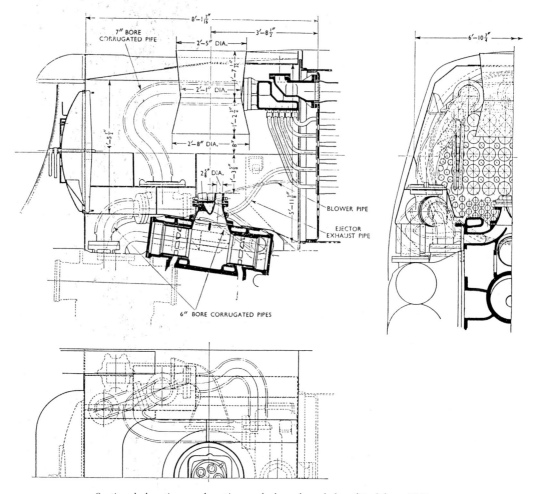

Sectional elevation, end section and plan of smokebox fitted from 1945

7 in diameter pipes and to the middle cylinder via two 6 in pipes branching off the outer 7 in pipes, feeding each end of the piston valve.

Bulleid chose three separate cylinders, which facilitated their casting and machining. The middle cylinder was positioned higher in the frames, inclined at 1 in 7¾ to give clearance to the inside connecting rod above the front coupled axle, and sited behind the two outer cylinders, which were set at 1 in 40. Drive from all three cylinders was taken to the centre coupled axle; with the differences in cylinder position, the length of the connecting rods were 8 ft for the inside cylinder and 11 ft for the two outside cylinders. All cylinders had a bore of 18 in with a 24 in stroke, these dimensions giving a tractive effort of 37,515 lb at 85 per cent boiler pressure. In the design of the cylinders allowance was made to bore the cylinder out to 19 in, which was more than the normal tolerance. The relatively small cylinders gave a cylinder clearance volume of 9.9 per cent, a higher value than normal which would not help overall locomotive efficiency.

The steam passages to the cylinders were as straight as possible, aided by outside admission valves. The design allowed the valve events to permit a high ratio of expansion without overheating and overstressing the big end brasses. The piston valves were 11 in diameter, with a maximum travel of 6¼ in, the heads being connected by a double girder. Although the valves were of the outside admission pattern the valve gear was arranged for inside admission, with the valves driven by rocker arms in order to multiply the valve movement. The arms were sited in the exhaust cavity and, in order to remove the angularity of the rocker, a short driving link connected the rocker to the front end of the valve, changing the orientation by 180 degrees. All three rocker arms were mounted on a shaft passing through the three cylinders. At first there was trouble with breakages of the driven arm and shafts of the piston valve rocker of the middle and outside cylinders, where, unknown to Bulleid, the balancing pipe between the front and back steam chests in the cylinders was omitted. Provision of the balancing pipe after a review of indicator diagrams reduced this problem. The balancing pipes fitted to the inside cylinder did not prevent the shafts breaking, but manufacturing the inside shaft from solid steel and the use of a longer double drive arm for the outside rocker shafts did cure the problem. In fact, a cylinder test rig driven by an electric motor was in operation at Eastleigh to prove the design of the rocker shafts, cylinders and lubrication to the motion, but some problems did not present themselves until the engines were in service.

One of the claims of Bulleid's Pacific design was to keep all routine maintenance as simple as possible and to reduce the daily chore of oiling. Bulleid did not favour divided drive, and of course did not wish his new engines to suffer from overheating of the inside big ends. The decision to have three cylinders with separate valve gear all driving the centre coupled wheel left very little space for conventional Walschaerts motion. This problem had been overcome by the Southern Railway on the three-cylinder 2–6–0 and the 'River' class 2–6–4 tanks by using a modification of the valve gear – Holcroft's conjugated valve gear with the centre motion derived from the outside gear. It is thought that Bulleid's first idea for the Pacifics' valve gear was to use a Caprotti type of rotary cam poppet gear as used on the LNER 2–8–2 engines, and designs were prepared in 1940 for such a system. However, with the pressure brought about by wartime shortages of materials and the dependence upon outside suppliers, Bulleid decided to proceed with his own ideas for the valve gear. His proposal for the valve gear involved its enclosure, together with the inside big end, in an oil bath, to produce a design that was free from dirt and which enabled the daily routine of lubrication to be forgotten. Bulleid himself believed that the system of lubrication of valve gear had remained unchanged since the early days and that poor hand-oiling of the motion was the cause of engine failures. Possibly influenced by his experiences with overheating of big ends on the Gresley engines, he admitted that the concept of total enclosure of the motion would result in reduced accessibility. He hoped that the reduced wear, freedom from heating and need for less routine maintenance would overcome this objection.

One of the main problems in enclosing the motion was that, unlike a motor vehicle, there was movement between the reciprocating and rotating masses and the locomotive frame. The three sets of valve gear, the middle connecting rod, slide bar, crosshead and crankpin, all sited between the frames, had to be enclosed in the lubrication system, with the three valve guides and middle piston rod taken through the front of the enclosure. Chain drive was the ultimate choice for actuation of the valve gear, after use of the cam valve gear had been discounted, and other possibilities such as derived motion had been ruled out. Bulleid patented his ideas regarding the valve gear under patent numbers 547,156 and 547,180 in 1942. The three sets of valve gear were operated by a secondary three-throw crankshaft sited below and in front of the crank axle on the middle driving wheel. This crankshaft was driven by two chains, a horizontal one from the crank axle to an intermediate sprocket and a vertical chain from the sprocket to the crankshaft. The inverted tooth chains were manufactured by Morse and were of 1.2 in

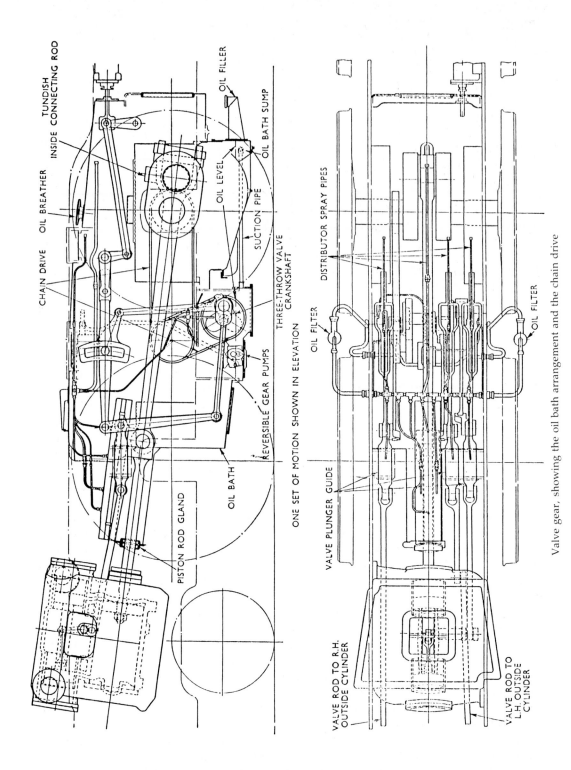

CHAIN DRIVE OIL BREATHER

TUNDISH INSIDE CONNECTING ROD

OIL FILLER

OIL BATH SUMP

OIL LEVEL

SUCTION PIPE

THREE-THROW VALVE CRANKSHAFT

ONE SET OF MOTION SHOWN IN ELEVATION

REVERSIBLE GEAR PUMPS

OIL BATH

PISTON ROD GLAND

DISTRIBUTOR SPRAY PIPES

OIL FILTER

OIL FILTER

VALVE PLUNGER GUIDE

VALVE ROD TO R.H. OUTSIDE CYLINDER

VALVE ROD TO L.H. OUTSIDE CYLINDER

Valve gear, showing the oil bath arrangement and the chain drive

12

The three-throw crankshaft, sited in the oil bath below the crank axle, and operating the three sets of valve gear and the oil pumps

Author's collection

pitch and 2 in width, with the original drawing for the intermediate sprocket dated June 1940. The horizontal chain consisted of 118 pitches with the shafts being 47.36 in apart giving a total chain length of 11.8 ft. The vertical chain had 73 pitches, operating on a shaft centre that could be adjusted from 20.4 to 22 in, and a total chain length of 7.3 ft. The tensioning of the two chains was achieved by movement of the intermediate sprocket, although in reality this only gave correct tensioning to the vertical chain drive. The three-throw crankshaft revolved at the same speed as the crank axle, with each crank being in phase with the appropriate big end.

To provide lubrication for the enclosed motion, two reversible gear pumps supplied oil at a pressure of 20 lb sq in. Each was driven by a $\frac{1}{2}$ in pitch Morse roller chain from the crankshaft. The oil was filtered before delivery to the enclosed parts of the motion and, to aid efficient lubrication of the middle big end, a collecting cup was provided on the big end to allow retention of the oil during the upper part of the revolution.

The enclosure of the valve gear in the space between the frames would only allow a restricted movement of the expansion links, which was limited to 37.5 per cent of the maximum valve travel. This movement was amplified by the proportional unequal length of the rocker arms, which multiplied the motion from the crank axle in the ratio of 8 to 3, giving the required 6 in of valve travel. One of the aspects of the valve gear of the class was that the timing was often 'out', with the blame being placed on the chain drive. Bulleid realized that one of the problems was the possibility of slackness developing in the chain, due to wear on the pins and sprockets. He suggested that a slack of 3 in would be absorbed when the chain was under load, and that any other irregularity affecting the valve events could be corrected by changing the cut off.

Frame flexure could not be compensated in the design of the sump and therefore, any movement of the sump in relation to the frame which formed the walls of the sump would result in cracks and oil leaking from the sump. Movement of the valve gear in the sump when the engine was in motion created pressure causing additional stress. Condensation and steam from the inside cylinder piston rod drain cocks and the steam brake cylinders was serious in the sumps of the Pacifics, and changes in oil specification did little to rectify the problem. The vents on top of the sump did not prevent the condensation problem, but the use of non-emulsifying red mineral oil enabled the water to be drawn off from the sump when the locomotive had been standing. Unfortunately the very purpose of the sump in preventing wear was now being thwarted, resulting in an increase in the wear of the motion pins. The oil capacity of the sump was 40 gallons, giving a depth of oil of about 8 in at the front end of the sump near the oil pumps. With the leaking of oil through the driving wheel seals and the poor joints between the sump and the frames, there was a constant need to check the oil level and for routine daily topping up of the sump.

Bulleid had to concede that examinations inside the sump could not be avoided. The issuing of protective clothing for repairs within the oil bath did little to help matters, and tales of the fitters' nightmares in trying to rectify faults within the sump are legion! The weight of oil in the sump of 330 lb added appreciably to the weight of the valve gear, which was quoted as 945 lb for each set, compared with that of a set of Walschaerts gear weighing 1,150 lb. Loss of oil caused slipping and in certain cases boiler lagging fires, not helped in some cases by oil thrown up by the coupling rods on the locomotives, as splashers were not fitted to the majority of the class. Some of the results of the tests carried out at Rugby Testing Station may well have been prejudiced by the oil loss from the sump coating the rollers and inducing power loss. Failure of the big end was noticed not by a smell of overheating but by the sight and sound of a connecting rod protruding through the sump with a concurrent loss of oil!

The use of a steam reverser was deemed necessary by the linkage required to circumvent the wide firebox; Bulleid preferred the steam reverser because he disliked the effort necessary to use a screw reverser. The reason for the adoption of the horizontal LSWR type of reverser rather than the better vertical SER Stirling version was a question of space. The LSWR reverser was in use on the T9, M7 and D15 classes with no major problems. Although there was a speeding up of the action of the steam reverser in later series of the locomotives its action was never precise. The reasons included inability to fix precisely the actual cut-off position, together with the creeping of the gear away from its set position, caused in some cases by use of the incorrect oil in the hydraulic cylinder, as well as the additional problems inherent in the chain drive of the valve gear. Drivers tended to adjust power output by changes in regulator opening, rather than by using changes in the cut-off with a fixed regulator opening. Modifications to the hydraulic locking mechanism of the reverser had little effect on the creep of the mechanism, although this did result in some decrease in the instability of the system.

The spacing of the frames, cut from $1\frac{1}{8}$ in plate, at 3 ft $3\frac{7}{8}$ in was much closer than normal. The purpose of the narrow spacing was to enable the oil bath to be fitted between the frames, and to centre the cast steel horn blocks bolted to the outside of the frame and thus ensure that the axlebox thrust was centrally applied. Additional reinforcement for the hornstays was provided in the form of cross stretchers bolted on to the horn cheeks, sited in front of the leading coupled wheel, between the leading and driving and the driving and trailing coupled wheels. All these stretchers were of cast construction, and to lighten them, additional holes were cut out which may have led to some of the frame fractures. The second and third series had fabricated stretchers which were lighter and equally robust. The hornstays provided further support at the forward end for the steam brake cylinder and the main brake shaft. The layshaft and the three-throw crank axle were carried by the hornstay between the leading driving and

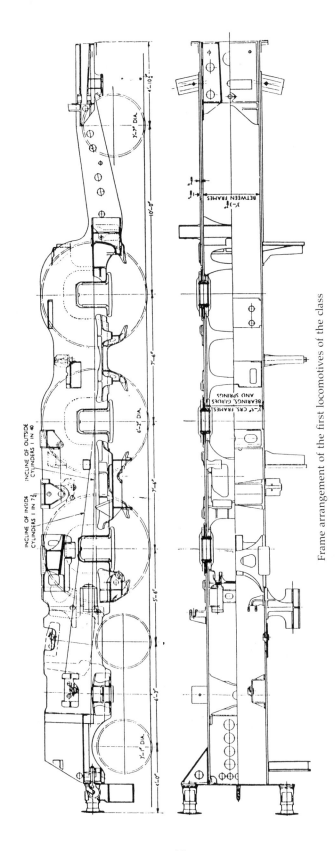

Frame arrangement of the first locomotives of the class

INCLINE OF INSIDE CYLINDERS 1 IN 7½

INCLINE OF OUTSIDE CYLINDERS 1 IN 40

3'-5" DIA.

2'-9" DIA.

3'-1" DIA.

3'-0½" DIA. BETWEEN FRAMES

3'-5" CRS. FRAMES, BEARINGS, GUIDES AND SPRINGS

15

Main frames laid out at Eastleigh Works
Author's collection

A January 1941 photograph at Eastleigh showing construction of No. 21C1 *Channel Packet*. This engine was fitted with splashers to the driving wheels. In the smokebox, the end of one of the main steampipes can be seen, sited on the superheater header. The narrow slot above the smokebox door was the subject of modification to improve smoke clearance

Author's collection

coupled wheels. The middle cylinder slide bar, the valve plunger guides for the three cylinders and the boiler front support were attached to the top cross stay over the leading coupled axle. The cast steel dragbox was bolted on to the trailing ends of the frames, with the steel casting behind the trailing coupled wheels used for support of the boiler. In addition, this casting carried the trailing spring hanger bracket and acted as the trailing truck pin anchorage.

The trailing truck was to provide much of the smooth riding of the locomotives and was later to be adopted almost totally for the BR standard designs. It was pivoted to the frame stretcher at the rear of the frame and was a one piece casting. The lateral control springs were located below the rear bearing pads with a maximum compression of 2 tons when the maximum transverse movement of 5 in was reached. The trucks of the last ten engines were fabricated rather than cast in an attempt to reduce weight. They were interchanged between engines in works and were thus to be seen on the earlier engines. Bulleid adopted the 'Lord Nelson' leading bogie designs for side control and suspension, although the the wheel base was shortened to 6 ft 3 in.

The driving wheels were 6 ft 2 in diameter and these, like all those for the locomotive and tender, were based on the American Boxpok idea. Bulleid, in collaboration with the Sheffield steelmakers Thomas Firth and John Brown, patented this design to give the BFB cast steel wheel, under patent 526, 518 issued in 1940. The wheels were lighter and stronger than the conventional spoked wheels providing continuous support for the tyre. The high tensile, alloy steel tyre was fastened to the wheel in a novel manner. The use of a turned lip on the outside, and one on the inside cold-rolled over the wheel after the tyre was in position, eliminated the use of the normal Gibson fastening ring.

One unusual feature of the Pacifics was that there was no reciprocating balance, although there was the normal balancing of the rotating parts of the engine. Indeed, the back of the driving wheels hid from view the steel plates used to hold the lead balance weights for dynamically balancing the wheels, with additional lead in the pockets formed by the profile of the wheels themselves. Speed tests over Barnes bridge observed

The trailing truck showing the cast construction, and the characteristic round-topped SR axlebox covers
Author's collection

17

The front bogie of No. 35011 *General Steam Navigation* at Eastleigh

B. Wright

by the CME demonstrated that there was no hammer blow. However, there may well have been an increase in stress in the frames and the driving axle to achieve this benefit.

The coupled wheel axle boxes were bronze, a material that Bulleid had had experience on the LNER. They gave very little trouble, but as a result of coupling rod breakage on No. 35016 *Elders Fyffes* in November 1955, it was discovered that the bronze boxes were cracked and brittle. It was decided to replace them with cast steel boxes.

The space between the wheels and the frames enabled clasp brakes to be fitted, actuated by the steam brake cylinders on the engine. This arrangement of braking increased the area of brake block surface in contact with the wheel and, in addition, reduced the unequal thrust on the horns which occurred when single blocks were used. The pull on the brake blocks from the two $6\frac{1}{4}$ in × 8 in steam cylinders was 57.4 tons – equal to 97 per cent of the braked wheel weight, but only 60 per cent of the locomotive weight. Nevertheless, braking on the locomotive itself was poor, and light engines had to proceed with caution. Braking on the tender was by vacuum with a brake cylinder at each end of the frames, in conjunction with a Westinghouse 'Westlak' slack adjuster, giving a brake pull of 24.7 tons.

The design of the three ashpans ensured that there would be a free flow of air over all the grate area, with ash disposal helped by the self-cleaning hoppers. These followed American practice, could be actuated from the ground, and eliminated part of the tiresome disposal duty normally associated with steam locomotives. There were no dampers fitted to the original engines but air doors were fitted at the front and the back; an additional door at the back of the middle ashpan ensured that the accumulated ash

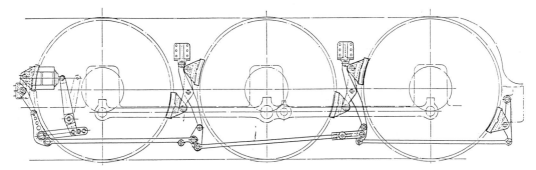

The brake gear showing the steam brake cylinder, hangers and clasp brakes

could be removed. The design, revised when the locomotives were rebuilt, was used as the basis of the three-compartment ashpan of the BR standard locomotives.

The mechanical lubrication of the cylinders, the valve chests and the rocker shafts was controlled by two six-feed Wakefield lubricators. These were sited below the smokebox door front plate and driven by ratchets off the valve rocker shafts. In this position they were prone to collect smokebox ash, although the single reservoir aimed at minimizing this. In addition there was a Detroit lubricator on the fireman's side of the cab on the first ten locomotives. The second and third series of locomotives were fitted with three mechanical lubricators all positioned below the smokebox door. Lubrication for the axleboxes was supplied by oil boxes with worsted trimmings sited on the footplate.

Steam sanding to the driving wheels was only applied to the front of the middle driving wheel on the first five engines. This proved to be totally inadequate in service, and resulted in additional sanding being fitted to the other driving wheels in the remaining engines of the first series of ten. The second and third series of locomotives had sanding applied to all the driving wheels with hand-operated sanding applied to the front tender wheels. The sandboxes were mounted in the only available space behind the air-smoothed casing and, in spite of various designs, were never easy to fill. Bulleid's idea was that the boiler heat would ensure a supply of dry sand to the sanders, but ladders were required to fill the sandboxes, and if no ladder was available the sandboxes went empty.

The idea of air-smoothed casing was to enable the engine to proceed through the carriage washing plant for cleaning – but the locomotives never entered such a domain! The casing, initially constructed of 16 swg steel sheeting, hid from view the glass fibre boiler lagging and the irregularly shaped fabricated smokebox. At the cab end the casing covered the shape of the Belpaire firebox. Bulleid was proud of his ergonomic cab design, which gave the crew a better standard of protection and comfort than the cabs of many other locomotives, although it was very hot in summer. The design and layout of the controls was to enable the driver and fireman to work efficiently as a team with the controls grouped on each side of the cab. The fittings on the driver's side of the cab were the regulator, the steam reverser, brake valve and ejector, blower, steam-chest pressure gauge, lubricating oil pressure gauges and cylinder cock gear. On the fireman's side of the cab were the boiler pressure gauge, firedoor treadle and control gear, steam heating controls, electric generator control and the water and steam controls for the two Davies

19

The cab of No. 21C1 *Channel Packet*. The driver's seat was similar to those found on some LNER Pacifics, but was soon replaced with a tip-up type. Note the inscription above this seat, commemorating the naming ceremony and unique to the engine, and the obstructed view forward for both driver and fireman. The regulator could be controlled from both sides of the cab. On the fireman's side is the Detroit displacement lubricator, and the injector controls under the seat. The Ajax firedoor could be controlled by the floor-mounted treadle, or by the lever on the operating mechanism. UV lamp bulbs are visible on the cab roof and over the pressure gauges

Author's collection

and Metcalfe No. 11 Monitor-type live steam injectors. The water supply from the injectors entered the boiler via clack valves mounted on the top section of the boiler, these valves later being adopted for the BR standard locomotives. Controls for the blower, whistle and the Klinger-pattern water level gauges were duplicated for driver and fireman, and on at least the first engine the regulator was positioned so control was possible on both sides of the cab. The fireman's control of the regulator was eventually removed. The manifold, mounted on the boiler backplate, supplied steam to the vacuum brake, injectors and other fittings, and its steam supply was controlled by a valve situated to the left of the steam dome. The vacuum brake ejector which partly obscured the driver's forward vision, was repositioned after completion of the first series, to improve the driver's view.

The black faces and luminous figures of the cab gauges were illuminated by lights in the cab roof, which were fitted with glass which only transmitted ultra violet light. Electrical power was supplied by a steam-driven Stone's turbo generator, of $\frac{3}{4}$ hp and rated at 350–500 W, initially mounted under the lubricators in front of the smokebox. It was repositioned below the driver's side of the footplate before the second series of locomotives was constructed. Electric lamps which could be switched on individually, were provided as route indicators on the front of the engine and on the rear of the tender. Further innovations were the fitting of lights to illuminate the injectors, inspection lights over the driving wheels, front and rear bogie and mechanical lubricators, and sockets for hand lamps situated over the centre driving wheel.

With the relatively wide firebox, forward vision from the cab was restricted, although when the wedge-shaped cabs were fitted the visibility was improved. The rear of the cab roof was connected to the front of the tender by a canvas screen and the lower side sheets were turned in at the rear to give additional protection for the crew. This was later supplemented when the complete rear of the cab sheeting was turned in, by the addition of a metal-framed, glazed window set in the upper part of the side sheet. On the cab of the first engine the driver's seat was of a bucket type similar to that found on the LNER A4 Pacifics, later to be altered to the tip-up type of seat provided for the fireman.

In the design of the Pacifics the estimated weight in working order was 92 tons 10 cwt, with 63 tons carried by the coupled wheels. The first two engines both weighed over 99 tons 10 cwt when built, with the tender weighing 47 tons 19 cwt; the axle loading was over 22 tons. This excess weight over the initial estimate, resulted in the Civil Engineer requesting that steps be taken to reduce the weight before construction continued. It was found that much of the weight was contained in the cast steel frame stretchers, later to be replaced by a fabricated design. A reduction in the thickness by $\frac{3}{16}$ in in the stretchers resulted in a saving of $23\frac{1}{2}$ cwt and, although the stretchers in the first two locomotives were not replaced, lightening holes were cut in them and in the main frames. The use of thinner plate for the air-smoothed casing, the replacement of the side casing with asbestos limpet board, the removal of the driving wheel splashers which had been fitted

The design of the cabs was modified, with the rear section being turned in and fitted with a framed glass window, as this 1945 photograph shows. The Detroit lubricator has been removed, and there are changes to the pipe layout, giving a less cluttered appearance. Below the cab floor, the draw bar is connected to the engine dragbox

Author's collection

to some engines, and the use of painted numbers rather than the cast gunmetal type, reduced the weight of the locomotives by a theoretical 4 tons. In practice, the third engine in working order weighed 96 tons 8 cwt, a reduction of 3 tons 4 cwt, with Bulleid's stipulation that the working order was a fully laden tender, a light fire burning, 3 in of water in the glass and 100 lb sq in boiler pressure. There was no clear agreement among Chief Mechanical Engineers as to the definition of the working order weight, but the modifications carried out to reduce the weight and to give an axle loading of a little over 21 tons with, of course, no hammer blow, appear to have satisfied the Civil Engineer. Although these were positive steps to reduce the weight, there were likewise further features added to the engines that increased the overall weight, including the addition of the front cowling, the smoke deflectors and the rear turned in section of the cab side sheets.

Bulleid based the numbering system for the class, commencing with 21C1, on a continental system. The figures 21 indicated the number of bogie and trailing axles, the letter C indicated the number of coupled axles, and the last number referred to the locomotive number in the class.

It would be foolish to suggest that the design of the class was perfect. The criticism that it should have been limited to an initial prototype before a full building programme commenced, did not take into account the nature of the Southern locomotive stock situation in the immediate pre-war period. When war broke out, orders for military and naval equipment were placed on all railway workshops. The staff at Eastleigh, where there were air raids in 1940, objected to working on a new-fangled locomotive not needed for the non-existent express trains. Bulleid then announced they could pull heavy freight trains, although they did not prove 100 per cent successful at this task. That the design was for a mixed traffic engine was borne out by correspondence in the period from April to September 1941 between Bulleid, Missenden, the General Manager of the Southern, and the Rt Hon Lord Leathers, Minister of War Transport. The case for the completion of the first ten members of the class was outlined and the usefulness by nature of their high tractive effort in the movement of war materials and military personnel throughout the Southern Railway emphasized. One criticism levelled against the locomotives was the additional cost of the air-smoothed casing over the ordinary boiler cladding.

But what of problems in the running department with the new locomotives? To spread the new design around the railway in time of war would be to invite disaster. It was deemed prudent to concentrate the class on the Salisbury–Exmouth Junction section of the system, where extra fitters could be based at the two sheds and parts could be readily obtained from Eastleigh Works. The provision of withdrawn locomotives for use as stationary boilers to supply steam to the first members of the class might now be considered a strange idea. However, it was considered necessary because of the high working pressure of the Pacifics, for the Southern was not used to a boiler pressure of 280 lb sq in. However, by 1943, with experience gained in the steel fireboxes and the high boiler pressures, the stationary boilers became redundant.

The initial failures of the driven arm of the piston valve rocker shaft of the middle cylinder, presenting as a sheared keyway, were quickly traced to a design fault. This was unnoticed by Bulleid, who had assumed that the pressures in the steam pipes feeding the front and back of the middle cylinder steam chests would equalize. It was not until 1943 that the rocker arm fractures became commonplace. A review of indicator diagrams revealed variable steam pressures in the front steam chest. The provision on No. 21C4, in January 1944, of a balancing pipe between the front and rear steam chests, and additional bearings for the enlarged rocker shafts, eased the problem. The rocker shafts were, furthermore, strengthened by increasing the diameter to 4 in.

The air-smoothed casing was fine in design, but in practice when leaks in the pipe runs occurred, the securing fasteners of the casing proved difficult to undo. The provision of opening apertures in the casing to allow access to the clack valves and the steam manifold valve was an attempt to alleviate some of the fitters' problems. The use of a steel boiler and firebox allowed the repairs to be carried out by conventional welding techniques.

Complaints from the footplate staff of drifting smoke and exhaust steam were investigated by the use of models in the wind tunnel of Southampton University. The result was a modification of the front end of the engines, and eventually the provision of a wedge-shaped cab, giving a clearer view ahead. The wheel slip on starting and running was never successfully cured, even with modification to the sanding arrangements. This problem, not uncommon with Pacific designs, was caused not only by the leakage of oil from the sump, picked up by the driving wheels, but also from the weight redistribution occurring when the locomotive started, the relatively soft springing of the locomotives and the low adhesion of the class. In addition, the drivers were used to locomotives with first and second regulators, whereas the Pacifics were designed with a pilot and then main valve on the regulator. The 'Merchant Navy' class has often been criticized, yet its initial introduction produced eulogies from the wartime press concerning the performance of the engines. Their haulage capacity was surpassing anything seen on the Southern – at the expense of coal and water consumption, and, of course, the liking of the locomotives for oil.

In 1948, it was proposed by R.A. Riddles, member for Mechanical and Electrical Engineering on the new Railway Executive, that there should be a series of Interchange Trials of locomotives between the various regions to decide the proposed standard BR locomotives. Realizing that its designs would have little chance of being put forward as the basis of the new standard design, the unwritten Southern law for the trials was to show the performance of the Southern engines. There was no briefing of drivers as to how to work, and the Southern men were used to working to time with little respect for coal consumption. The 'West Country' Pacifics held the limelight regarding performances in Scotland during the trials. The 'Merchant Navy' class engines were, however, among

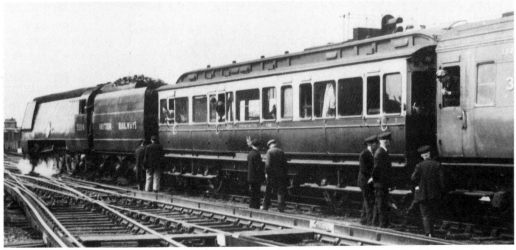

No. 35018 *British India Line* about to leave Waterloo on 1 June 1948 for a test run with the down 'Atlantic Coast Express'. The WR dynamometer car is next to the engine

The late G. Reynolds

the leaders for the listings of the most powerful locomotive related to db hp, at the expense of coal and water consumption. The trials were somewhat inconclusive, but Riddles launched his programmme of standard BR locomotives. The opening of the Rugby locomotive testing station, designed to obtain scientific knowledge of the locomotives, came too late to have much influence apart from improvement in front end design.

In December 1951 the Southern Region was asked to provide a suitable member of the class for testing at Rugby, and after a light intermediate repair No. 35022 *Holland America Line* was chosen. This engine may well have been selected as the Southern was asked for a random locomotive in workaday condition. It had run a comparatively high mileage of 188,928 miles with no general repair undertaken. The tests were conducted at a constant rate of evaporation, combustion and speed, with the cut-off between 10 and 50 per cent, and from 10,000 to 42,000 lb per hour of feed water, with, in the majority of cases, the regulator fully opened. The use of a fixed regulator setting was not the Southern practice; a partly closed regulator and a longer cut-off had developed with the use of the Maunsell locomotives. The maximum steaming rate was never reached, although 42,000 lb per hour was attained for 20 minutes. In addition to the test plant trials, the engine ran a series of controlled road trials over the Skipton–Carlisle route, with 594 ton trains of twenty coaches. The engine proved to have a superb boiler, but the reversing gear left room for improvement and there were problems with buckled coupling rods. The design of the front end was also in doubt and it was felt that there could be enhancements to the draughting arrangements and possible use of a boiler without thermic syphons. No. 35019 *French Line C.G.T.* had earlier run with a single blastpipe, and No. 35022 *Holland America Line* was similarly fitted in March 1953. The single blastpipe results did not improve the engine's performance, having reduced the

No. 35019 *French Line C.G.T.* fitted with the single blastpipe pulls into Salisbury in 1952. The Flaman speed recorder, fitted for the 1948 Interchange Trials, is still present
G. Heiron

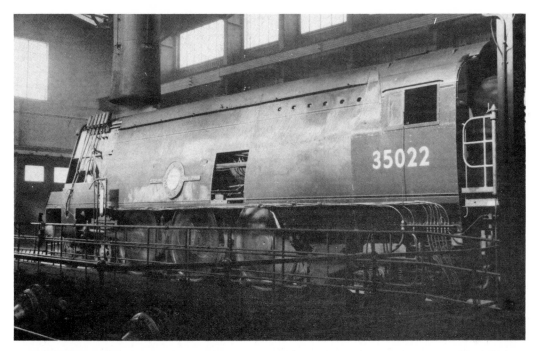

These two photographs show No. 35022 *Holland America Line* at Rugby locomotive testing station. In March 1952, the engine is on test, and a year later, in March 1953, fitted with the single blastpipe, is tenderless and in light steam outside the plant. The whistle is sited behind the safety valves on the top of the casing
J.B.C. McCann

maximum boiler output and increased the fuel consumption, although there were in fact limitations imposed by the loading gauge regarding the single blastpipe. The Southern people regarded this as academic, and were more concerned that the class had had over 165 modifications since it was built, and still had a low availability.

The usefulness of thermic syphons to the boiler was often questioned, and in August 1951 No. 35014 *Nederland Line* was fitted with a boiler without syphons in the firebox. After problems with the design of a suitable brick arch, a modified design was established, the boiler transferred to No. 35022 *Holland America Line* in November 1953, and the engine proceeded to Rugby in December 1953. The report was inconclusive and suggested that the removal of the syphons would not be an economic proposition. Overall, the Rugby tests showed that the design of the locomotive was difficult to test, owing to its inconsistent performance, although the one interesting facet was that there was no mechanical trouble other than the buckled coupling rod, caused by slipping at speed on the test plant rollers! The locomotive was effective and capable as designed but unfortunately uneconomical, and during the two years that it was under test no attempt was made to investigate fully the inherent weakness shown by the tests on the Bulleid valve gear. The report of the investigations could almost be stated as a summation of the different types of coal on the steaming of the locomotive; the initial brief for the testing fell short of any real scientific investigation into the shortcomings and solutions to the locomotive's problems.

In January 1947 a series of haulage tests were carried out using a dynamometer car to compare the performance of one of the 'Merchant Navy' class, No. 21C13 *Blue Funnel*, 'West Country' class locomotive, No. 21C140 *Crewkerne*, and an electric locomotive, No. CC1, on the Central section of the Southern. The conclusions reached were that the boiler efficiency of both steam locomotives was not satisfactory, with high coal consumption rates in relation to the rate of water evaporation. These tests were very similar to those carried out by Bulleid between 'Merchant Navy' class, No. 21C14 *Nederland Line*, 'Lord Nelson' class, No. 861 *Lord Anson*, and 'King Arthur' class, No. 789 *Sir Guy*, in the summer of 1946, when there was talk of the excessive coal and water consumption of the class. The runs were made on the West of England main line between Waterloo, Salisbury and Exeter, with loads of up to eighteen coaches, but with no dynamometer car.

The firebox grate area of the class, at $48\frac{1}{2}$ sq ft was close to the maximum that could be handled by a single fireman, and in October 1947 Bulleid purchased a reconditioned Berkley mechanical stoker. This was fitted to No. s21C5 *Canadian Pacific* in March 1948, with the thought that mechanical firing might permit the use of lower grade coal, although the use of pulverized coal on the Great Central in 1922 and the Southern in the 1930s had not proved very successful. The mechanical stoker was driven by a steam engine fitted to the front of the tender coal space, which drove a flexible and reversible Archimedian screw and coal crusher feeding coal to the distribution plate inside the firebox. In case of failure of the stoker, hand-firing could be used, since the Ajax firedoors were still in place. The coal fed to the distribution plate was delivered to the appropriate sections of the firegrate by four separately controlled steam jets. The maximum rate of coal supply was 5 tons per hour, and after initial problems the locomotive was based at Nine Elms and rostered on the Bournemouth and West of England expresses. The coal supply had to be of a standard size, even though a coal crusher was incorporated to deal with any large lumps, and to reduce dust from the tender the bunker was covered with a canvas sheet. To combat spark throwing, the Lemaître blastpipe nozzles were increased in size to $2\frac{7}{8}$ in diameter and a thinner fire employed, although there were still tales of the table-cloths in the dining car being

The cab of No. s21C5 *Canadian Pacific*, showing the positioning of the stoker conduit. The Ajax firedoors are still in place

Author's collection

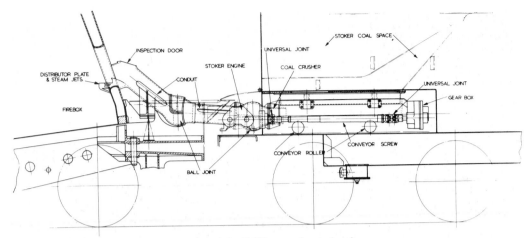

Diagram of the Berkley mechanical stoker

The crank axle, No. E4237, of No. 35020 *Bibby Line* fractured on 24 April 1953 through the sprocket seating of the left-hand axle section, when the locomotive was travelling at between 70 and 80 mph approaching Crewkerne

Author's collection

The Crewkerne station canopy sustained damage, as a result of No. 35020 becoming partly derailed
K. Robertson collection

covered with coal dust and unburnt coal. In February 1950, after a heavy intermediate repair at Eastleigh, the engine, now renumbered No. 35005, ran trials at the Rugby locomotive testing station and over the Rugby–Euston and Waterloo–Salisbury line attached to the LMR mobile testing unit. The stoker was removed for comparative trials in April and May 1950, and then refitted in June 1950 before the trials were concluded in April 1951, after a mileage of 77,338 miles. The mechanical stoker was generally liked by the footplate crew, but the need to pick coal of a size less than 6 in square was impractical with the use of coaling plants.

Bulleid had left the Southern in 1949. He had never shown much interest in locomotive maintenance, and was more interested in the designs for 'Leader' in his last years on the Southern. With his departure, the Southern works managers and motive power officers felt free to give vent to criticism and to formulate a financial case for rebuilding the locomotives to the BR board. H.H. Swift, Bulleid's successor, was an electrical engineer, but his deputy W.G. Burrows (son of Churchward's chief draughtsman at Swindon) started the ball rolling. Correspondence took place between the locomotive accountant at Brighton and the locomotive works manager at Eastleigh setting out the proposal for rebuilding the 'Merchant Navy' and 'West Country' classes. The problems of the Pacifics were compounded in 1953 with the crank axle failure of No. 35020 *Bibby Line* at Crewkerne, resulting in the redesign of the axle as a modified balanced pattern. The failure of the axle on No. 35020 at Crewkerne was traced to corrosion under the chain sprocket, and served to alert the BR board to the Southern's need to spend money on rebuilding the Pacifics. In addition, there were more failures,

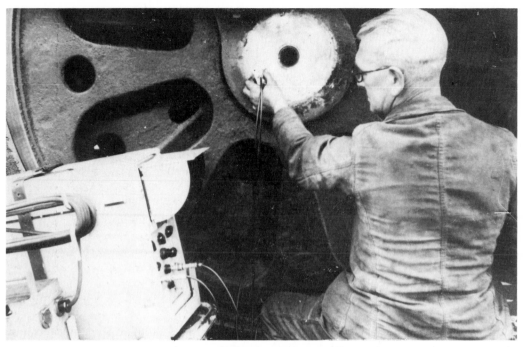

A coupled axle on one of the 'Merchant Navy' class being ultrasonically tested at Eastleigh Works after the Crewkerne incident

Author's collection

No. 35009 *Shaw Savill* is photographed at Eastleigh with the centre driving wheels and axle removed for testing. This engine was one of those found to have a flawed crank axle

B.I. Fletcher collection

with the coupling rod incidents of No. 35025 *Brocklebank Line* in 1954, and No. 35016 *Elders Fyffes* in 1955; the latter also resulted in the substitution of steel axleboxes for the bronze boxes. The coupling rod problems had been a trouble for many years, with the tests at Rugby being interrupted by the need to restraighten the rods, and stories from the sheds of the rods being straightened by the use of a jack against the rod and the shed wall.

R.G. Jarvis, the Chief Technical Assistant (Locomotives) on the Southern Region, based at Brighton, was invited to prepare designs for the modification of the Pacifics. The main features for redesigning were the valve gear, the intermediate drawbar gear between the engine and tender, the elimination of problems with the mechanical lubricators (whose drive was not satisfactory and whose location was entirely unsuitable), the steam reversing gear and the unsuitability of the air-smoothed casing in relation to overall accessibility and repair. Reliability and availability were low, and running costs were high, as were the costs of repair and maintenance. One of the original ideas for modifying the locomotives was as a two-cylinder type, based on the 'Britannia' design. Luckily this proposal by M. Lockhart, who was in charge of the section of the Brighton drawing office involved with the modifications, did not extend beyond the drawing board. The report setting out the proposed modification to the class reviewed their design and performance and then set out the poor availability and cost of repair and maintenance of the engines, showing that they cost about 20 per cent more in maintenance than the 'Lord Nelson' class. Jarvis' proposals for the engine modification retained the boiler, frames, outside cylinders, wheels and cab, and removed or replaced the following items: valve gear and rocker shafts, inside cylinder, smokebox, super-heater header, steampipes, reversing gear, piston heads and rods, oil bath, air-smoothed casing, mechanical lubricators, regulator, ashpan and grate, cylinder cocks and sandboxes. In addition, the tender would be modified by the removal of the raves and the provision of a tunnel for the fire irons and a cover for the vacuum cylinders. Tank sieves would be fitted outside the tender tank and a tender water gauge would be added. The intermediate drawbar gear between the engine and tender would be redesigned, as drawbars were bent when travelling over sharp curves.

Prior to rebuilding the class Jarvis prepared drawings for an initial series of modifications, carried out on three members of the class, No. 35012 *United States Lines*, No. 35013 *Blue Funnel* and No. 35021 *New Zealand Line*. These modifications included the strengthening of the 3:8 valve operating levers and bearings, strengthening of the mechanical lubricator drives, the fitting of LNER-type cylinder cocks and LMS-type automatic steam chest drains to replace the plug-type cocks, and the strengthening of the frame stretchers. One of the problems with the engines had been the drawbar, connecting the engine to the tender, which was frequently found to be bent or flawed. It was pin-jointed at the engine dragbox, but at the tender end there was a spherical bearing surface to transmit the load in the drawbar to the tender underframe. The curved rubbing surface on the tender rubbed against the flat block on the engine dragbeam, producing a high loading of the drawbar. The modification consisted of the replacement of the flat surface of the engine dragbeam with a curved rubbing surface faced with manganese steel to reduce wear. The pin-jointed plunger, similar to that in use on the LNER and sliding in guides, was now cushioned by a rubber spring and, in addition, safety links were fitted between the engine and tender. The modified locomotives were a definite improvement, and the design changes were incorporated in the rebuilding of all members of the class.

The problem of bent coupling rods was overcome by the use of a different class of steel, and a plain section replaced the earlier I-section design. The existing rods were of class C steel of low tensile strength, 32 to 38 tons sq in, and were replaced by plain section rods of high tensile, 50 tons sq in, fine grain steel. With a coupling rod it was important to use a steel capable of absorbing as much energy as possible under the conditions normally causing a bending moment, such as when the wheels are slightly out of phase as the engine slips. The new design of rod was utilized on all the rebuilt engines and also on some of the unrebuilt members of the class. In addition, manganese steel liners were introduced between the horn-guides and coupled axleboxes. A redesigned sprocket fixing on the right-hand section of the crank axle enabled replacement by an eccentric, when Walschaerts valve gear was used in the rebuilding. These crank axles also incorporated balanced crank webs, although this design feature increased the unsprung weight of the engine. The BFB wheels remained but outside balance weights were added, as a result of changes to the valve gear.

One of the characteristics of the locomotives was the securing cap for the coupling rods. The design, due to R.G. Curl, a senior locomotive draughtsman, was a complex and ingenious yet effective fastening, whose genesis was brought about by Bulleid's dislike of a split-ended taper pin. Replacement of the hexagonal-pentagonal securing cap, by a plate washer and large nut with a split taper pin, commenced in early BR days. However, by 1954, No. 35003 *Royal Mail* appeared with the LMS style of four studs and nuts securing the large washer. On rebuilding, the driving wheels with the four studs provided a convenient method of securing the return crank of the Walschaerts valve gear. The leading driving wheel pin was a similar, yet simpler design of the hexagonal-pentagonal cap, consisting of a dished or recessed plate washer, a stud set into a bored out crankpin and a nut, secured by a split pin or cotter through the stud. The trailing driving wheel used a large plate washer, a nut and a split taper pin.

The steam reversing gear had given a lot of trouble, and the inability of the driver to make fine adjustments or to keep the engine at one set cut-off was a major problem. Attempts to provide a cure by the addition of a modified locking cylinder had not been successful, since the device relied upon absolute oiltightness. Although the steam reverser would be useful on a shunting locomotive, on a locomotive such as this Pacific class where frequent reversing was uncommon and where adjustment of cut-off was more important, it was a troublesome piece of equipment. The replacement was a BR-type screw reverser, with the reversing handle face-on to the driver and cut-off indicator of the drum type. The operation of the gear was transmitted by means of a universally jointed shaft to the screw located on a bracket attached to the outside of the main frames, midway between the left-hand driving and trailing wheels. A short bridle rod connected the reversing screw to the reversing shaft. With multi-cylindered locomotives having independent sets of valve gear it is normally necessary to use an auxiliary reversing shaft to the inside reversing gear. However, it was found possible with the 'Merchant Navy' class to use a single shaft for all the three gears. The radius rods were lifted by an arrangement in which a slide block worked in a slot in the rod itself, with the slide block being attached directly to the reversing shaft arm.

The outside cylinders remained but there was a new inside cylinder fitted with a cast steel liner, with the steam chest, also with a cast-iron liner, moved to the right to be in line with the valve gear and arranged for inside admission. Bulleid's piston rods were forged with the crosshead, and the pistons attached with lock nuts; the pistons had a habit of working loose and breaking through the cylinder covers. The rebuilt engines had pistons riveted on the rods, the latter being cottered onto separate crossheads. In addition, a means of transmitting the actuation from the plane of the valve gear to the steam chest centre line was incorporated. The new rods were provided with United Kingdom-type cast-iron packings, which were also used for the valve spindles of the outside cylinders.

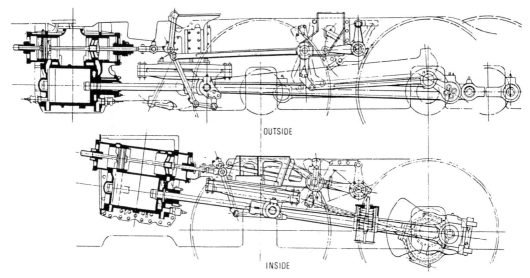

OUTSIDE

INSIDE

Walschaerts valve gear arrangements for the rebuilt engines

The Bulleid valve gear and sump were removed and replaced by three sets of Walschaerts valve gear, with the outside gear being driven by return cranks on the driving crankpins and by arms attached to the crossheads. The outside valve gears with outside admission, similar to those on the Standard class 4 2–6–4 tank engines, transmitted the motion by means of a 9:8 rocker to the valve spindle from the top of the combination lever. Due to the offset between the centre line of the valve gear and the axis of the steam chest, a suspension link carried the weight of the valve gear. A short link connected the suspension link to the valve spindle crosshead. The maximum travel of the piston valves was $6\frac{3}{4}$ in, and the return crank rod was attached to the return crank through an SKF self-aligning roller-bearing. The inside valve gear was driven by an eccentric mounted on the right-hand crank web of the driving axle, and followed the basic idea of the 'Schools' class of locomotives. A spigot and five studs were used for attachment of the eccentric to the drive sprocket of the crank axle, a design feature that was incorporated in the redesign of the crank axle after the Crewkerne accident involving No. 35020 in 1953.

The oval smokebox door was retained, but the lightly fabricated smokebox, of irregular shape, was replaced by a cylindrical-shaped design, resting on a saddle formed by the upper part of the new inside cylinder and the new fabricated stretcher. The saddle stretcher was, in addition, bolted on to the front of the cylinder casting and the frames, giving a further rigidity to the front of the locomotive. The saddle gave access to the front cover of the inside cylinder to allow removal of the piston and rod. The stovepipe chimney was replaced by a new cast-iron type of the same diameter of 2 ft 5 in, similar in design to that fitted to 'Lord Nelson' class No. 30852 *Sir Walter Raleigh* in 1956, and fitted with a petticoat and exhaust ejector ring. The Lemaître multiple-jet blastpipe was retained but the height of the chimney choke was reduced by 7 in and the choke diameter by $1\frac{1}{2}$ in. There was a new superheater header, having three flanges for individual direct steampipes to each cylinder; the right-hand pipe fed the middle cylinder, the inside the right-hand and the left-hand the left-hand cylinder. All the steampipes passed outside the smokebox through stuffing boxes on the smokebox wrapper. With the new superheater header the superheating surface was 612 sq ft, as against a figure of 665 sq ft for the original locomotives. The figure of 822 sq ft often quoted as the original superheating surface area was derived from the outside surface area of the elements. Correspondence between Jarvis and D. Carling, the Superintendent Engineer at Rugby locomotive testing station, in May 1955 stated that the superheater elements had been shortened by 1 ft in an attempt to reduce damage to the spear ends due to burning. This could in addition account for the differences in the superheater surface area, although the new elements were of 9 swg thickness, as against the 10 swg of the originals.

The boiler itself was unaltered, although the air-smoothed casing which previously enveloped the boiler was removed. Insulation was provided by glass fibre mattresses, although asbestos was sometimes used, and normal boiler clothing supported on crinolines provided easier access to the pipework. One of the problems with the original engines was the absence of running plates along the side of the locomotive and with the rebuilding and the use of normal boiler cladding these were incorporated, carried on brackets supported on the main locomotive frame. The original smoke deflector plates were replaced by those of more orthodox shape, with the lower edge mounted on the front of the side running plate. There was a new design for the three-section ashpan; the central section was fitted with two hoppers each with bottom doors, and the two outer sections each fitted with a single hopper and door. The ashpan hopper doors were operated from the ground by means of a common linkage, providing an easier means of ash disposal. The cast-iron rocking grate sections were of the Hulson grate/BR standard type and divided into two groups, which could be moved separately from the footplate. These would allow two types of grate movement – a small movement for fire cleaning while running, and a larger movement for fire dumping when on shed. The front and rear damper doors on each of the three sections of the ashpan were not a feature applied by Bulleid; they were incorporated into the rebuilt design and could be operated by two screw controls from the footplate in two groups, each group consisting of front or rear opening dampers. Provision was made in the design of the damper control linkage to eliminate any problems which might arise due to deformity in the ashpan itself. The thermic syphons were retained despite their usefulness being questioned by the Rugby tests; to remove them would have been an unnecessary expense.

The sanding to the coupled wheels had been modified in a number of ways since the first locomotive had been built and sanding had been provided on the tender for tender-first running. On the rebuilt engines sanding was restored to the leading wheels, with the sandbox being mounted on the footplating to the rear of the smoke deflectors. Sand pipes which had initially led to the trailing coupled wheels were reversed and provided sanding behind the centre driving wheels for tender-first running, the tender sandboxes having been blocked off. The sandboxes for the centre driving wheel were placed between the frames, with the twin box ahead of the wheel providing sand for the forward and a similar box behind the wheel providing sand for the rearward sanding gear. This system, although not ideal, was a great improvement on the original design.

When the engines were rebuilt, the three six-feed Wakefield lubricators supplying the cylinders and the steam chests were moved to a new position on the side running plate; two on the left and one on the right-hand side. A fourth ten-feed lubricator, mounted on the right-hand running plate, was added to supply oil to the slide bars, the coupled axleboxes and the inside valve spindle crosshead guides, replacing the cab-mounted oil boxes. All the lubricators were driven from small levers attached to the expansion links of the outside valve motion. Lubrication to the steam chests of the outside cylinders was atomized, but atomized feeds to the inside valve were introduced into the steampipe, because of the position of the steam chest under the smokebox. The cylinder barrels were lubricated by non-atomized feeds introduced at the top and bottom, and the remaining non-atomized feeds were to the piston rod packing and the valve spindle rear bush. Axlebox guides and the piston rod swab boxes were lubricated with trimming feeds, and the connecting and coupling rods remained oil-lubricated. One of the changes in the rebuilt locomotives was the wide use of grease lubrication, which was used for the valve gear, the rubbing blocks, the spring and hanger pins and the springing to the leading and trailing trucks.

The structure of the cab remained essentially the same, although the cab side panel contour followed the pattern of Nos 35021–35030, with an access hole cut in the lower part of the side panel for one of the boiler mud hole doors. The sliding roof ventilator was replaced by one supported on brackets, which was easier to use and ensured improved ventilation to the cab. With the exception of the reversing screw handle, the driving controls remained similar to the original engines, although the reversing screw position resulted in the driver's seat being placed further back. The Ajax steam-operated firedoor was a feature not universally liked or used by the fireman, and only a small number of crews used the system. Problems arose with its use in that a partly open door would not open further, and there were complaints about the fumes from the system's operating mechanism. The modified locomotives retained the door itself, but the door-opening was now carried out by the lever attached to the right-hand side of the door and not by depression of the foot-operated opening mechanism. With the elimination of the oil bath there was a nasal indication of overheating of the inside big end, with a sign on the cab roof indicating that the aniseed or garlic odour was from an overheating big end, an LNER idea. The centre crank pin contained a metal cylinder which included a glass bulb designed to burst should the temperature rise above 160 °F, containing either garlic or aniseed fluid. When Bulleid heard of this, he suggested in a letter to R.C. Bond, the Chief Mechanical Engineer of BR, that the inside connecting rod should be enclosed in an oil bath!

The tenders had produced a variety of critical comments and in reality they were not strong enough for the buffeting received. Earlier attempts at strengthening the tender tank were not completely successful, and initial modification was carried out in 1952 on the tenders of Nos 35012, 35013 and 35021. Details of the modified tenders can be found on p. 116. The modified tenders were not without fault, since the drainage holes provided in the tender shovelling plate became blocked with small coal, causing corrosion of the platework and increased wear of the intermediate drawbar rubbing block. Jarvis proposed that a chute be designed to remove the coal to a point below the dragbox, out of the way of the drawbar mechanism.

The proposal for the rebuilding of the locomotives was not solely concerned with mechanical reliability, for it also covered the expense of engines awaiting repairs. In 1952 the average number of weekdays the class was out of traffic for running repairs and examinations was sixty-two days per locomotive, compared to the 'Lord Nelson' class with thirty-nine days. Financially, this was £650 or 20 per cent per locomotive greater than the 'Lord Nelson' class. The gross cost of the rebuilding, £5,615 per locomotive, i.e. £168,450 for the class, would be recouped from operating and staff savings and increased availability, which was estimated to be £11,770 per annum simply for coal, water and oil. When the deductions were made for the recovered materials during the rebuilding of £5,500, and the cost of repairs avoided, £16,350, the outlay would be £146,600, or £4,887 per locomotive. These figures were submitted by H.H. Swift, the Chief Mechanical Engineer of the Southern Region, in his initial report on the proposed modifications, dated January 1955. In the financial aspects of the report he showed that the whole cost of rebuilding the class would be recovered by 1962, if rebuilding commenced in 1955.

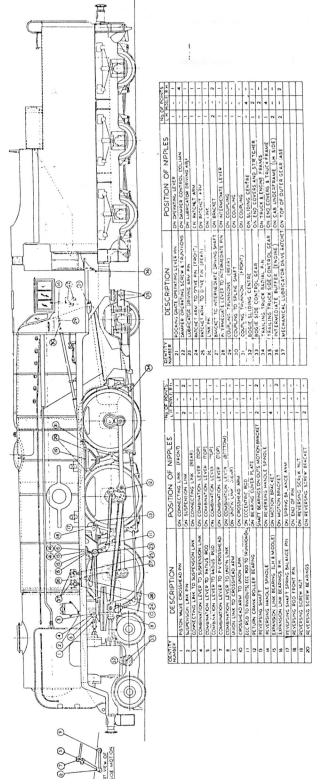

Grease lubrication chart of the rebuilt locomotives

IDENTITY NUMBER	DESCRIPTION	POSITION OF NIPPLES	NO OF POINTS LH MODEL	RH
1	PISTON VALVE CROSSHEAD PIN	ON CONNECTING LINK (FRONT)	1	1
2	SUSPENSION LINK PIN	ON SUSPENSION LINK	2	2
3	CONNECTING LINK TO SUSPENSION LINK	ON CONNECTING LINK (REAR)	1	1
4	COMBINATION LEVER TO SUSPENSION LINK	ON COMBINATION LEVER (TOP)	1	1
5	COMBINATION LEVER TO RADIUS ROD	ON COMBINATION LEVER (TOP)	1	1
6	COMBINATION LEVER TO RADIUS ROD	ON COMBINATION LEVER (TOP)	1	1
7	COMBINATION LEVER TO PV CROSSHEAD	ON COMBINATION LEVER (BOTTOM)	1	1
8	COMBINATION LEVER TO UNION LINK	ON UNION LINK (REAR)	1	1
9	UNION LINK TO CROSSHEAD ARM	ON CROSSHEAD ARM	1	1
10	CROSSHEAD ARM TO UNION LINK	ON UNION LINK	1	1
11	ECC ROD TO PIN/OUT'S ECC ROD TO TRUNNION	ON ECCENTRIC ROD	2	2
12	RETURN CRANK ROLLER BEARING	ON BEARING COVER PLATE	1	1
13	RETURN CRANK SHAFT	SHAFT BEARINGS ON OUT'S MOTION BRACKET	2	2
14	REVERSING HANDLE SPINDLE	ON REVERSING HANDLE SPINDLE	1	1
15	EXPANSION LINK BEARING (LH & MIDDLE)	ON MOTION BRACKET	4	4
16	EXPANSION LINK BEARINGS RH	ON MOTION BRACKET	1	2
17	REVERSING SHAFT SPRING BALANCE PIN	ON SPRING BALANCE ARM	1	1
18	REVERSING ROD FRONT PIN	ON END OF PIN	1	1
19	REVERSING SCREW NUT	ON REVERSING SCREW NUT	2	2
20	REVERSING SCREW BEARINGS	ON REVERSING SCREW BRACKET	1	1

IDENTITY NUMBER	DESCRIPTION	POSITION OF NIPPLES	NO OF POINTS LH MODEL	RH
21	ROCKING GRATE OPERATING LEVER PIN	ON OPERATING LEVER	-	4
22	DAMPER OPERATING SCREW & TRUNNIONS	ON DAMPER CONTROL COLUMN	-	-
23	LUBRICATOR DRIVING ARM PIN	ON LUBRICATOR DRIVING ARM	1	1
24	RATCHET ARM TO D'VE PIN (FRONT)	ON RATCHET ARM	-	-
25	RATCHET ARM TO D'VE PIN (REAR)	ON RATCHET ARM	-	-
26	LINK PIN	ON LINK	-	2
27	BRACKET TO INTERMEDIATE DRIVING SHAFT	ON BRACKET	2	-
28	INTERMEDIATE LEVER TO INTERMEDIATE PIN	ON INTERMEDIATE LEVER	-	-
29	COUPLING TRUNNIONS (REAR)	ON COUPLING	-	-
30	COUPLING TO SPLINE SHAFT	ON COUPLING	-	-
31	COUPLING TRUNNION (FRONT)	ON COUPLING	-	-
32	BOGIE SLIDING CENTRE	ON SLIDING CENTRE	4	4
33	BOGIE SIDE CONTROL GEAR	ON END COVERS AND STRETCHER	2	2
34	TRAILING TRUCK SIDE RADIAL PIN	ON TRUCK & ENGINE FRAMES	1	1
35	TRAILING TRUCK SIDE CONTROL GEAR	ON TRUCK & COVERS & TRUCKFRAME	4	4
36	INTERMEDIATE BUFFER (ENGINE)	ON CAB UNDERFRAME (LH SIDE)	2	2
37	MECHANICAL LUBRICATOR DRIVE RATCHET	ON TOP OF OUTER GEAR CASE	2	2

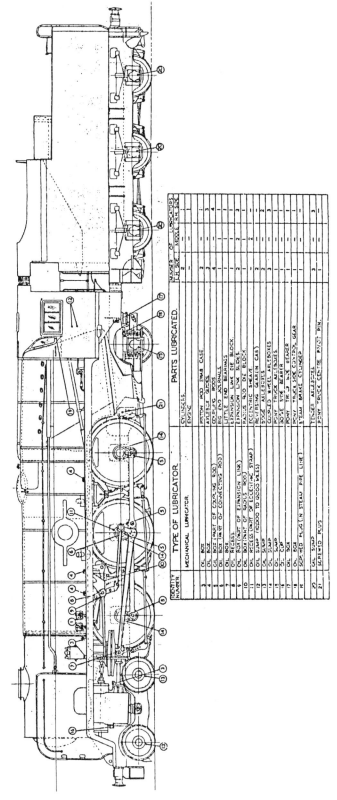

Oil lubrication chart of the rebuilt locomotives

IDENTITY NUMBER	TYPE OF LUBRICATOR.	PARTS LUBRICATED.	NUMBER OF LUBRICATORS. L.H. SIDE	MIDDLE	R.H. SIDE
	MECHANICAL LUBRICATOR.	CYLINDERS	2	1	1
		ENGINE		1	
3	OIL BOX	PISTON ROD SWAB CASE	2		1
4	OIL BOX	AXLEBOX GLASS	2		3
5	OIL BOX (PART OF COUPLING ROD)	COUPLING RODS	3	1	4
6	OIL BOX (PART OF CONNECTING ROD)	BIG END JOURNALS	1		1
7	OIL BOX	LITTLE END BEARINGS	1	1	1
8	OIL RECESS	EXPANSION LINK DIE BLOCK	2		2
9	OIL BOX (PART OF EXPANSION LINK)	EXPANSION LINK SLIDES	2	2	2
10	OIL BOX (PART OF RADIUS ROD)	RADIUS ROD DIE BLOCK			
11	OIL RECESS (PART OF ECCENTRIC STRAP)	ECCENTRIC STRAP	2	2	2
12	OIL SUMP (10,000 TO 15,000 MILES)	REVERSING GEARBIN CASE	1		1
13	OIL SUMP	BOGIE AXLEBOXES	2		2
14	OIL SUMP	COUPLED WHEEL AXLEBOXES	3		3
15	OIL CUP	PONY TRUCK AXLEBOXES	1		1
17	OIL BOX	BOGIE SIDE BEARER	1		1
18	OIL BOX	PONY TRUCK SIDE BEARER	1		1
	SCREWED PLUG (IN STEAM PIPE LINE)	PONY TRUCK SIDE CONTROL GEAR			
		STEAM BRAKE CYLINDER		1	
20	OIL SUMP	TENDER AXLEBOXES	3		3
21	SCREWED PLUG	PONY TRUCK CENTRE PIVOT PIN.	1		1

37

To enable the first modified locomotives to be completed on schedule by late 1955, there was agreement that the assistance of the other regions in British Railways should be sought. Crewe provided the new inside cylinder and some of the valve gear and Swindon supplied the return cranks, expansion links, piston rods and valve spindles.

LEADING DIMENSIONS OF 'MERCHANT NAVY' ENGINES

		First 10 after 1945	Rebuilt 1955–9
Cylinder bore and stroke (three)	in	18 × 24	18 × 24
Cylinder slope:			
inside		1 in 7.75	1 in 7.75
outside		1 in 40	1 in 40
Coupled wheel diameter	in	74	74
Boiler pressure	lb/sq in	280	250
Maximum axle load	ton	21.0	22.0
Adhesion weight	ton	63.0	65.0
Locomotive weight in working order	ton	94.2	97.9
Locomotive weight empty	ton	84.45	88.4
Coupled wheelbase	ft in	15 0	15 0
Locomotive wheelbase	ft in	36 9	36 9
Engine and tender wheelbase	ft in	59 6*	61 6†
Length over buffers	ft in	69 7¾*	71 7¾†
Boiler pitch	ft in	9 5¼	9 5¼
Maximum height	ft in	12 11	12 11
Boiler: maximum diameter	in	69.75; 75.5	69.75; 75.5
Length between tubeplates	ft in	17 0	17 0
No. and outside diameter of tubes	in	124 @ 2¼	124 @ 2¼
No. and outside diameter of flues	in	40 @ 5¼	40 @ 5¼
Evap heating surface:			
tubes	sq ft	1,242	1,242
flues	sq ft	934	934
firebox	sq ft	275	275
total	sq ft	2,451	2,451
Grate area	sq ft	48.5	48.5
No. and outside diameter of elements	in	40 @ 1½	40 @ 1½
Superheating surface	sq ft	665‡	612
Free gas area through boiler	sq ft	6.4	6.4
Tender:			
water capacity	Imp gall	5,100	6,000
coal capacity	ton	5	5
tare weight	ton	20.5	21.5
full weight	ton	48.5	53.5
Engine and tender full weight	ton	142.7	151.4
Tractive effort at 85 per cent boiler pressure	lb	37,515	33,495

* With 5,100 gallon tender
† With 6,000 gallon tender
‡ Usual figure given, 822 sq ft, is surface area on outside of elements

Order No. HO 7998 provided for the rebuilding of fifteen locomotives, with the necessary material being assembled at Eastleigh. On 16 November 1955, No. 35018 *British India Line* was accepted in the works and a start was made on rebuilding. The engine left the erecting shop on 9 February 1956 for official photographs, complete except for the handrails on the smoke deflectors. A trial run to Botley was undertaken the following day and the running-in was continued to Brockenhurst and Basingstoke, successfully apart from the occasional overheating of bearings and adjustment to piston valve clearances. The official inspection was made by Sir Brian Robertson, Chairman of the British Transport Commission, at Waterloo on 13 February 1956, and rostered duties commenced on 17 February. The remaining days of the month were not without drama, for there were a number of minor mechanical failures which resulted in a return to Eastleigh Works for attention before the engine was rostered for regular duties, being allocated to Nine Elms. The rebuilding produced a division among the footplate crews, with the rebuilt locomotives being preferred by some and the original locomotives by others, although the testimonial by the Salisbury, Nine Elms and Exmouth Junction drivers to Bulleid in 1966 showed that most were in favour of the original engines. The weight in working order of the rebuilt engines varied between 96 tons 1 cwt and 97 tons 16 cwt, less than the original weight of No. 21C1, which weighed 99 tons 12 cwt. With the attempts at weight reduction for the other members of the class when built, producing a figure of approximately 94 tons in working order, the rebuilt series were heavier. The financial savings produced by the rebuilding programme were £550 per locomotive per year for works repairs, with coal and water economies of nearly 10 per cent over the original locomotives, and savings in the oil consumption of 100 per cent for the sump oil and further savings for superheater oil.

No. 35018 differed from the other rebuilds in having a high swan neck to the front sand fillers. In practice the swan neck proved difficult to use, and was not perpetuated in the other members of the class. The two left-hand lubricators were mounted further back on the running plate when the other members of the class were rebuilt. Rebuilding of the Pacifics went ahead steadily, the programme being undertaken on two orders for the works: order No. HO 7998 covering the initial fifteen locomotives was completed by May 1957; order No. HO 9199 the remaining fifteen, completed with the last two locomotives to be rebuilt, No. 35006 *Peninsular & Oriental S.N. Co.* and No. 35028 *Clan Line* emerging from Eastleigh Works in October 1959. The pioneer locomotive, No. 35001 *Channel Packet*, rebuilt in August 1959, had the longest life in the original condition of $18\frac{1}{2}$ years, during which time it ran 807,318 miles.

The second member of the class to be rebuilt in April 1956, No. 35020 *Bibby Line*, was used to undertake a series of trials to compare the performance of the rebuilt locomotives with the original engines. For the testing of No. 35020 the modified 6,000 gallon tender was exchanged for one of the original 6,000 gallon type with high side raves, which would simplify the run of the cables to the dynamometer car. In contrast to the LMS tenders used during the Interchange Trials of 1948 this tender was repainted with the panelling and emblem lowered, and a broad band of black added to the top of the side raves. The trials, with the Western Region dynamometer car, were under the direction of S.O. Ell of the Swindon testing section, and consisted of a series of controlled road test runs over the West of England main line in both directions between Salisbury and Exeter. The tests were both of an analytical nature, when the rate of working would be controlled by means of a gauge in the blastpipe to give a constant rate of steaming, and tests on revenue-earning trains running in normal service. For the normal service trains there would be no control of the engine working by the dynamometer car staff. The highest rate of working on the controlled road workings was 32,000 lb of steam per hour,

No. 35020 *Bibby Line* on test with the WR dynamometer car between Salisbury and Exeter in June 1956
Author's collection

No. 35025 *Brocklebank Line* on the locomotive test plant at Swindon, 12 August 1957
Author's collection

with a coal usage rate of 4,780 lb per hour, with the limitation imposed by the capacity of the tender to provide for minimum test and warming up periods. After the controlled road trials there were a series of service train workings, including the 'Atlantic Coast Express' trains between Waterloo and Exeter, with loadings varying between 390 and 500 tons. Throughout, the locomotive steamed freely, with the coal consumption very little different from that of the original members of the class involved in the 1948 Interchange Trials. It has to be conceded that the calorific value of the fuel in 1948 was higher. Further tests were made with No. 35025 *Brocklebank Line* at Swindon in 1957 on the stationary testing plant, to investigate the knock which had developed after running approximately 35,000 miles. It was concluded that revised settings were needed for the inside and outside valve heads, since the pressures developed at the front and the back of the cylinders differed by up to 100 lb sq in. The valve settings were made when the engine was cold and it was found that the valves of the middle cylinder required setting back by $\frac{1}{16}$ in, and those of the outside cylinder needed to be set forward by $\frac{1}{16}$ in. The valve setting was a critical factor in the efficient performance of the rebuilt engines, and the valve events were checked at intermediate repair.

It is clear that the Southern Region now possessed a class of locomotive of performance and reliability equal to any other in the country, with engine crews who delighted in demonstrating the ability of their machines. Bulleid may well have been a disappointment to some of the Southern locomotive officers, as he was by nature a loner who did not readily invite the opinion of others. However, as an innovative Chief Mechanical Engineer with an almost compulsive obsession to try out new ideas, regardless of production requirements, he was encouraged by the Chairman of the Southern, Sir Robert Holland-Martin, to show that this railway needed the Pacifics in the first place. The discussions, as to the merits of the original engines in comparison with the rebuilds, will be for ever a topic for discussion among railway enthusiasts.

LOCOMOTIVE HISTORIES

Built at Eastleigh works, No. 21C1 was the first locomotive of order No. 1068, and was fitted with a 5,000 gallon water capacity tender, No. 3111, constructed at Ashford Works, and boiler No. 1090, one of the ten fabricated by the North British Locomotive Works at Glasgow for the first series. The first main-line outings were a test run on 18 February 1941 to Winchester, and to Bournemouth on 22 February, hauling ten coaches. The engine was named *Channel Packet* in the works yard by the Minister of Transport, Rt Hon J.T.C. Moore-Brabazon, on 10 March 1941, after which a three-coach special train, including a restaurant car and directors' saloon, was worked as far as Alresford before returning to Eastleigh. The locomotive was finished in matt malachite green livery with three horizontal yellow bands. Cast number plates were affixed to the cab sides and sloping front above the buffer beam, although the latter plate was refixed on the vertical face immediately below its initial position soon after construction.

Cast plates carrying the word 'Southern' were fixed to the tender sides in a horizontal form, and on the smokebox door in the shape of an inverted horseshoe. Tender No. 3112 was fitted in May 1942, to allow repairs to the tank welding and the axleboxes of the original tender, which was refitted later that month. The engine underwent extensive trials from Eastleigh Works before being placed in traffic at Salisbury shed on 5 June 1941, from where it was employed for some months on freight work to Eastleigh and Southampton. It was transferred in the autumn of 1942 to Exmouth Junction shed. The inverted horseshoe plate was replaced by the standard circular type at the beginning of 1942, and the smokebox casing amended with a hood in October 1943. Although repainted black in January 1944, the engine re-emerged from Eastleigh Works in December 1945 in full malachite green livery, still retaining cab and tender side plates.

After being fitted with new inside and outside cylinders, No. 21C1 was allocated to the Eastern section in April 1946, working from Stewarts Lane shed, and underwent tests in which it was reputed to have attained 98 mph near Paddock Wood. No. 21C1 hauled a special publicity working of the 'Golden Arrow' on 13 April, and then headed that train on the re-inauguration trips of 15 April and for the remainder of that and the following week, before returning to Exmouth Junction, still retaining the side arrows. Boiler No. 1102 was fitted in August 1947.

The engine was renumbered as No. 35001 with a further boiler change to No. 1107, and repainted in blue livery in October 1949, losing smokebox door, cab and tender side plates in the process. The inaugural train was hauled to the new Ocean Terminal at Southampton docks on 31 July 1950. Another boiler change to No. 1115 occurred in

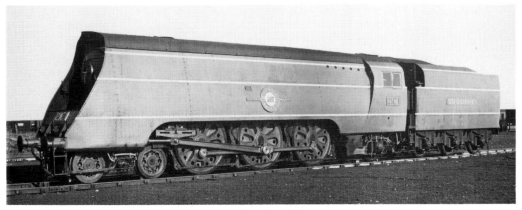

No. 21C1 *Channel Packet* stands at Eastleigh in original condition, in March 1941, painted in matt malachite green with three yellow lines. The front number plate is on the sloping front portion of the sheeting below the smokebox, and a single footblock is positioned on the left-hand buffer casing, with a footstep below. The widow's peak can be seen at the front of the top casing, with the circular disc used to cover the chimney just visible. The horseshoe-shaped ownership plate is attached to the smokebox door, the cast number plate to the cab side and the 'Southern' plate to the tender side. The coupling rods were secured by a hexagonal-pentagonal cap, which can be seen on the middle driving wheel. Sanding is to the front of the middle driving wheel only

G. Shelley

In rebuilt condition, No. 35001 *Channel Packet* is photographed at Eastleigh in 1963, with the headcode of a relief Bournemouth to Bradford train. The tender is a rebodied first series tender, now of 5,250 gallon capacity, with the final version of the BR emblem displayed on the sides. The pockets for the valve guides protrude into the bottom part of the smoke deflectors in the form of a step, and the AWS battery box is mounted between the front of the frames below the smokebox. Balance weights are fitted to the driving wheels, and a layer of oily grime is accumulating on the brake rigging and the front bogie frames. The clack valves, whistle, snifting valves and sand fillers are now more readily visible and accessible than in the previous photograph

F.R. Sherlock

December 1950, when a modified cab was fitted. The locomotive was repainted in BR green in May 1952. The driving axle was replaced in June 1953, and in March 1955 the boiler pressure was reduced to 250 lb sq in. The tender was modified and the safety valves resited in June 1956, and the locomotive transferred to Stewarts Lane in January 1957 where, appropriately, it was employed principally on boat trains to the Channel ports.

In June 1959 No. 35001 was re-allocated to Nine Elms, shortly before being rebuilt at Eastleigh Works in August 1959, having covered 807,318 miles, when AWS gear was fitted. In December 1960 a speedometer was fitted, the tender rebodied in February 1963 with an increased water capacity of 5,250 gallons and the engine finally transferred to Bournemouth in September 1964. No. 35001 was withdrawn in November 1964, having run 1,095,884 miles, and sold to Birds (Swansea) Ltd, Morriston, Glamorgan, with acquired tender No. 3349. Before steps to preserve the locomotive could be firmly made, engine and tender were scrapped in 1965.

No. 21C2

Built as the second locomotive of order No. 1068 at Eastleigh Works, and fitted with boiler No. 1091 and tender No. 3112, No. 21C2 appeared in early June 1941 in a condition similar to No. 21C1. However, the livery lacked the horizontal bands, and the narrow slit in front of the chimney had given way to a large unobstructed area. A trial train was worked to Bournemouth on 7 June 1941 and freight duties carried out on the Salisbury – Eastleigh route, before No. 21C2 was officially placed in traffic on 16 June 1941, at Salisbury shed. The yellow horizontal bands were painted on before 4 July 1941, when the official naming of the locomotive as *Union Castle* took place on platform 7 at Victoria station, with the ceremony performed by Mr Robinson F. Gibb, director of the shipping line. After the ceremony the engine worked a four-coach special train as far as Earlswood. The inverted horseshoe smokebox plate was replaced by the standard circular type in February 1942. In the following autumn the engine was transferred to Exmouth Junction shed, and the locomotive was repainted black in May 1944, when the hooded smokebox deflector was fitted.

New inside and outside cylinders were fitted in July 1945, and in mid-August 1945, test trains, consisting of ten Pullman and two corridor vehicles, were hauled on an 85 minute schedule between Victoria and Dover Marine. Similarly, on 17 October 1945, a sixteen-coach train was hauled from Waterloo to Bournemouth Central and back, running non-stop each way, and for these tests No. 21C2 was fitted with a Flaman speed recorder. In July 1946, the engine was repainted in malachite green, and in November 1947 fitted with boiler No. 1096.

The cast plates on cab, smokebox door and tender, were removed when the engine was renumbered as No. 35002, fitted with boiler No. 1090 and repainted in blue livery in January 1950, only to lose this colour in June 1951 when BR green livery was applied. For a short time in March 1952 the engine ran with tender No. 3115, still painted blue and earlier used for the mechanical stoker experiments, but later the same month it reverted

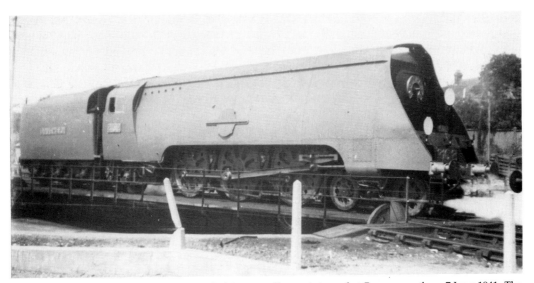

No. 21C2 *Union Castle*, in unlined matt malachite green livery, is turned at Bournemouth on 7 June 1941. The cut-out above the smokebox door is now larger, and the front number plate is mounted vertically above the front buffer beam, with the repositioned route lamps and brackets above. Front steps and buffer footblocks are now provided to both sides. The nameplate is covered up, and the number and 'Southern' name appear as on No. 21C1. The rain gutter is visible above the cab window, and inside the curved raves on the tender is the area used for storage of fire irons. Sanding is to the middle driving wheel. The holes in the lower cab side and in the casing behind the rear driving wheel were to provide access for boiler washing out

The late G.O.P. Pearce

No. 35002 *Union Castle*, shedded at Bournemouth, is photographed at Weymouth on 6 July 1962. A speedometer is fitted to the rear coupled wheel. The steam manifold control valve is visible adjacent to the steam dome, and the cut-out on the cab side provides access to the boiler for wash purposes. The coupling rods are of rectangular cross-section, as fitted to the rebuilt locomotives. Below the tender tank is the vacuum brake pipe

C.L. Caddy

to its original tender No. 3112. The cab was modified in January 1954, and the engine transferred to Bournemouth in May 1954, but returned to Exmouth Junction a month later. Boiler No. 1121, with pressure reduced to 250 lb sq in, was fitted in September 1954 and the safety valves resited in August 1955.

The engine was rebuilt in May 1958, having covered 776,797 miles, the tender modified and boiler No. 1114 fitted. A speedometer was fitted at Eastleigh Works in April 1960, when the tender was rebodied with a water capacity of 5,250 gallons. Re-allocated to Nine Elms (November 1960), to Bournemouth (January 1961) and back to Nine Elms (January 1964), No. 35002 was withdrawn in February 1964, after a total of 1,101,914 miles, and disposed of to Slag Reduction Company Ltd, Holmes Farm, Rotherham, Yorkshire where it was scrapped in December 1964.

MERCHANT NAVY CLASS

No. 21C3

Constructed under order No. 1068 at Eastleigh Works with boiler No. 1092 and tender No. 3113. After being photographed in grey livery, No. 21C3 worked from Salisbury in mid-September 1941 in matt finish malachite green livery with yellow bands. Various alterations to the design had been made to reduce weight and these included the omission of the cab and tender side plates, although these had already been cast, as well as the front number plate. The cab end of the tender had metal sliding panels to reduce the glare from the firebox, and a small window was fitted high above the main windows on the fireman's side of the cab to illuminate the Detroit lubricator. The inverted horseshoe smokebox plate appeared as a complete circle however – an increase in weight! – to mollify superstitious enginemen who considered the original arrangement ill-chosen. No. 21C3 was named *Royal Mail* by Lord Essendon, chairman of Royal Mail Lines, at Waterloo station on 24 October 1941 in full malachite green livery.

On 9 November 1941, a sixteen-coach special train was hauled from Waterloo to Salisbury, one of a number of trips by the initial members of the class to supply Bulleid with data on coal and water consumption and haulage capacity. No. 21C3 started the regular passenger working for the class early in January 1942 on the 9.00 a.m. ex-Waterloo between Salisbury and Exeter Central, and the 2.30 p.m. return as far as Salisbury. A transfer to Exmouth Junction shed occurred in the autumn of 1942, and No. 21C3 was repainted in black livery in May 1943. In February 1944 tender No. 3117 was acquired, and a hood over the smokebox fitted in September 1944. A new left-hand cylinder was fitted in October 1945, when the engine was repainted in malachite green. Boiler No. 1095 was fitted in May 1947.

No. 21C3 was renumbered as No. 35003 in May 1948, and given blue livery when the cab was modified in May 1950. In August 1953 it was repainted in BR green livery, and in March 1955 fitted with boiler No. 1094, with pressure reduced to 250 lb sq in and resited safety valves. No. 35003 was rebuilt in August 1959, having run 859,784 miles, and tender No. 3117 rebodied and water capacity increased to 5,250 gallons. AWS gear was fitted at rebuilding and a speedometer added in September 1961. The engine passed into the Western Region stock on 1 January 1963. A spark arrester was fitted in May 1963 and

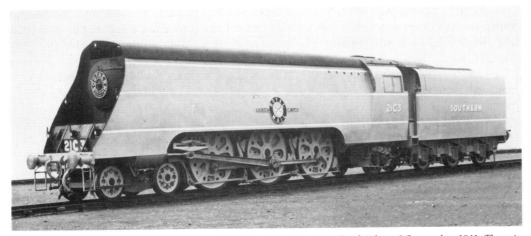

No. 21C3 *Royal Mail* in photographic grey with white side stripes is at Eastleigh on 9 September 1941. There is no reverse curve to the base of the cylinder cladding, and the smokebox door roundel is now a full circle with place and date of building added. The numbers are painted, and the 'C' in the numbers is in sunshine lettering, being depicted as a letter and not as a number. The rear truck is covered with canvas or rexine to prevent the ingress of ash from the ashpans on to the bearing surfaces. Visible on the tender are the front water filler, and the sliding cover to reduce the glare from the firebox in wartime conditions

B.I. Fletcher collection

The dirt and grime of the engines in the 1960s is shown in this photograph of No. 35003 *Royal Mail* at Southampton Central on the evening of 31 December 1965, heading a London-bound train. This engine remained in service until the end of steam in July 1967. The timed exposure shows up the glow from the firebox and the impressive headlight effect from the front electrically illuminated route lamps. Also visible is the bent front buffer-mounted step – reputedly named the 'Salisbury shunt'. The Salisbury turntable was initially 65 ft long – a little too short for the 'Merchant Navy' class – and the front steps of the engine fouled protruding brickwork, giving them the characteristic backward bend

D. Mackinnon

in June 1964 No. 35003 returned to Southern Region stock, and was allocated to Nine Elms. Further transfers took place to Bournemouth (September 1964), Weymouth (October 1966) and finally Nine Elms (March 1967). The engine was withdrawn at the cessation of steam traction on the Southern Region in July 1967 after a total mileage of 1,131,793, disposed of as scrap to John Cashmore Ltd, Newport, Monmouthshire and cut up in December of the same year.

No. 21C4

Built in October 1941 as part of order No. 1068 at Eastleigh Works and fitted with boiler No. 1093 and tender No. 3114, No. 21C4 was taken into stock in December 1941, finished in full malachite green livery and allocated to Salisbury. On 30 November 1942 the engine was shot at by a low-flying German aircraft at Crannaford, west of Whimple, with the 10.10 a.m. Plymouth–Brighton passenger train. No. 21C4 was named *Cunard White Star* at Charing Cross station on New Year's Day 1942 by Sir Percy E. Bates,

No. 35004 *Cunard White Star* approaches Salisbury on a down West of England express with the tender of a 'West Country' class Pacific visible on the left. On No. 35004 the horizontal strengthening rib is visible, a feature of those locomotives fitted with limpet board for the casing. The casing ahead of the cylinders has now been removed, and there are footholes in the front sloping panel above the buffer beam. This locomotive was one of those fitted with a catch on the fireman's side of the smokebox door. The steam manifold cover is of the sliding type, and is visible above the nameplate on the top of the air-smoothed casing. The Salisbury East signal-box on the right was built by the LSWR in 1902, although the original roof was replaced by a flat roof in 1928 when the electro-pneumatic signalling equipment was installed. The box served this section of the station and the freight yard opposite, which frequently included army vehicles among the goods traffic

Author's collection

No. 35004 *Cunard White Star* stands at her home shed of Salisbury, 72B, on 1 October 1961. The engine was not fitted with AWS at this date, and had normal valve spindle guides. The boiler water supply to the clack valves mounted on the top of the boiler is visible on the rebuilt locomotives, and is fed from the twin pipes from the injectors sited below the cab

G.W. Morrison

chairman of Cunard White Star. The engine was transferred to Exmouth Junction shed in the autumn of 1942, repainted black in July 1943, and smokebox hood and tender No. 3113 were acquired in January 1944. A new left-hand cylinder was fitted in February 1945, and the engine repainted in malachite green livery in April 1946, when boiler No. 1093 was exchanged for No. 1110. A special Pullman train was hauled from Waterloo to Southampton docks for the first ordinary passenger sailing of RMS *Queen Elizabeth* on 16 October 1946.

In April 1948 the engine was renumbered as No. 35004, re-allocated to Salisbury shed in November 1948, and back to Exmouth Junction in February 1950. A modified cab and boiler No. 1123 were fitted in October 1950 and the engine repainted in blue livery at the same time. On 21 November 1951, No. 35004 hauled a special boat train for the Netherlands Royal Family from Dover Marine to Victoria. The engine was repainted in BR green livery in February 1953 and, in June 1954, boiler pressure was reduced to 250 lb sq in. In October 1955, boiler No. 1095, with resited safety valves, was fitted, and the engine transferred to Salisbury in April 1957.

In July 1958, the engine was rebuilt and the tender modified after a total of 750,886 miles. A speedometer was fitted in January 1960, and spark arrester acquired in April 1963. No. 35004 was transferred to Bournemouth in September 1964, and was withdrawn from service from there in October 1965, attached to tender No. 3121, with a total mileage of 1,131,417. The engine was cut up at Eastleigh shed in February 1966 by Cohen's.

No. 21C5

No. 21C5 was constructed as the fifth engine of order No. 1068 at Eastleigh Works, fitted with boiler No. 1094 and tender No. 3115, and taken into stock in December 1941, although not appearing in traffic until 13 January 1942. Finished in full malachite green livery and allocated to Salisbury shed, No. 21C5 was repainted in March 1942 in black livery especially for its naming ceremony at Victoria station on 27 March, when it was named *Canadian Pacific* by Mr F.W. Mottley, the acting European manager. Transfer to Exmouth Junction shed occurred in the autumn of 1942 and on 4 May 1943, No. 21C5 headed the first regular sixteen-coach train out of Exeter Central, the 10.35 a.m. to Salisbury and Waterloo. The smokebox hood was fitted in March 1944 and the engine returned to malachite green livery in January 1946, when the left-hand cylinder was replaced.

In January 1948, boiler No. 1091 was fitted, and the *s* prefix added to the number in March 1948, the only member of the class to run with this prefix. Renumbered as No. 35005 the next month, and at the same time a Berkley mechanical stoker and Flaman speed recorder were fitted. A transfer to Nine Elms took place in November 1948, and the engine took part in assessment trials with the mechanical stoker, including through trips from Waterloo to Exeter. Following cab modification in February 1950, the engine

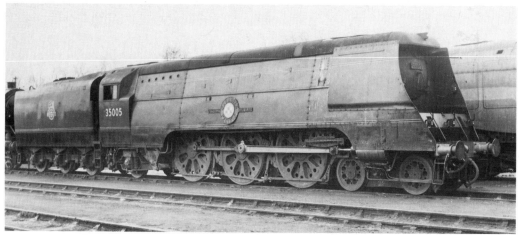

No. 35005 *Canadian Pacific* is ex-works at Eastleigh in blue livery on 18 November 1950 after a six-week repair following the parting of the chain drive on a Waterloo–Bournemouth working the previous September. The marks on the side casing were the attachment points for the recording equipment used for the Rugby tests with the Berkley mechanical stoker. The slide bars were covered to prevent ingress of sand from the sand fillers. The upward-opening hatch for the whistle was sited on the top of the casing, above the nameplate. On the tender, the curvature at the rear of the coal bunker was to attach the cover enclosing the coal space used during the mechanical stoker experiments, and reduce the amount of dust. The tender emblem is the original BR version. To the right of the engine is No. 36001, which had been undergoing tests from Eastleigh, and was on this date only two days away from being cancelled and ultimately scrapped on the orders of R.A. Riddles in his memorandum to the Railway Executive of 20 November 1950

L. Elsey

Rebuilt No. 35005 *Canadian Pacific* waits at Waterloo, with the 'Bournemouth Belle' headboard and train working number 208 en route to Nine Elms. The locomotive looks remarkably clean, and the lining is visible on both the engine and tender. The tender was rebodied in May 1959, when the engine was rebuilt, and was fitted with a 5,250 gallon capacity tank. Sanding was to the front and middle driving wheels, with the sanding for tender-first running provided by the sand pipe to the rear of the middle coupled wheel

Author's collection

was repainted in blue livery and sent to Rugby locomotive testing station late in the same month, returning in mid-March to Nine Elms. Further trials were worked from London to Salisbury with the LMR mobile testing unit. In September 1950 the chain drive parted while travelling on a Waterloo–Bournemouth working, completely destroying the oil bath and the enclosed motion. A new right-hand cylinder and rods and LMR self-cleaning smokebox equipment were fitted while the engine was undergoing repairs at Eastleigh in November. The Berkley stoker was finally removed during April 1951 and the locomotive transferred back to Exmouth Junction shed.

In February 1954, boiler No. 1093 with resited safety valves was fitted and No. 35005 was painted in BR green livery. Boiler pressure was reduced to 250 lb sq in three months later, when a new inside cylinder was fitted. The right-hand cylinder was replaced in September 1956, after cracks had been found.

In May 1959, having covered 632,322 miles, No. 35005 was rebuilt and the tender rebodied, with the water capacity increased to 5,250 gallons. In November 1959 the engine was re-allocated to Bournemouth, a speedometer fitted in November 1960 and spark arrester in January 1964. Transfer to Weymouth occurred in September 1964, and the engine and tender No. 3348 were withdrawn from service after 976,806 miles in October 1965, to be disposed of to Woodham Bros, Barry. The engine was rescued from the scrap-holding yard by Steamtown, Carnforth, where it arrived on 4 April 1973, attached to tender No. 3119. Seventeen years later its restoration is still not complete.

MERCHANT NAVY CLASS
No. 21C6

No. 21C6 was built at Eastleigh Works under order No. 1068, fitted with boiler No. 1095 and tender No. 3116, and taken into stock in December 1941 in malachite green livery, although not placed in traffic until 14 January 1942, when it was allocated to Salisbury shed. Repainted black in May 1942 and named *Peninsular & Oriental S.N. Co.* at Ashford Works on 4 June 1942, by Sir W. Currie, chairman of the line. No. 21C6 was one of the locomotives involved in smoke clearance experiments in the autumn of 1942. A hood over the smokebox was fitted in April 1944, a new left-hand cylinder in February 1946, and in September 1946, when boiler No. 1093 was fitted, the engine regained malachite green livery.

In December 1948 the engine was renumbered as No. 35006, still lettered 'Southern', when a boiler change to No. 1111 also occurred. Blue livery and a modified cab were fitted in March 1951. The engine was painted in BR green livery in September 1953 when boiler No. 1100, with the pressure set to 250 lb sq in, was acquired. A further boiler change occurred in July 1955, when boiler No. 1119 was fitted with resited safety valves.

No. 35006, having run 962,757 miles, was rebuilt and the tender modified in October 1959, and boiler No. 1096 and AWS gear fitted. A speedometer was acquired in January 1961, and the locomotive withdrawn in August 1964, after a total mileage of 1,134,319. This engine was the sole member of its class to remain at one shed, in this case Salisbury, throughout its career, and in addition it was attached to the same tender throughout. Disposed of to Woodham Bros, Barry, and purchased during 1982 for £7,245 by 35006 P & O Loco Society (later 35006 Association), arriving at Toddington on the Gloucestershire–Warwickshire Railway in mid-March 1983 for a very extensive restoration, including the construction of a new tender.

No. 21C6 *Peninsular and Oriental S.N. Co.* in malachite green and with the 'Southern' smokebox roundel in place, climbs the 1 in 90 gradient of Honiton bank with a Waterloo-bound train in the summer of 1948, a few months before the locomotive had a third boiler change. This engine was one of those involved in the smoke clearance trials in the autumn of 1942, and is now fitted with smoke deflectors and a hood over the smokebox. The original cab is still fitted

Author's collection

Immediately to the east of Honiton is the 1 in 80 gradient of Honiton bank flanked by telegraph poles and marking the seven miles of ascent to the 1,345 yd long Honiton tunnel. No. 35006 *Peninsular & Oriental S.N. Co.* hauls an Exeter-bound train up the gradient in the summer of 1960. With scenes of hard work by the locomotive, this section of the line was a popular place for photography. Some way up the bank was the diminutive Honiton incline signal-box. The locomotive, rebuilt in 1959, remained at Salisbury all its working life, and also ran with the same tender throughout. It is now being restored at Toddington

A.C. Cawston

No. 21C7 was built at Eastleigh Works as part of order No. 1068 early in 1942, fitted with boiler No. 1096 and tender No. 3117. Finished in unlined malachite green livery, but not placed in traffic until June 1942, when it went to Salisbury shed in black livery. No. 21C7 was named *Aberdeen Commonwealth* on 30 July 1942 at Victoria station by Lord Essendon, chairman of the line, in company with No. 21C9. A new right-hand cylinder was fitted in July 1943, tender No. 3114 in May 1944 and a hood over the smokebox in August 1944. The engine worked over the Eastern section during October 1944 – on the 8.35 a.m. Victoria–Ramsgate on the 11th and between Victoria and Dover via Ashford two days later – the first appearance of the class in Kent other than for naming ceremonies. A new left-hand cylinder was fitted in August 1945 and the engine repainted in malachite green livery in July 1947, when the inside cylinder was replaced and boiler No. 1108 fitted.

The engine was renumbered as No. 35007 in December 1948 and in February 1949 the fractured inside cylinder was replaced. In March 1950 a modified cab and boiler No. 1105 were fitted, and the engine repainted in blue livery. No. 35007 was reliveried in BR green in December 1952, and in June 1955 fitted with boiler No. 1118, with resited safety valves and pressure reduced to 250 lb sq in. In September 1956 tender No. 3114 was modified.

No. 21C7 *Aberdeen Commonwealth*. In spite of the initial design being for the Eastern section boat trains, it wasn't until 1944 that the class first appeared here, other than for naming ceremonies. This rare photograph shows one of the first workings of the class, with the engine being prepared at Dover on 30 October 1944. On the tender, a 5,000 gallon type, the crew are at work in the coal space. The engine is in wartime black livery, and fitted with a hood over the smokebox and smoke deflectors, these modifications being carried out in July 1943
H.W. Attwell

No. 35007 *Aberdeen Commonwealth* basks in the lighting at Nine Elms on 13 November 1966. The contours of the engine show up well, with the additional balance weights added after rebuilding visible on the driving wheels. The characteristic round top to the tender and bogie axleboxes can be seen, and running below the tender tank is the lagged steam heat pipe. The rear truck is of the cast type
J.R. Carter

During May 1958, having covered 799,299 miles, the engine was rebuilt and boiler No. 1106 fitted. AWS gear was fitted in September 1959 and a speedometer in April 1961. Transfer to Weymouth occurred in January 1965, tender No. 3127 was fitted in September 1966 and finally the engine was transferred to Nine Elms in March 1967. In July 1967, at the end of steam traction on the Southern Region of BR, the engine was withdrawn with a mileage of 1,318,765. Sold for scrapping to J. Buttigieg, Newport, Monmouthshire it was cut up during April 1968.

No. 21C8

Constructed under order No. 1068 at Eastleigh Works with boiler No. 1097 and tender No. 3118. Entering traffic in black livery in June 1942 at Salisbury shed, No. 21C8 was officially named *Orient Line* by Mr I.C. Geddes, chairman of Orient Line, at Waterloo station on 2 November 1942 and not 1 November as is often stated. The engine took part in the smoke clearance trials with Nos 21C6 and 10 in the autumn of 1942. A hood over the smokebox was fitted in May 1943, and a new left-hand cylinder in November 1944. No. 21C8 was damaged in collision with an electric train at Waterloo station in June 1947

On 10 June 1947, No. 21C8 *Orient Line* collided with electric stock while running into Waterloo with a West of England train. The engine is photographed at Eastleigh on 19 June 1947 awaiting repairs without the connecting rods. Considerable damage occurred to the front section of the air-smoothed casing, the smokebox door and buffer beam. Just visible among the mass of lubrication pipes between the main frames, which have had lightening holes cut in them, is the Stone's turbo generator. This was eventually moved to a more convenient position under the driver's side of the cab. In addition to repairs to the locomotive after the collision, it was also given a general overhaul. Sanding on the locomotive was to all coupled wheels

Author's collection

On 2 July 1967, with the end of steam in sight on the Southern, No. 35008 *Orient Line* is approaching Weymouth with one of the 'Farewell to Steam' specials from Waterloo. The nameplate is in place but the front number and shed code plates are missing, and one of the covers to the lubricators on the running plate has been left open. Fitted with a rebodied 5,250 gallon tender, this photograph shows that locomotives could still appear in a relatively clean condition for special events. Set slightly forward of the steam dome is the whistle, operated by a rod linkage running across the top of the firebox casing, and behind the dome are the three safety valves

B. Morrison

and repaired, fitted with boiler No.1092, a modified two-window cab and repainted in malachite green livery in August 1947, the last of the class to be reliveried. The engine was renumbered as No. 35008 and finished in blue livery in July 1949, when the cab was altered to the standard three-window type at the same time. A new left-hand cylinder was fitted in January 1950, the engine was painted in BR green livery in May 1952, and boiler No. 1106 with resited safety valves fitted during October 1953. Transferred in February 1954 to Bournemouth and in the following August to Exmouth Junction shed. In September 1954 the boiler pressure was reduced to 250 lb sq in.

No. 35008 was rebuilt during May 1957 with a mileage of 730,712, and boiler No. 1102 fitted and tender No. 3118 modified at the same time. Re-allocated to Bournemouth in March 1960 and AWS gear and speedometer fitted in April 1960. Tender No. 3443 was attached in February 1962, having been rebodied with a water capacity of 5,250 gallons, with a boiler change to No. 1112 occurring at the same time. In October 1964, the original tender No. 3118, now rebodied with a water capacity of 5,250 gallons, was refitted at Nine Elms. A transfer to Weymouth occurred in October 1966 and finally, in March 1967, to Nine Elms. Withdrawn in July 1967 at the end of Southern Region steam, after a total mileage of 1,286,418, No. 35008 was disposed of to J. Buttigieg, Newport, Monmouthshire where it was cut up during October 1968.

No. 21C9

Built as part of order No. 1068 at Eastleigh Works in June 1942, finished in black livery, and fitted with boiler No. 1098 and tender No. 3119, No. 21C9 was allocated to Salisbury shed. No. 21C9 was named *Shaw Savill* on 30 July 1942 by Lord Essendon, chairman of the line, at Victoria station in company with No. 21C7. In the autumn of 1942, the engine was one of those involved in initial experiments to improve smoke clearance. No. 21C9 hauled the first regular sixteen-coach train to operate from Waterloo, the 10.50 a.m. to Exeter Central on 4 May 1943, the wartime equivalent of the 'Atlantic Coast Express'. A smokebox hood deflector was fitted in June 1943, a new left-hand cylinder in September 1945 and the engine repainted in malachite green livery in November 1946. The first boiler change occurred in November 1947, when boiler No. 1097 was fitted.

Renumbered as No. 35009, a new inside cylinder was fitted and the locomotive finished in blue livery in August 1949, and in February 1952 a new right-hand cylinder was fitted. In February 1953, the cab was modified, boiler No. 1102 acquired and the locomotive repainted in BR green livery. Boiler pressure was reduced to 250 lb sq in during June 1954.

Rebuilt, having covered 684,482 miles, the tender modified and boiler No. 1117 fitted in March 1957, the engine was immediately transferred to Exmouth Junction shed. A speedometer was fitted in February 1960, and AWS gear eight months later. A further

No. 21C9 *Shaw Savill* heads the up 'Devon Belle' at Sidmouth Junction in 1947, passing the M7 tank awaiting to depart with the Sidmouth branch train. The 'Merchant Navy' is in malachite green livery, with the full smokebox roundel giving the date and place of building. The poor lookout for the crew from the original cab can be seen here, with the smoke deflectors not assisting the forward vision. The lower route disc has been mounted in reverse, and sits above the first type of headboard carried by this service. In addition to the headboard, the characteristic 'Devon Belle' wings were attached to the smoke deflectors

P. Short

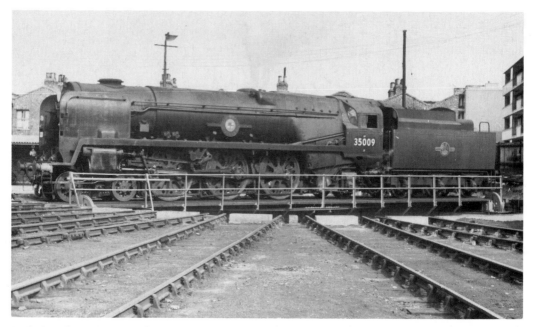

With the safety valves providing a chorus for the adjacent flat-dwellers, No. 35009 *Shaw Savill* resides on the turntable at Nine Elms in the late 1950s, with an oil lamp in position on the front. The yellow disc sited below the cab number denoted that water treatment was fitted to the locomotive. The engine was at this time shedded at Exmouth Junction, and eventually passed into Western Region stock. It is now at Brighton awaiting possible restoration

Author's collection

boiler change occurred in September 1961 when boiler No. 1108 was fitted. No. 35009 passed into Western Region stock on 1 January 1963 and was withdrawn by that region in September 1964, having run a total of 1,127,452 miles with the same tender. It was sold to Woodham Bros, Barry and eventually reserved for the Wessex Railway Society, but was resold to the Barry Steam Loco Action Group in 1982, and is now at Brighton.

No. 21C10

Built as the last unit of order No. 1068 at Eastleigh Works in July 1942, with boiler No. 1099 and tender No. 3120, No. 21C10 was placed in traffic in black livery at Salisbury. It operated twenty-coach test trains from Waterloo to Exeter Central (12.50 p.m. ex-Waterloo) on 2 December 1942, returning the following day with the same load on the 12.50 p.m. ex-Exeter Central. On 18 December 1942 the locomotive was named *Blue Star* at Waterloo station by the chairman of the shipping company, Lord Vestry, after which it returned to Eastleigh to act as a mobile test bed in an attempt to cure the problem of drifting smoke obscuring the driver's vision. It was fitted with an experimental hood over

Photographed on 15 December 1942, the lines of No. 21C10 *Blue Star* are accentuated by the wartime black livery, and with the naming ceremony two days away the cleanliness is obvious! At this time sanding was to the front and middle driving wheels, with the sandbox covers visible on the air-smoothed casing. The horizontal strengthening rib on the casing shows that this engine was one of those fitted with limpet board for the casing. The increased cut-out above the smokebox door was one attempt to improve smoke clearance, and below the smokebox door is the circular apperture providing access to the middle cylinder. The additional small window on the cab roof above the forward side window, may well have been installed to provide illumination for the hydrostatic lubricator in the cab, since steel-sheeted side windows have been fitted

B. Morrison

the smokebox and later separate smoke deflectors during March 1943. A new right-hand cylinder was fitted in June 1947 when the engine was repainted in malachite green livery.

Boiler No. 1090 was acquired in January 1948 and the engine renumbered as No. 35010 in December 1948, still lettered 'Southern'. The cab was modified and the locomotive repainted in blue livery in November 1949, when boiler No. 1101 was fitted. A transfer to Nine Elms shed took place in February 1950, and boiler No. 1124 was fitted in May 1951. No. 35010 was repainted in BR green livery in November 1952, and in May 1954 the boiler pressure was set at 250 lb sq in. The engine was re-allocated to Bournemouth in January 1956.

No. 35010 was rebuilt in January 1957, after 663,174 miles, when extensive replacement of the main frames ahead of the cylinders was undertaken, boiler No. 1112 with resited safety valves fitted and the tender modified. AWS gear was fitted in August 1959. A transfer to Exmouth Junction occurred in March 1960, at which shed it passed into Western Region stock on 1 January 1963. Speedometer and boiler No. 1105 were acquired in November 1961, and a spark arrester fitted in September 1963. The engine returned to the Southern Region in September 1964 when steam traction ceased on the Salisbury–Exeter route, and was allocated to Bournemouth. A tender change to No. 3122 occurred at Nine Elms in December 1964. No. 35010 was withdrawn in September 1966 due to damage to the right-hand outside cylinder, having covered 1,241,929 miles, and sold as scrap to Woodham Bros, Barry. However the engine was resold to the Blue Star Association, part of the British Enginemen Steam Preservation Society in 1982, and is now undergoing restoration at King George V dock in London.

A grimy No. 35010 *Blue Star* waits to come off Nine Elms to work the 'Bournemouth Belle' on 8 August 1957, seven months after being rebuilt

D. Gomersall

No. 21C11

Constructed as the first of order No. 1189 at Eastleigh Works in December 1944, fitted with boiler No. 1100 and attached to tender No. 3121 of 5,100 gallon capacity. All the boilers for this order were constructed at Eastleigh and all the tenders at Ashford. The engine entered traffic in black livery, working from Nine Elms shed, and was named *General Steam Navigation* at Waterloo station on 20 February 1945 by Mr R. Kelso, chairman and managing director of the line. In January 1947, boiler No. 1111 was fitted, and the engine repainted in malachite green livery.

Renumbered as No. 35011 and receiving boiler No. 1112 in November 1948, it was fitted with modified cab in September 1950, when boiler No. 1104 was fitted. No. 35011 was repainted in BR green in November 1951 without acquiring the BR blue livery, transferred to Bournemouth in February 1954 and back to Nine Elms in May of the same year. The boiler pressure was reduced to 250 lb sq in during June 1954, and the boiler

The all-Pullman 'Devon Belle' was one of the post-war efforts of the Southern to attract the war-weary British back to the delights of luxury travel by train. Inaugurated on 20 June 1947, the noon departure of the first working from Waterloo had four cars for Plymouth and eight for Ilfracombe, including an observation car. The novelty for the Southern was the omission of the Salisbury stop, with the engines being changed at Wilton South. However, a stop was officially made at Sidmouth Junction. This photograph shows No. 35011 *General Steam Navigation* coasting into Wilton South for the engine change-over with No. 35009 *Shaw Savill* on 26 July 1952. The engine, in Brunswick green livery, is carrying both the 'Devon Belle' headboard and the side wings attached to the smoke deflectors, the latter having special attachment points on the top of the deflectors. While the guard and driver exchange greetings, the railway employee standing between the tracks with his bucket and step-ladder awaits the engine change-over to clean the observation car windows

L. Elsey

No. 35011, *General Steam Navigation*, an Exmouth Junction engine with a full tender of coal, starts the up 'Atlantic Coast Express' from Exeter Central in the autumn of 1959, and is just passing Exeter Central 'A' signal-box. The Padstow coaches have already covered nearly 88 miles, and the train has a further 172 miles to travel before Waterloo is reached. Bulleid coach set 64 is immediately behind the locomotive. In this photograph taken from Howell Road bridge, the contour of the Belpaire firebox is visible and the shape of the chimney fitted to the rebuilt locomotives can also be seen

Author's collection

changed for No. 1090 in March 1956. The engine was transferred to Exmouth Junction in June 1957 and two months later the tender was modified.

Rebuilt in July 1959, having run 670,782 miles, and fitted with boiler No. 1097. In March 1960 No. 35011 was re-allocated to Bournemouth. AWS gear and speedometer were fitted in May 1961, and a spark arrester acquired in June 1963. Tender No. 3129 was fitted in October 1965, and the locomotive withdrawn from traffic in February 1966 with a total mileage of 1,069,128. It was sold to Woodham Bros, Barry as scrap, reserved for the Barry Steam Loco Action Group, and is now at Brighton.

MERCHANT NAVY CLASS
No. 21C12

Built at Eastleigh Works with boiler No. 1101 and tender No. 3122 during December 1944, as the second of order No. 1189, No. 21C12 emerged in black livery to traffic in January 1945, and was allocated to Nine Elms shed. Repainted grey in February 1945 and then in April, in malachite green, it was the first member of the class to regain this livery after the war. No. 21C12 was named *United States Lines* on 10 April 1945 at Waterloo station by Adm. Schuirman, USN. On the arrival of the liner *America* on its maiden voyage to Southampton, on 21 November 1946, the locomotive worked a boat train to Waterloo.

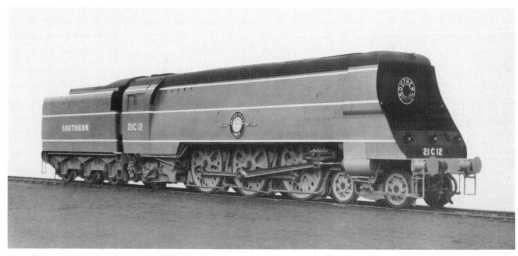

The photographic grey livery accentuates the outline of No. 21C12 *United States Lines* on 10 February 1945. The engine is fitted with short smoke deflectors and smokebox hood, a full-circle Southern roundel on the smokebox door and sanding to all driving wheels. On the second series the base of the air-smoothed casing was cut off almost at right angles at the front and rear, in comparison with the curves of the first ten locomotives. The pipes from the injectors feeding the clack valves on the boiler can be seen at the base of the cab. The rear bogie is partly covered by sheeting, a characteristic of many of the engines when built. On the cab roof is a small rectangular window, seen earlier in the photograph of No. 21C10

Author's collection

No. 35012 *United States Lines*, in need of a clean, passes Radipole Halt with a Bournemouth to Weymouth local service in the early 1960s. The engine is fitted with AWS, and the battery box is sited between the frames above the buffer beam. The pockets for the valve spindle guides can be seen on both sides of the smoke deflectors. The coach behind the tender is a BR Mk 1, in red and cream livery, followed by two Bulleid coaches in green

B. Morrison

Fitted with boiler No. 1106 in January 1947, renumbered as No. 35012, and having a modified cab and boiler No. 1104 fitted in March 1949. In February 1950 boiler No. 1096 was fitted. In February 1951 the locomotive was painted in blue livery, and during August 1951 the vitreous enamelled section of the nameplates was altered from the flag hitherto depicted, to that of a ship's wheel with flag superimposed, and underneath, on a scroll, the name of the Lines. No. 35012 was coupled to the newly modified self-weighing tender No. 3343 for official photographs and test weighings for two weeks in July 1952. Tender No. 3122 was modified in July 1952 and at the same time the locomotive was repainted in BR green livery and boiler No. 1101, with pressure reduced to 250 lb sq in, fitted. The crank axle was replaced in June 1953, the engine transferred to Bournemouth in February 1954 and to Nine Elms in the folllowing May.

The engine was rebuilt in February 1957 with a mileage of 564,821, and boiler No. 1124 fitted. AWS gear was acquired in November 1959, and a speedometer fitted in September 1960. A further boiler change occurred in April 1962 when boiler No. 1120 was fitted. In July 1964 it covered the 17.45 miles from Appleby to Ais Gill on a gradient of 1 in 100 in 17.41 minutes during the Solway Ranger rail tour. Re-allocated to Weymouth in September 1964, tender No. 3120 was acquired in December 1964, and finally, in March 1967 was transferred to Nine Elms. No. 35012 was withdrawn in April 1967, after a total mileage of 1,134,836, sold for scrapping to John Cashmore Ltd, Newport, Monmouthshire, and cut up during October of that year.

No. 21C13

Built as the third locomotive of order No. 1189 at Eastleigh Works, with boiler No. 1104 and tender No. 3123, and placed in traffic in black livery at Nine Elms in February 1945. No. 21C13 was officially named at Waterloo station on 17 April 1945 by Mr L. Holt, the senior partner of Alfred Holt and Co. Reports gave the name bestowed as *Blue Funnel* and although the nameplates carried *Blue Funnel Line* for the ceremony, these plates were removed shortly after the naming, and replaced by others with the lettering *Blue Funnel Certum Pete Finem*. The engine was repainted in malachite green livery in November 1946, and in company with No. 21C140 and No. CC1, was employed on fifteen-coach, 500 ton, test trains between Brighton and Norwood Junction on 19 January 1947. A boiler-lagging fire resulted in a return to the works for examination in May 1947.

Renumbered as No. 35013 in July 1948 and fitted with boiler No. 1093 in February

Displaying the original 'Bournemouth Belle' headboard and still fitted with the Southern smokebox roundel, No. 21C13 *Blue Funnel* departs from Waterloo on 15 July 1947 with the steam sanders in operation. The driver's forward visibility was not helped by the original cab fitted to the locomotive. The middle route disc brackets have been transferred to the smokebox door, since in their earlier position adjacent to the electric route indicator lamps the disc projected outside the air-smoothed casing. The all-Pullman 'Bournemouth Belle' was introduced on 5 July 1931, and then re-introduced after the war on 7 October 1946. The 'Merchant Navy' class took over the train from the 'Lord Nelson' class soon after its re-introduction, and carried on almost until the demise of the service in July 1967. The additional metal sections to the top of the smoke deflectors of No. 21C13 indicate that the engine was also involved in haulage of the 'Devon Belle'

J.P. Wilson

Although No. 35013 *Blue Funnel* looks in a grimy state at Weymouth, with one of the middle electric lamps missing on 29 March 1965, the engine survived until the end of steam on the Southern in July 1967. Having been transferred to the Western Region in January 1963, she returned to Southern care in September 1964 at the cessation of steam on the West of England main line. The angled front cab window offered improved visibility, in comparison with the photograph of the engine in its original condition, and the engine is now fitted with plain section coupling rods, AWS and a speedometer

C.L. Caddy

1949, the locomotive was repainted in blue livery in August 1950, and at the same time tender No. 3124 was fitted. In December 1952, BR green livery was acquired, boiler No. 1112 fitted and the cab and tender modified. Transfer to Exmouth Junction took place in March 1954, after acquiring a new inside cylinder, and in October 1954 the boiler pressure was reduced to 250 lb sq in.

No. 35013 was rebuilt in May 1956, having run 517,915 miles, and fitted with boiler No. 1105. AWS gear was fitted in November 1959, boiler No. 1119 and a speedometer in May 1961 and a spark arrester in March 1964. The engine passed into Western Region stock on 1 January 1963, but returned to the Southern Region in September 1964, at the end of steam working of main-line services in the West of England, and was allocated to Bournemouth. Transferrred to Weymouth (October 1966) and finally to Nine Elms (March 1967) it lasted until the end of steam on the Southern in July 1967, having covered a total of 1,114,658 miles. No. 35013 was disposed of for scrapping to J. Buttigieg, Newport, Monmouthshire where it was cut up in April 1968.

No. 21C14

Built, under order No. 1189, at Eastleigh Works with boiler No.1106 and tender No.3124, No. 21C14 entered traffic in black livery in February 1945, and was allocated to Nine Elms. A new inside cylinder was fitted in April 1945, and the engine repainted in malachite green livery in November 1945. It was named *Nederland Line* at Waterloo station on the 27th of that month by Mr A.F. Bronsing, managing director, in a joint ceremomy with No. 21C15. In mid-1946, the locomotive was involved in a series of fuel and haulage trials in comparison with engines from the 'Lord Nelson' and 'King Arthur' classes; the trials took place over the West of England main line, in some cases with sixteen-coach loads. Boiler No. 1100 was fitted in February 1947, and the cab and firebox sheeting were damaged in a collision at Nine Elms in September 1947, with repairs and part repainting carried out at that shed. It was renumbered as No. 35014 and fitted with a modified cab in May 1949, when boiler No. 1106 was fitted, and in June 1950, tender No. 3123 was fitted.

Boiler No. 1107 was acquired, without thermic syphons, and the engine repainted in BR green livery in August 1951, never having received the BR blue livery. In October 1952 the engine was paired with the modified coal- or self-weighing tender No. 3343. The thermic syphonless boiler was removed and replaced by No. 1103 in October 1953, and boiler No. 1107 transferred to No. 35022 in November 1953. Four comparatively quick

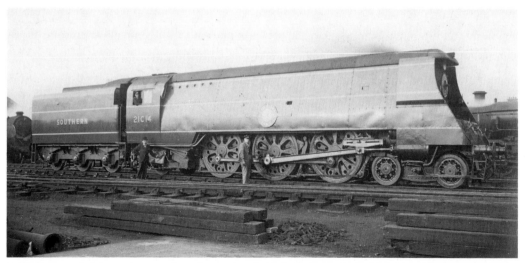

J. Morris was a Salisbury photographer who produced classic photographs such as this of No. 21C14 *Nederland Line*, taken at Salisbury on 30 November 1945, three days after the naming ceremony. The engine is outside the shed, and has the short smoke deflectors and smokebox hood fitted. Sanding is to all driving wheels, with the sandbox cover to the central driving wheel open. The additional cab roof window has been fitted, and the angle of the photograph shows the small sun shields fitted to the side of the cab front windows, which, in some cases, helped to trap steam and smoke. The attractive profile of the BFB wheels and the Reg Curl-designed securing caps for the rods are well profiled here

Author's collection

No. 35014 *Nederland Line* on the down 'Atlantic Coast Express' leaves Honiton tunnel on a hot 3 August 1964, with Bulleid coach set No. 845 behind the engine, and just a slight smoke haze from the chimney. With the hardest part of the journey behind them, life is now a little easier for the crew on the remaining 18 miles to Exeter Central. The descent is almost 1 in 90 to Honiton station, and then to Sidmouth Junction, initially named Feniton and then Ottery St Mary, until the branch to Sidmouth opened in 1874. The station closed with the closure of the Sidmouth branch in 1967, to open again four years later as Feniton!

P.W. Gray

transfers occurred between 1954 and 1956; to Exmouth Junction (May 1954), Bournemouth (August 1954), Stewarts Lane (June 1955) and Nine Elms (June 1956). During this period, in July 1954, boiler pressure was reduced to 250 lb sq in and the safety valves resited.

Rebuilt in July 1956, having run 516,811 miles, it was coupled to tender No. 3126 and fitted with boiler No. 1123. AWS gear was fitted in October 1959, and a speedometer in November 1960. A new right-hand cylinder was fitted in July 1961, and in March 1962 boiler No. 1116 acquired. The final transfer to Weymouth was made in September 1964, tender No. 3345 fitted there in March 1965, and in September the locomotive acquired tender No. 3115. The locomotive was withdrawn in March 1967, after 1,062,394 miles, and sold for scrapping to John Cashmore Ltd, Newport, Monmouthshire where it was cut up during September of that year.

No. 21C15

No. 21C15 was constructed as part of order No. 1189 at Eastleigh Works, with boiler No. 1105 and tender No. 3126, and placed in traffic at Nine Elms in black livery in March 1945, although it was repainted in malachite green livery in September 1945. Named *Rotterdam Lloyd* at Waterloo station on 27 November 1945 by Mr W. Ruys, managing director, at a joint ceremony with No. 21C14. Boiler No. 1107 was fitted in February 1947. No. 21C15 headed the inaugural 'Devon Belle' on 20 June 1947, both ways between Waterloo and Wilton. In October 1947, it was fitted with a new right-hand cylinder.

Photographed at Sevenoaks in 1956, No. 35015 *Rotterdam Lloyd* shows some of the external changes that the engines underwent. The casing in front of the cylinders has been removed and the engine has normal length smoke deflectors, standing proud of the casing sides with the 'Devon Belle' mounting strip on their upper section. The wedge-shaped cab has a larger front window and improved forward visibility. Although all the rebuilt engines had non-fluted coupling rods, these were in some cases fitted to the original engines as seen here. From July 1956 until June 1958, the engine ran with the coal- or self-weighing tender, No. 3343, which can just be seen in this photograph

H.A.P. Browne

Rebuilt No. 35015 *Rotterdam Lloyd* stands at Bournemouth shed on 21 February 1959, the engine paired with modified 5,100 gallon tender, No. 3123. The additional rivets below the smoke deflector handrails were for attachment of the 'Golden Arrow' insignia, carried on the original locomotives on the casing above the nameplate. When rebuilt, the irregularly shaped smokebox door was retained, its shape giving almost a smile to the locomotive

A. Swain

Renumbered as No. 35015 in June 1949 and fitted with modified cab, boiler No. 1121 and a new inside cylinder. A second new right-hand cylinder was fitted in February 1950. No. 35015 was repainted in blue livery in February 1951, and BR green livery in May 1953. Boiler No. 1099 with resited safety valves and 250 lb sq in pressure was acquired in April 1954. No. 35015 was transferred to Stewarts Lane in June 1956, and tender No. 3343, of modified type and fitted with coal-weighing apparatus, was coupled in July 1956. The left-hand cylinder was replaced in August 1957, this cylinder coming from No. 35016.

Rebuilt in June 1958 after 549,706 miles, paired with tender No. 3123 and boiler No. 1113, and fitted with a new left-hand cylinder, No. 35015 was re-allocated to Nine Elms in June 1959. AWS gear was fitted in November 1959, a speedometer in June 1960 and boiler No. 1091 in June 1962. Withdrawn from traffic in February 1964, having completed 813,950 miles, the locomotive was sold for scrapping to Slag Reduction Company Ltd, Holmes Farm, Rotherham, Yorkshire where it was cut up in December 1964.

No. 21C16

Built at Eastleigh Works, with boiler No. 1107 and tender No. 3125, as part of order No. 1189, No. 21C16 entered traffic in black livery in March 1945, working from Nine Elms. On 5 July it was named *Elders Fyffes* at Waterloo station, by Mr H. Stockley, managing director. The engine was repainted in malachite green livery in January 1947, when boiler No. 1112 was fitted and all the cylinders were rebored.

It was renumbered as No. 35016 in October 1948, when boiler No. 1094 was acquired, and the cab was modified in June 1949. The locomotive was repainted in blue livery in May 1950 and in BR green in March 1953. In August 1954, boiler No. 1111, with 250 lb sq in pressure and resited safety valves, was fitted. On 16 November 1955 near Gillingham, Dorset, fractures occurred of all four coupling rods and cracks appeared in the axleboxes. This resulted in the redesigning of the rods and use of steel axleboxes on rebuilt engines.

In malachite green livery No. 35016 *Elders Fyffes*, still with Southern-style number on the cab side, is at Salisbury shed on 21 August 1949, flanked by two of her light Pacific sisters. The wedge-shaped cab had been fitted in June 1949, but as yet the casing in front of the cylinders has not been removed. The route disc brackets are now mounted on the smokebox door, but although fitted with a smokebox number plate, no shed plate is as yet fitted. Visible on the sloping front below the smokebox are the two footholds, added soon after the cast number plates of the first locomotives were repositioned. Centrally positioned below the smokebox door dart is a metal protrusion, whose function has eluded the author, although it appears on many of the locomotives with the additional 'Devon Belle' smoke deflector sections

J.H. Aston

The West of England car carrier was a short-lived experiment and one of the few motorail services on the Southern. Photographed near St James Park, Exeter on a dismal 3 August 1963, No. 35016 *Elders Fyffes* has some hard work ahead, with the Bulleid coaches having left Okehampton at 3.55 p.m. Except for the fitting of AWS, with the battery box visible behind the lower route disc, and a speedometer, the locomotive is in the condition as rebuilt

W.L. Underhay

Rebuilt with the mileage at 467,091, a new left-hand cylinder and boiler No. 1110 were fitted and the tender modified in April 1957. AWS gear was fitted in November 1959 and a speedometer in March 1961. Boiler No. 1124 was acquired in August 1962, and the locomotive transferred to Weymouth in September 1964. No. 35016 was withdrawn from service in August 1965, after 900,637 miles, having run with the same tender since being built. It was disposed of for scrapping to Birds (Swansea) Ltd, Bridgend, Glamorgan where it was cut up in December 1965.

Constructed under order No. 1189, at Eastleigh Works, having boiler No. 1108 and tender No. 3127, No. 21C17 was allocated to Nine Elms on being placed in service, in black livery, in April 1945. It was repainted in malachite green livery in October 1945 and named *Belgian Marine* by Monsieur G. Rongvaux, the Belgian Minister of Communications, at Victoria station on 22 October 1945. The following day, the engine worked the inaugural post-war continental boat train from Victoria to Folkestone Junction sidings, although this task was then taken over by the 'King Arthur' class. The boiler was changed for No. 1101 in May 1947.

In April 1948 the engine was renumbered as No. 35017, and fitted with Flaman speed recorder, modified cab and LMS tender No. 10123. The locomotive worked between King's Cross and Leeds, and also Euston and Carlisle, during the course of the 1948 Locomotive Interchanges. The LMS tender was replaced by the original tender, No. 3127, still lettered 'Southern', in June 1948. The engine was repainted in blue livery in July 1949, when boiler No. 1122 was acquired, and in July 1950 a new left-hand

With the last design of train headboard, No. 35017 *Belgian Marine* heads west from Southampton Central to Bournemouth with the down 'Bournemouth Belle' on 17 March 1956. The engine, which took part in the 1948 Locomotive Interchanges, is in lined Brunswick green with a black splash skirt to the lower part of the casing, the cylinder and the tender, and with the early BR lion-over-wheel emblem on the tender. The casing has been removed from the front of the cylinders, and part of the cylinder drain cock mechanism is visible. The hatch giving access to the steam manifold valve is now fitted with a sliding cover, replacing the earlier hinged type. Rectangular-section coupling rods have been fitted. The famous signal gantry at Southampton and the clock tower, both visible in the background, are now but memories

Author's collection

Preparations go ahead at Branksome on 15 September 1964 for No. 35017 *Belgian Marine* to haul the up 'Bournemouth Belle'. The tender tank is being filled and attention given to the coal bunker. The front route lamps are showing signs of poor maintenance with broken lamp glasses and lamp housings left open, yet the engine still has two years of active life before being withdrawn. The smokebox was fitted with a spark arrester, and both AWS and speedometer have been fitted. The actuating shaft for the screw reverser can be seen extending from the cab to the running plate, and although the original steam reverser was not universally liked, it did have its devotees among the drivers. Below the handrail on the boiler are the large pipe for the brake ejector and the smaller one for the blower, supplying steam to the blastpipe to create a smokebox vacuum, and give enhanced combustion

G.W. Morrison

cylinder was fitted. BR green livery was applied in April 1953, and boiler No. 1114, with resited safety valves and pressure of 250 lb sq in, fitted in July 1954.

No. 35017 was rebuilt after 594,522 miles and fitted with boiler No. 1107 without thermic syphons, and the tender was modified in March 1957. The engine was involved in track and vehicle tests with locomotives No. 10203 and No. 20003 between Redhill and Three Bridges in the spring of 1957 and on 16 June worked the Newhaven Harbour–Victoria boat train. AWS gear was fitted in October 1959, a speedometer in March 1961 and spark arrester in September 1963 when boiler No. 1109 was acquired. Transferred to Weymouth in September 1964, the locomotive was withdrawn from that shed in July 1966, having run a total of 1,017,754 miles, and sold to J. Buttigieg, Newport, Monmouthshire paired to tender No. 3114 where it was cut up in September 1966.

No. 21C18

No. 21C18 was built as part of order No. 1189 at Eastleigh Works, fitted with boiler No. 1109 and tender No. 3129, and placed in traffic in black livery in May 1945 at Nine Elms. The coupled wheels differed from the remainder of the class in being fabricated and not cast. It was repainted in malachite green livery in August 1945 and named *British India Line* at Waterloo station on 13 December 1945 by Mr A.J. Lang, managing director. The engine worked the first post-war 'Bournemouth Belle' on 7 October 1946. In April 1947 the fabricated driving wheels were replaced by the standard cast type, and boiler No. 1105 was fitted.

The locomotive was renumbered as No. 35018, fitted with a Flaman speed recorder and the cab modified in May 1948, prior to taking part as the Southern engine over the Waterloo–Exeter line in the Locomotive Interchanges. It was repainted in blue livery in September 1949 when boiler No. 1100 was acquired, and a new right-hand cylinder fitted in August 1950. In July 1951, BR green livery was applied and boiler No. 1109 fitted, and in July 1952, No. 35018 was coupled to modified coal-weighing tender No. 3343 for a period of approximately three months, after which tender No. 3346 was attached. A new driving axle was fitted in June 1953, and the boiler pressure reduced to 250 lb sq in, in August 1954.

The engine was rebuilt, fitted with boiler No. 1116 and the tender modified at Eastleigh Works early in 1956, the first of the class to be so treated, having covered 504,900 miles. No. 35018 was released to service in February of that year, initially with

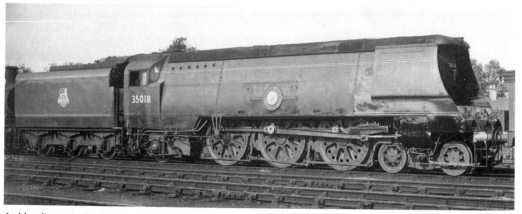

In blue livery with black and white lining, No. 35018 *British India Line* is at Eastleigh on 19 August 1950, the same month that a new right-hand cylinder was fitted. The splash skirt, on the bottom of the engine's casing and on the tender and the cylinders, was painted black. Although the sandbox to the front driving wheels has been blocked off, a cover has been fitted to the slide bars in an earlier attempt to reduce the effects of sand abrasion on the motion. The triangular mounting on the casing adjacent to the rear driving wheel is for the Flaman speed recorder, whose drive shaft can be seen entering the rear of the cab. The recorders were fitted to the engines taking part in the Locomotive Interchanges, but were not always removed immediately on completion of the trials

W. Gilburt

The first of the class to be modified, No. 35018 *British India Line* is passing Allbrook, with smoke hanging around the chimney, en route to Nine Elms and an official inspection at Waterloo on 12 February 1956. The uncharacteristic sheen on the paintwork was produced by the application of tallow and neatsfoot oil. The air-smoothed casing has been removed, the engine now appearing in a more conventional silhouette, and is fitted with rectangular-section coupling rods. This locomotive differed in a number of details from the remainder of the class when rebuilt. The feed pipes to the clack valves were normally a straight run from the running plate to the valves, whereas a right-angle curve was present on No. 35018. The pipes for the blower and brake ejector on the driver's side of the casing had a lower curve introduced above the nameplate, whereas on the other members of the class this occurred at the junction of the smokebox and boiler barrel. The front sand fillers were positioned higher on this engine than on the other rebuilds, but proved difficult to replenish and were repositioned lower on the other engines. The handrails on the smoke deflectors were added later, as the lower holds cut in the deflectors proved insufficient to permit safe access to the running plate. On the rear of the tender is the TIA box, containing the water treatment fluid

L. Elsey

no handrails to the smoke deflectors, and with odd swan necks to the front sandboxes. A rare visit to the Central section was made in September 1956, when the locomotive visited Brighton Works. A speedometer was fitted in February 1960, AWS gear in December 1960, and the engine was transferred to Bournemouth in November 1960 and back to Nine Elms in January 1961.

In December 1961, boiler No. 1117 was fitted and tender No. 3346 was exchanged for No. 3118, a rebodied tender of 5,250 gallons capacity. Withdrawn from service in August 1964, having completed a total of 956,544 miles, the locomotive was sold to Woodham Bros, Barry as scrap, attached to tender No. 3343. Rescued by the Mid-Hants Railway in 1980 with tender No. 3350, it arrived at Alresford on 14 March and was propelled to Ropley the next day, to commence the long process of restoration.

No. 21C19

No. 21C19 was the penultimate locomotive of order No. 1189, built at Eastleigh Works carrying boiler No. 1103 and tender No. 3128, and entering traffic in black livery in June 1945, allocated to Nine Elms. It was repainted in malachite green livery in September 1945 and named on the 22nd of that month, *French Line C.G.T.* at Southampton docks, by Monsieur de Malglaive, director of the line. In August 1947 all cylinders were rebored due to excessive wear.

The *s* prefix to the number was added in the works in March 1948, but the engine was renumbered as No. 35019 before emerging in April 1948. For the Locomotive Interchanges, the engine was fitted with a modified cab, Flaman speed recorder and LMS tender No. 10219. During these trials, No. 35019 operated between King's Cross and Leeds – for two days only, due to firebox defects – and Paddington and Plymouth. The

No. 35019 *French Line C.G.T.*, hauling a Waterloo to Plymouth train, awaits the guard's signal at Axminster on 16 August 1956. A number of locomotives had additional strengthening rods added to the top and bottom of the smoke deflectors, and these are shown here. The fastenings for the 'Devon Belle' wings have not been removed from the smoke deflectors, although this train had not run for almost two years at this time. The coupling rods are of rectangular cross-section. Axminster was the junction station for the Lyme Regis branch, with the branch-line trains starting from the bay platform on the up side of the station

L. Marshall

With the safety valves just feathering, No. 35019 *French Line C.G.T.* hauls the 11.46 a.m. Plymouth to Waterloo train on 14 July 1962, through the glorious Devon countryside approaching Seaton Junction station. In comparison with No. 35018, the feed pipe to the clack valves rises vertically from the running plate, and the front sand fillers are positioned nearer the running plate, making refilling easier. This engine was one of those fitted with extended valve spindles, and the step formed by the valve spindle cover can be seen on the sloping section of the running plate adjacent to the smoke deflectors

W.L. Underhay

original tender was re-instated in May 1948, still lettered 'Southern'. Boiler No. 1102 was fitted in January 1950, when the locomotive was repainted in blue livery. The engine worked the French Presidential train from Dover Marine to Victoria on 7 March 1950 and the Royal train from Waterloo to Sherborne on 1 June 1950.

A single-nozzle blastpipe and chimney and boiler No. 1108 were fitted and the engine repainted in BR green in June 1951. Sundry modifications were made on empirical lines before the multi-nozzle blastpipe was refitted in January 1952; the lack of height between the top of the inside valve chest and the top of the chimney being a limiting factor in obtaining good results with this design. Boiler pressure was reduced to 250 lb sq in during August 1954, and boiler No. 1100 with resited safety valves acquired in October 1955.

Rebuilt, having run 617,368 miles, No. 35019 was fitted with three new cylinders, boiler No. 1092 and the tender modified in May 1959. AWS gear was acquired in October 1959, and a speedometer fitted in February 1961. Transferred to Weymouth in September 1964, and withdrawn from service one year later with a total mileage of 947,344, the locomotive was sold to John Cashmore Ltd, Newport, Monmouthshire for scrapping, which occurred in January 1966.

No. 21C20

No. 21C20 was turned out from Eastleigh Works as the last of order No. 1189, with boiler No. 1102 and tender No. 3130, and placed in traffic in black livery in June 1945 at Nine Elms. It was repainted in malachite green livery in August 1945, and named *Bibby Line* on 18 October 1945 at Waterloo station, by Mr H. Bibby, chairman of the line. Fitted with boiler No. 1109 in July 1947 and in May 1948, for the Locomotive Interchanges, renumbered as No. 35020, the locomotive was fitted with a modified cab, Flaman speed recorder, extra-long smoke deflectors – unique for the class – and LMS tender No. 10373, but in the event it did not participate. Original tender No. 3130 was restored in June 1948, still lettered 'Southern'. The engine was repainted in blue livery in May 1950, when a new inside cylinder and boiler No. 1103 were fitted. In June 1952 it was repainted in BR green livery, and received tender No. 3347.

On a misty morning, 6 November 1955, No. 35020 *Bibby Line* passes Allbrook with a down Waterloo to Bournemouth train. The locomotive was unique among the Pacifics in having extra-long smoke deflectors fitted for the 1948 Interchange Trials, which were retained until the engine was rebuilt in April 1956. As this engine hauled the 'Devon Belle', the fastening for the wings can just be seen on the top front section of the smoke deflectors. The tender, one of the first to be modified, is seen here with the cut-down side raves

L. Elsey

On a sunny 5 May 1957, a well-cleaned No. 35020 *Bibby Line*, the second member of the class to be rebuilt, passes Allbrook with a Waterloo to Bournemouth train and Bulleid set No. 351 behind the engine. The modified tender seen here was visually more suited to the rebuilt engines

L. Elsey

The driving wheel axle fractured at Crewkerne on 24 April 1953, causing the immediate examination of the whole of the Southern Pacifics with a view to discovering similar latent defects. The tender was modified in June 1953 while the engine was undergoing repairs following the Crewkerne accident, and boiler No. 1096, with repositioned safety valves, was fitted at the same time. In April 1954, boiler pressure was reduced to 250 lb sq in, and in August 1955 a new inside cylinder was fitted.

Rebuilt in April 1956, having run 507,958 miles, it was fitted with boiler No. 1108. The engine was sent to Swindon test plant shortly afterwards in connection with tests on the 'Atlantic Coast Express' in May 1956, for which an unmodified tender, No. 3345 with adaptations, was used from 25 May until 11 July. After the tests, in July 1956, modified tender No. 3344 was coupled to the locomotive. No. 35020 was fitted with AWS gear in August 1959, and a speedometer in April 1961, when boiler No. 1100 was fitted. The engine was transferred to Weymouth in September 1964 and withdrawn from that shed in February 1965 with a total mileage of 981,479, to be cut up at Eastleigh Works a month later – the only member of the class to be cut up by BR.

No. 35021

Built at Eastleigh Works, No. 35021 was the first of order No. 3393, with boiler No. 1098, previously fitted to No. 21C9 from June 1942 until November 1947, when the firebox had been renewed. This third series of engines was all fitted with wedge-shaped cabs and three side windows from the outset, and in addition the rear or delta truck was fabricated rather than cast as had been the practice in the first twenty engines. Construction of the major components was split between Ashford, where the frames and cylinders were built, Brighton, where the boilers and tenders were built, and Eastleigh where the remaining parts were manufactured and where the locomotives were assembled. The engine visited the works again shortly after construction, to rectify damage sustained after derailment on a trial run at Fratton. No. 35021 was placed in service at Exmouth Junction shed in September 1948 in unlined malachite green livery and attached to light Pacific tender No. 3333, of water capacity 5,500 gallons. The engine was coupled to 6,000 gallon capacity tender No. 3342 in November 1948, which like the other tenders of this capacity constructed at Brighton, was fitted with TIA water treatment when built, and fully lined out. It was named *New Zealand Line* at Waterloo station on 24 November 1948, by Mr H.S. Whitehouse, chairman of the line.

The engine was repainted in blue livery in November 1950 and transferred to Nine Elms in May 1951. In February 1952, No. 35021 was repainted in BR green livery and the

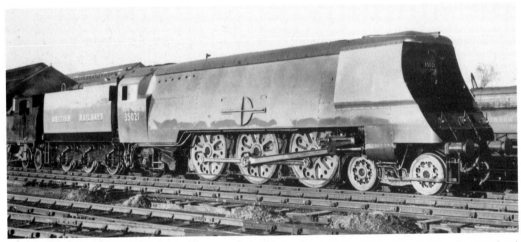

No. 35021 *New Zealand Line*, the first locomotive of the third series, initially fitted with a 5,500 gallon 'Battle of Britain' tender lettered 'British Railways', is photographed at Eastleigh on 2 November 1948 in unlined malachite green, eleven days before the 6,000 gallon tender was fitted. This series were all built with wedge-shaped cabs, three side windows and smokebox number plates. The cab guttering is now directly over the cab windows, and below the cab the cover to the trailing truck has disappeared. With the higher base of the casing on this and the second series, the feed water pipes from the injectors to the clack valves are visible. The rear truck was fabricated rather than cast, as had been the practice in the first twenty engines. On the casing, the nameplate is covered, the practice until the naming ceremony had taken place
W. Jackson

Framed by two water columns, and almost at the end of her working life, No. 35021 *New Zealand Line* waits at Basingstoke on 7 June 1965 with a train for Waterloo; behind the tender is Bulleid set No. 886. Signs of distortion are visible on the lower part of the smokebox door. The engine was fitted with AWS, and the battery box is visible between the front frames. The pockets and footstep for the valve spindle guides can be seen on the inside and outside of the smoke deflectors

D. Gomersall

tender was modified. Boiler No. 1091 – pressure 250 lb sq in and with resited safety valves – was fitted in October 1954 and the engine transferred to Bournemouth in June 1957.

It was rebuilt in June 1959, having run 575,993 miles, when boiler No. 1098 was acquired, and in April 1961 AWS gear and a speedometer were fitted. The locomotive was withdrawn from service in August 1965 with a total mileage of 859,661 and sold to Birds (Swansea) Ltd, Bridgend, Glamorgan for scrapping in October 1965, attached to tender No. 3126.

No. 35022

No. 35022 was built under order No. 3393 at Eastleigh Works with boiler No. 1099, which had been fitted with a new firebox and had originally seen service with No. 21C10. No. 35022 entered traffic in unlined malachite green livery attached to light Pacific tender No. 3335 of water capacity 5,500 gallons, and was allocated to Exmouth Junction in October 1948. Lined out and fitted with 6,000 gallon capacity tender No. 3345 in January 1949, it was named on the 24th of that month, *Holland America Line* at Southampton docks by Mr W.H. deMonchy, managing director, in a joint ceremony with No. 35023.

Ready to depart for Waterloo, No. 35022 *Holland America Line* waits at Exeter Central in the summer of 1949, while in the background is 'West Country' class Pacific, No. 34007 *Wadebridge*. The casing contours of the third series were similar to those of the second series, although the smoke deflectors were longer, extending almost to the middle of the slide bar. The 6,000 gallon tenders fitted to this series had no front water fillers, but space was provided for storage of the fire irons between the side rave and the coal bunker. The coal space looked comparatively small, but was of standard 5 tons capacity. On the rear of the tender tank top, is the TIA water treatment tank, which contained the appropriate chemicals for automatic addition to the tender water. The pipe below the base of the tank is the lagged steam heat pipe. One of the characteristic Southern route discs is still in place on the rear of the tender

J.H. Aston

The engine was then repainted in blue livery in May 1950 and in BR green in January 1952.

No. 35022 underwent tests at Rugby locomotive testing station during the period March 1952–January 1954 and also on the Carlisle–Hellifield route, and during this time buckled a coupling rod due to slipping. A single-nozzle blastpipe was fitted between February and May 1953 and tests were carried out with this system, reaching similar conclusions to those carried out earlier with No. 35019. Boiler No. 1107 without thermic syphons was acquired from No. 35014 in November 1953. No. 35022 was transferred to Bournemouth in June 1954 and boiler pressure set to 250 lb sq in during February 1955.

The locomotive was rebuilt in June 1956 after 329,083 miles, and fitted with boiler No. 1109 with resited safety valves and modified tender No. 3347. AWS gear was fitted in October 1959, and a speedometer acquired in October 1960. Re-allocated in March 1960 to Exmouth Junction shed, and having boiler No. 1123 fitted in July 1962, the engine passed into Western Region stock on 1 January 1963. However, it was transferred back to the Southern Region in February 1964 and allocated to Nine Elms. No. 35022 hauled the last down 'Atlantic Coast Express' on the 80 minute schedule between Waterloo and Salisbury on 4 September 1964. The final shed transfer to Weymouth occurred in September 1964, and No. 35022 was withdrawn in May 1966 after running 903,542 miles and sold as scrap to Woodham Bros, Barry. The engine was purchased by the Southern Steam Trust, Swanage in 1983.

With the rebuilding of the Pacifics, and the removal of the sump, it was necessary for the driver to manually lubricate parts of the motion. The driver of No. 35022 *Holland America Line* oils round, as the engine awaits the signals at Salisbury on 5 September 1964 with an Exeter-bound train, and a good fire. To the driver's right is the flexible shaft drive for the Smiths speedometer. The previous day this engine, immaculately cleaned, had hauled the last down 'Atlantic Coast Express', with its tight 80 minute Waterloo to Salisbury timing. The rear turn-in of the cab, the inset window and handrails can be seen. Below the yellow triangle on the cab, denoting that the engine has BR boiler water treatment, is a brass plate recording all the tests currently being carried out on the engine

D. Mackinnon

No. 35023

Built as part of order No. 3393 at Eastleigh Works, with boiler No. 1113 and tender No. 3341, No. 35023 was outshopped in malachite green livery and placed in service in November 1948 at Exmouth Junction shed. The boiler was one of twelve built at Brighton. The official naming ceremony took place with that for No. 35022 at Southampton docks, when the name *Holland–Afrika Line* was bestowed on 24 January 1949 by Mr M.A. Pelt, managing director. In March 1952 the engine was repainted in BR green livery, being the last of the 'Merchant Navy' class to retain Southern malachite green livery, having never received the BR blue livery. Boiler pressure was reduced to 250 lb sq

At Eastleigh, on 1 May 1954, No. 35023 *Holland–Afrika Line*, an Exmouth Junction engine in Brunswick green livery, awaits resetting of the safety valves to 250 lb sq in. All the upper three lamp brackets are now mounted on the smokebox door, together with a handle to assist door manipulation. Below the shed plate is a small metal protrusion, shown earlier in the photograph of No. 35016, whose function is unknown. The cowl over the smokebox provided improvement in smoke clearance, and the additional top metal section on the deflectors indicates that the engine was used on the 'Devon Belle'. The sliding cover to the whistle is mounted on the top of the casing above the front wing of the nameplate. The hasp, closing the cover to the mechanical lubricators, is above the lower middle route lamp, and the steps cut into the sloping front plating aided access to the smokebox. The casing in front of the cylinders has been cut away, and the drain cock operating mechanism is now more readily visible

Author's collection

in during May 1954, and in October 1954 boiler No. 1092 was fitted with resited safety valves.

Rebuilt in February 1957, having run 433,833 miles, the locomotive was fitted with boiler No. 1115 and tender No. 3341 was modified at the same time. In February 1960, No. 35023 was transferred to Bournemouth. AWS gear and speedometer were fitted in October 1960, a spark arrester in October 1961 and boiler No. 1102 in November 1962. The engine was re-allocated to Weymouth in October 1966 and to Nine Elms in March 1967. It was withdrawn at the end of Southern Region steam operation in July 1967 after 941,326 miles and sold for scrapping to J. Buttigieg, Newport, Monmouthshire being cut up in April 1968.

In spite of the premier train being hauled, there is no headboard for the 'Bournemouth Belle' awaiting departure from Waterloo on 17 March 1962. The engine, No. 35023 *Holland–Afrika Line*, is in need of a clean, and attention is required to one of the electric route lamps. Although the record cards state that AWS and the speedometer were fitted in October 1960, no evidence of the AWS can be seen in this photograph! The 6,000 gallon modified tender still carries the small BR totem, with the fire iron tunnel, rear spectacle and inset coal bunker visible. The sand fillers, the repositioned lubricators and the steam manifold valve adjacent to the steam dome can also be seen

G.M. Cashmore

No. 35024 was built at Eastleigh Works, part of order No. 3393, with boiler No. 1114. Placed in traffic temporarily with tender No. 3333, previously coupled to No. 35021, and in unlined malachite green livery, in November 1948, it was allocated to Exmouth Junction shed. In February 1949, it was the first of the class to be painted blue, with red lining bands, when the engine visited Brighton for an inspection of the livery by the Railway Executive. A 6000 gallon capacity tender, No. 3346, was fitted at the same time. During March the lining was amended to black and white. No. 35024 was named *East Asiatic Company* on 5 May 1949 at Waterloo station, by HRH Prince Axel of Denmark,

With the popularity of the West Country as a holiday area, the Southern Region was forced to run additional trains both to and from this area in the summer season. The second part of the up 'Atlantic Coast Express' is seen east of Basingstoke on August Bank Holiday, 4 August 1958, hauled by No. 35024 *East Asiatic Company*. The coal- or self-weighing tender is paired to the engine, and the small additional side raves for storage of the fire irons can be seen. The sliding cover to the whistle is on the top of the casing, and below this are the open covers to the sand fillers. Clearly visible is Bulleid's stovepipe chimney, with a fairing behind it and the safety valves, now resited, behind the chimney fairing

M. Mensing

With the steam sanding in operation, No. 35024 *East Asiatic Company* pulls away from Southampton Central hauling the down 'Bournemouth Belle' on 7 May 1960. Coupled to the engine is the coal- or self-weighing tender which, in comparison with the previous photograph, has the latest BR emblem on its side. When rebuilt, No. 35024 was one of the two locomotives fitted with open-ended guides for the valve spindles. The steps over the guides can be seen on the inner sloping section of the running plate inside the smoke deflectors

Author's collection

who was also chairman of the shipping company. In May 1951, it was repainted in BR green livery, again the first of the class to be so treated. Tender No. 3123 was acquired in November 1952, and the driving axle replaced in May 1953. Boiler No. 1097 was fitted in May 1954, with pressure set at 250 lb sq in, and modified coal-weighing tender, No. 3343, was fitted in May 1958.

The locomotive was rebuilt in April 1959, after 552,053 miles, acquiring boiler No. 1099 with repositioned safety valves, and was immediately transferred to Bournemouth. AWS gear was fitted in October 1959, speedometer in November 1960 and tender No. 3346 in December 1961. Re-allocated to Nine Elms in January 1962, in July 1963 it was fitted with a spark arrester. Transfer to Weymouth shed took place in September 1964, and withdrawal from that shed occurred in January 1965, with the total mileage being 839,415. The engine was sold for scrapping to Ivor C. Woodfield and Sons, Newport, Monmouthshire and cut up in May 1965.

No. 35025

Constructed as part of order No. 3393 at Eastleigh Works, with boiler No. 1115 and tender No. 3343, No. 35025 entered traffic in malachite green livery in November 1948, being allocated to Bournemouth shed. In September 1949, repainted in blue livery, it was named *Brocklebank Line* on 20th of that month at Waterloo station, by Col D.H. Bates, chairman of the line. Transferred to Stewarts Lane in March 1950, in November it

Departing from Salisbury, No. 35025 *Brocklebank Line* uses the steam sanding to gain adhesion with an Exeter to Waterloo special, probably in 1952. The engine is in Brunswick green, with the 'Devon Belle' wing supports fixed to the top of the smoke deflectors. The sand filler covers have been left open, as has the hatch to the whistle, but despite this the locomotive looks well cared for

Author's collection

The general grime of a steam shed is depicted in this photograph of No. 35025 *Brocklebank Line* at Weymouth on 28 April 1963. The coaling stages on the Southern used a variety of methods for filling the locomotive tenders, with that at Weymouth employing small four-wheeled hoppers which emptied directly into the tender coal bunker. Although over a year away from withdrawal, the engine is showing signs of neglect, with the edge of the running plate and the cylinder casing having a battered appearance. The pockets for the valve spindles are visible adjacent to the AWS battery box

C.L. Caddy

was fitted with boiler No. 1110. The locomotive was repainted in BR green livery in June 1952 and re-allocated the same month to Exmouth Junction shed. Tender No. 3350 was acquired in June 1952, when the original tender No. 3343, was modified to become the self-weighing tender. In May 1953 the driving axle was replaced, and boiler pressure set to 250 lb sq in during October 1953. The locomotive was transferred to Nine Elms in June 1954. In December 1954, the inside coupling rod fractured, damaging the track and the oil bath, with the leaking oil igniting and setting the boiler lagging alight. No. 35025 was re-allocated in June 1956 to Bournemouth.

Rebuilt in December 1956, having run 419,374 miles, boiler No. 1104 with repositioned safety valves was fitted and the tender modified. The engine was sent to Swindon Works for testing purposes in August 1957. AWS gear was fitted in October 1959 and a speedometer in June 1960. In March 1960 the engine was transferred to Exmouth Junction shed, and then passed into Western Region stock on 1 January 1963. No. 35025 was withdrawn on the cessation of main-line steam traction on the Salisbury–Exeter route in September 1964, and disposed of to Woodham Bros, Barry for scrapping, with a total mileage of 884,081. The engine was purchased in 1984 by Brocklebank Line Rescue and moved to the Great Central Railway in February 1986.

No. 35026

The locomotive was constructed as part of order No. 3393 at Eastleigh Works, fitted with boiler No. 1116 and placed in service in December 1948 in unlined malachite green, coupled to light Pacific tender No. 3260, of 4,500 gallons capacity, and allocated to Bournemouth. In July 1949 the engine was repainted in blue livery and received a 6,000 gallon capacity tender No. 3350. It was transferred to Stewarts Lane in March 1950 and remained unnamed until 15 Janauary 1951 when, in a joint ceremony with No. 35028 at Southampton docks, it received the name *Lamport & Holt Line*, the ceremony being

With the footplate crew viewing the photographer from the cab, No. 35026 *Lamport & Holt Line* makes a spirited ascent from Folkestone Junction on 25 July 1953 with a 12.35 p.m. special whose headcode indicates a route to Victoria via Maidstone East. This engine was one of the first members of the class to return to traffic after the crank axle failure at Crewkerne in April 1953. A self-cleaning smokebox is fitted, with the SC plate visible just above the shed plate on the smokebox door. The handles for the sliding cover to the main steam manifold valve can be seen on the top of the casing above the nameplate

A.C. Cawston

carried out by Mr S.H. Mercer, London manager of the line. Fitted with a self-cleaning smokebox and repainted in BR green livery in June 1952, it received tender No. 3130 at the same time. In January 1955, boiler pressure was reduced to 250 lb sq in.

Rebuilt with a mileage of 311,063, boiler No. 1103 with resited safety valves was fitted and the tender modified in January 1957, the engine being transferred to Exmouth Junction. It was re-allocated to Bournemouth in June 1957 and then back to Exmouth Junction in May 1959. AWS gear was fitted in November and a speedometer acquired in October 1960. No. 35026 passed into Western Region stock on 1 January 1963, but was transferred back to the Southern Region in February 1964 when it was allocated to Nine Elms. Final transfer was to Weymouth in September 1964, where tender No. 3349 was acquired in March 1965 and No. 3111 a month later. The locomotive was withdrawn in March 1967 after a total mileage of 858,784. Sold for scrapping to John Cashmore Ltd, Newport, Monmouthshire, it was cut up in September 1967.

During the last years of steam traction, the Pacifics travelled to foreign metals. No. 35026 *Lamport & Holt Line* is photographed at Stockport, prior to working an enthusiasts' train from Manchester to Doncaster on 20 November 1966. Visible within the cab are the vacuum brake ejector and speedometer, the drive for the latter being taken from the trailing driving wheel. In front of the tender step is the Stone's turbo generator, supplying lighting for the cab and route lamps, with the fuse box immediately above it. The characteristic round-topped 'Merchant Navy' axlebox covers are fitted to both the tender and the rear bogie, the latter being of the fabricated type

J.R. Carter

Built at Eastleigh, part of order No. 3393 with boiler No. 1117, and coupled to light Pacific tender No. 3288, of 4,500 gallons capacity, No. 35027 entered traffic in December 1948 in unlined malachite green livery and was allocated to Bournemouth. The engine received a 6,000 gallon capacity tender No. 3349 and lining to the livery in April 1949, and was transferred to Stewarts Lane in March 1950. Repainted in blue livery in April 1950, it was named *Port Line* at Southampton docks on 24th of that month by Mr W. Donald, chairman. In November 1953, the engine was repainted in BR green livery and during November 1954 fitted with boiler No. 1098 set at 250 lb sq in. Transfer to Bournemouth occurred in June 1955.

Rebuilt and the tender modified in May 1957, having run 363,351 miles, the

The 'Golden Arrow' was one of the Southern's most prestigious trains, with both the engine and rolling stock immaculately turned out. Driver J. Durrant and his fireman of No. 35027 *Port Line* pose for the camera before departure from Victoria station on 16 August 1951. The locomotive is in blue livery, with black and white lining, and a black splash skirt and cylinders. The smokebox arrow was frequently stuck vertically into the ground before being mounted on the smokebox, hence the discoloured tip! The international nature of the train was enhanced by the Union and Tricolor flags, which were carried on a holder mounted on the central lamp bracket below the smokebox

J. Kent

An unusual sight is a main-line train passing over the flyover near Wimbledon. No. 35027 *Port Line* hauling the up 'Bournemouth Belle' leaves the flyover by the Railway Staff Halt on 3 June 1965, the diversion caused by a broken toe on the up main-line points. The engine is attached to 5,100 gallon modified tender No. 3130. This tender is now attached to 'Battle of Britain' class Pacific No. 34067. With the rebuilding of the engines, the resited safety valves could be seen more clearly, and they are just feathering in this photograph. No. 35027 was rescued from Woodham's yard at Barry, and has now been restored to become the first Barry 'Merchant Navy' locomotive to return to steam, currently being based on the Bluebell Railway

G.M. Cashmore

locomotive was fitted with boiler No. 1101, with resited safety valves, and a new left-hand cylinder. In April 1959 it achieved the rare honour for a member of this class of hauling the Royal train from Windsor to Hamworthy Junction, where the train was berthed overnight. It was fitted with AWS gear and a speedometer in May 1960, and a spark arrester in September 1963. Boiler No. 1115 was fitted in October 1963, and tender No. 3130 in March 1965. Withdrawn in September 1966 with a final mileage of 872,290, No. 35027 was sold to Woodham Bros, Barry for scrapping. Resold to the Port Line Locomotive Project, it left Barry on 18 December 1982 for the Swindon and Cricklade Railway, Blunsdon, Wiltshire. Restoration was completed at Swindon, and the loco-motive was the first Barry 'Merchant Navy' class to be steamed, this being achieved in 1988.

No. 35028

Constructed as part of order No. 3393 at Eastleigh Works, with boiler No. 1118 and tender No. 3344, it entered service at Bournemouth shed in malachite green livery in December 1948. Transfer to Dover occurred in October 1949 and to Stewarts Lane in March 1950. The locomotive was repainted in blue livery in January 1951 and named *Clan Line* on 15 January 1951 at Southampton docks by Lord Rotherwick, chairman of the shipping line, on the same occasion as the naming of No. 35026. A new left-hand cylinder was fitted in October 1951. In June 1953, it was repainted in BR green livery, boiler No. 1120, with resited safety valves set at 250 lb sq in, was fitted in December 1954, and tender No. 3345 in July 1956. This unmodified tender from rebuilt engine No. 35020 was finished in that engine's livery, and looked a little out of place behind unrebuilt No. 35028. Because of stage 1 of the Kent coast electrification, No. 35028 was transferred to Nine Elms in June 1959.

Rebuilt, with the mileage at 401,005, in October 1959, it was the last of the class to be dealt with, having boiler No. 1094 and AWS gear fitted and tender No. 3345 modified. Fitted with a speedometer in July 1961, on the down 'Atlantic Coast Express' on 23 September of that year it attained 104 mph near Axminster. In February 1964 boiler No. 1121 and spark arrester were fitted, and re-allocation to Weymouth followed that

Photographs of original and rebuilt Pacifics together are rare. No. 35028 *Clan Line* waits at Folkestone Junction with No. 35015, her rebuilt sister, behind her, in late 1958. The engine is in Brunswick green livery, with the characteristic black splash skirt and cylinders, and the casing ahead of the cylinders has by this time been removed. The cover to the steam manifold valve is now the sliding type, and, like the sandbox covers, is partially open. The coupling rods are of rectangular cross-section, not frequently found on the original locomotives. The fastening cap for the rods is the later design, consisting of a large washer and four nuts, used on the rebuilt locomotives

D.W. Winkworth

A splendid sight as No. 35028 *Clan Line* heads a down express at Parkstone near Poole on the fine summer day of 19 July 1966. The engine, shedded at Weymouth, was fitted with AWS, and the protection plate for the detector can be seen behind the coupling on the buffer beam. The final version of the valve spindle pockets are visible on both sides of the smoke deflectors. The locomotive was initially the only member of the class to be preserved, although now one third of the 'Merchant Navy' class have escaped the cutter's torch. It remains to be seen how many will in fact steam again

G.W. Morrison

September. Two further tender changes were made, No. 3126 in March 1965 and No. 3342 seven months later. No. 35028 was transferred to Nine Elms in March 1967, having run a total of 794,391 miles, before being withdrawn at the end of Southern steam in July 1967.

Purchased on withdrawal on 9 July 1967, by the Merchant Navy Locomotive Preservation Society for £2,200, it was towed from Nine Elms to Longmoor Downs on 13 August 1967 and moved to Liss station on the Longmoor Military Railway on 28 May 1970. It left there on 28 August 1971 for Ashford, Kent, where it arrived the next day, having travelled by rail via Guildford, Redhill and Tonbridge. In February 1972 the engine was accepted by British Railways as being suitable to operate special trains over its system, with the inaugural run from Basingstoke via Salisbury to Westbury and return taking place on 27 April 1974. No. 35028 departed from Ashford on 19 April 1975 to be based in Hereford at the Bulmer Railway Centre, from whence it made a great variety of special railtour trips, mainly in the north of England. The locomotive also participated in the Rail 150 celebrations at Shildon in 1975 and the Rainhill Rocket 150 cavalcade in 1980, fitting in a visit to Swindon Works in 1975 for attention to the springs. Taken out of service on 3 September 1980 for a major overhaul at Hereford, it was re-rostered to main-line service in 1984. Its recent main-line runs include a return to the old LSWR line from Salisbury to Yeovil Junction, and the 'North Wales Coast Express'.

No. 35029

Built at Eastleigh Works, the penultimate locomotive of order No. 3393, and fitted with boiler No. 1119 and tender No. 3347, No. 35029 entered service in February 1949 in malachite green livery. The locomotive was allocated at first to Bournemouth, but in October 1949 transferred to Dover. A derailment at London Bridge in February 1950 necessitated a visit to the works to rectify damage to tyres and wheel flanges. In January 1951 it received blue livery, and was named *Ellerman Lines* on 1 March 1951 at Southampton docks by Mr A.F. Hull, chairman. On 8 May of that year it headed the special Royal train conveying the King and Queen of Denmark from Dover Marine to Victoria. Repainted in BR green in July 1952, when it acquired tender No. 3129 and in December 1954, boiler No. 1122, with a pressure of 250 lb sq in and resited safety valves. Transferred in June 1958 to Nine Elms, in December of that year it was fitted with a new right-hand cylinder.

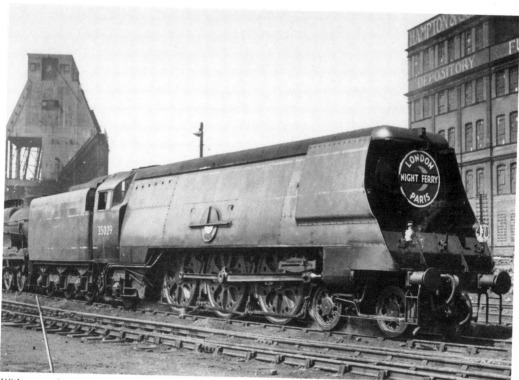

With nameplate half uncovered and the coaling stage in the background, No. 35029 *Ellerman Lines*, in malachite green, awaits the next duty at Stewarts Lane on 10 June 1950. It was customary on the Southern to cover the nameplates until the engine had been named; in this case the naming ceremony did not take place until 1 March 1951, by which time the locomotive was in BR blue livery. The sliding covers to the three sandbox fillers can be seen, and the wedge-shaped cab gave improved forward vision for the crew. With the heavy load of sleeping cars, the 'Night Ferry' was often double-headed, with an L1 class 4-4-0 frequently being the pilot

W. Gilburt

On the damp evening of 16 September 1965, No. 35029 *Ellerman Lines* waits to leave Waterloo with the 5.30 p.m. for Bournemouth West. The battery box for the AWS is visible between the frames below the smokebox, the door of which is fitted with a handle. Below the smokebox, the bolted panel allows access to the inside cylinder. The pockets for the valve spindle guides can be seen on both sides of the smoke deflectors, with the steampipes for the right-hand cylinder passing through the deflector at its junction with the running plate. It was a characteristic of the last years of steam that with neglect, small items such as the electric route lights on the Pacifics were frequently broken or misaligned. No. 35029 is today sectionalized at the National Railway Museum, showing the paying public the workings of a steam engine

C. Haydon

The engine was rebuilt, having completed 428,621 miles, and fitted with boiler No. 1090 and AWS gear and the tender modified in September 1959. In June 1960, it worked the inaugural Surbiton–Okehampton car carrier service. A speedometer was fitted in May 1961, and a spark arrester in November 1963, when the boiler was changed for No. 1103. Re-allocated to Weymouth in September 1964, tender No. 3113 was fitted in October 1965 and the locomotive withdrawn in September 1966, with a total mileage of 748,343, the lowest of any member of the class. Disposed of as scrap to Woodham Bros, Barry, it was acquired together with its tender for the National Railway Museum and removed from Barry in January 1974. No. 35029 was sectionalized by Flying Scotsman Enterprises and placed on exhibition in the museum for the opening on 27 September 1979.

No. 35030

Built as the last of order No. 3393 at Eastleigh Works No. 35030 was fitted with boiler No. 1120 and tender No. 3348. It was placed in service at Bournemouth in April 1949, in malachite green livery. Transferred to Dover in October 1949, it was repainted in blue livery in May 1950. The locomotive was named *Elder–Dempster Lines* on 5 June 1950 at Southampton docks by Mr G.H. Avezathe, director of the line. A series of haulage trials with loads of approximately 725 tons was undertaken on the Eastern section in the spring of 1952, to compare the different classes of Bulleid Pacifics with the 'Britannia' Pacifics. Repainted in BR green in May 1953, No. 35030 was fitted with 250 lb sq in boiler No. 1113 during October 1954. In June 1955, it was re-allocated to Nine Elms.

No. 35030 was rebuilt in April 1958, having run 351,234 miles, and fitted with boiler No. 1111 with resited safety valves, and tender No. 3348 modified at the same time. AWS gear and speedometer were acquired in May 1960. Boiler No. 1122 was fitted in May 1962, and a spark arrester in December 1963. The engine was transferred to

No. 35030 *Elder–Dempster Lines*, the last member of the class, stands outside the shed at Stewarts Lane on 22 May 1954, with the tender being replenished. In fully lined Brunswick green with black to the cylinder casing and splash skirt, the tender carries the first of the BR emblems. The casing ahead of the cylinders has been cut away in an attempt to ease maintenance procedures. Above the open sandbox covers on the casing are the three attachment points for the side arrows for the 'Golden Arrow'. The engines at Stewarts Lane were always immaculately turned out, the care and attention being the result of the presence of R.H. Hardy as shed master, who was not averse to taking over the driving and firing when the opportunity arose!

J. Kent

With the snow falling, No. 35030 *Elder–Dempster Lines*, shedded at Weymouth, is photographed at Eastleigh on 16 January 1966. One month later the light casual overhaul was the last recorded mechanical repair for the locomotive, but it was one of those which remained working until the end of steam in July 1967. In fact, No. 35030 had the honour of hauling the last passenger train of the Southern steam era on 9 July 1967
B. Eagles

Weymouth in September 1964, fitted with tender No. 3345 in October 1965 and re-allocated back to Nine Elms in March 1967. No. 35030 hauled the last passenger train of the Southern steam era, the 2.07 p.m. Weymouth–Waterloo, on 9 July 1967, and immediately afterwards was withdrawn with a mileage of 850,876, sold to J. Buttigieg, Newport, Monmouthshire and cut up there in November 1968.

TENDERS

For a class of only thirty, the 'Merchant Navy' locomotives had a diverse collection of tenders, with each of the three series of locomotives constructed having a distinct style of tender:

1st series (Nos 21C1–10), tender Nos 3111–20, 5,000 gallon; built at Ashford 1941–2.
2nd series (Nos 21C11–20), tender Nos 3121–30, 5,100 gallon; built at Ashford 1944–5.
3rd series (Nos 35021–30), tender Nos 3341–50, 6,000 gallon; built at Brighton 1948–9.

All three series of tenders had a double-framed chassis, the outer frames being set 6 ft ½ in apart with the inner frames 4 ft ½ in apart. The six wheels of the tender were of the Bulleid-Firth-Brown pattern, each 3 ft 7 in diameter, running in axleboxes whose round tops were lettered S/E\R after the war. The self-trimming coal bunker of 5 ton capacity and three vacuum reservoir cylinders, cab steps and a water capacity plate, were again common to all three series. The self-trimming bunker had already been tried by Bulleid in the 'Lord Nelson' class tenders and one 'Schools' class tender. The upper section of the tender sides, which curved to match the profile of the Bulleid coaches, and which were technically termed raves, the sides themselves, the coal bunker and the base of the tender tank were fabricated from $\frac{3}{16}$ in steel. The top section of the raves varied in shape with each series of tender, with a tendency to become less streamlined with each batch. In March 1948, one of the first series of locomotives, No. 35005 and its tender, No. 3115, were modified to accommodate a mechanical stoker; in 1948 three locomotives temporarily acquired LMS tenders for the Interchange Trials and five locomotives of the third series borrowed four 'West Country' and 'Battle of Britain' tenders while awaiting delivery of their own 6,000 gallon tenders.

Starting in 1952, but not getting into full production until 1956, the Bulleid tenders were modified to assist taking water. All the tenders were eventually so treated, except for two 5,000 gallon tenders which were rebodied with new tanks of 5,250 gallon capacity, and all the tenders were fitted with BR-pattern rear ladders.

One of the 6,000 gallon tenders, No. 3343, was modified in 1952 to become a self- or coal-weighing tender, which then ran behind a variety of 'Merchant Navy' locomotives. In Southern Railway days, tenders generally remained with one locomotive but this was no longer so when modification occurred to both locomotives and tenders. In the final years, locomotives exchanged tenders with withdrawn engines to run with a serviceable tender.

FIRST SERIES TENDERS

Nos 3111–20, fitted to locomotives Nos 21C1–10
5 tons coal, 5,000 gallons water
Tare weight: Nos 3111–2, 20 tons 13 cwt; Nos 3113–20, 20 tons 10 cwt

The rear view of the 5,000 gallon tender No. 3111 attached to No. 21C1 *Channel Packet*, taken at the naming ceremony on 10 March 1941, shows the cast ownership plate on the side of the tender, long spring hangers and front footstep at the cab end of the tender. On the rear of the tender are the footsteps on the right-hand side, the vertical handrails, the electric route lamps and connecting conduit, and the high swan neck of the vacuum brake hose. A two-step ladder runs down from the buffer beam

Author's collection

Fully laden weight: Nos 3111–2, 47 tons 19 cwt; Nos 3113–20, 47 tons 16 cwt
6 wheels on equal wheelbase, 6 ft 6 in + 6 ft 6 in

These tenders were based on Maunsell's practice and externally the frames were almost identical to the 'Schools' class tenders. The first tenders, like the engines, were soon modified in several respects, especially at the cab end and, to a lesser extent, at the rear of the tender. The basic design remained, adapted after further experience with the Q1 class tenders, to give towards the end of the war the second series tenders (Nos 3121–30).

At the front, the tender profile matched that of the engine's cab and was connected to it with flexible sheeting. The top of the side raves curved downwards, to be approximately in line with the top of the cab windows, continuing at this height to the rear of the tender. The coal bunker was hidden from view by the raves and on the first two tenders, Nos. 3111 and 3112, it extended right across the width of the tender. Immediately behind the bunker were the three uncovered vacuum reservoir cylinders, each 1 ft $4\frac{1}{2}$ in diameter and 3 ft 9 in long, mounted on wooden beams and held in position by metal bands. The cylinders were interconnected by external pipes, and a pipe led down through the tender tank to the braking system. Below the tender were two 1 ft 9 in diameter vacuum braking cylinders for the tender brakes – the operating cylinder at the front of the tender actuated brake blocks on the rear of the wheels while that at the rear of the tender operated the brake blocks on the front of the wheels.

Set centrally between the frames was the well to the tender tank, 13 ft long, 4 ft wide and about 1 ft 5 in deep, holding approximately 400 gallons of water. A strainer was fitted inside the well in an attempt to provide relatively particle-free water for the injectors. However, with no external access to the strainer, blockages resulted in the tank itself being drained, since cleaning was only possible via the inside of the tank.

The long link hangers of the tender springs were only present on this first series. They

At the cab end of tender No. 3111 are the two front water fillers positioned inside the raves, the two lockers on the right, door to the coal space and brackets for the helmets worn by the crew in the wartime situation. The shovelling plate for the coal is centrally situated adjacent to the handle for the hand brake. The canvas covers for the roof and the side raves have been rolled back. The steam heat and vacuum brake hoses are on the left and right of the photograph below the cab floor, and between them are the tender to engine water hoses. One of the brake operating cylinders is seen below the draw bar aperture on the tender front

Author's collection

were removed in the 1950s and replaced by normal spring brackets, when British Railways commenced alteration of the 5,000 gallon tenders.

The lower edges of the tender tank overhung the top of the frames, were in line with the bottom of the cab casing and hid from view two pipes; the lagged steam heating pipe on the right and on the left the vacuum brake pipe. These pipes ran beside the paired brackets set between the tender wheels supporting the tender tank, and curved down and turned in behind the buffer beam to emerge and end in the familiar flexible connecting hoses. When tender No. 3111 was built in 1941, the vacuum brake hose had a high swan neck but this was modified after a short time in service to almost match the steam heat connection set below the buffer beam.

The layout of the rear of the first three tenders, Nos 3111–3, was a blend of Maunsell and Bulleid ideas. The rear of the tender was very high and three footsteps were provided on the right-hand side, and to assist the crew to mount the steps there were four handrails, as well as very useful lamp irons! Two vertical handrails were positioned towards the outside edge of the tender, running almost from the buffer beam to just above the middle lamp brackets; the top handrail ran horizontally and was positioned centrally just below the top lamp, with the fourth handrail off-set to the right and positioned below the middle step. To these Maunsell traditions, Bulleid had added his own ideas in the form of a ladder of rectangular steel section with two steps running down from the tender buffer beam face beside the right-hand buffer, and electric lighting for the route indicator lamps. A turbo generator, initially mounted between the frames in front of the smokebox, provided electric power for engine and tender lights and the matt black painted brass lamps could be switched on individually to indicate the engine or train route. These lamps became standard fitting for all Bulleid Pacifics, although modifications occurred in their design. They were positioned immediately below the six route lamp brackets which were still provided either for the route disc boards used in daylight or for oil lamps. In the late 1940s a centrally placed coupling light was introduced with a separate switch and a hood on the lamp to direct the light downwards onto the couplings. The third series tenders had these from new, while the other series of tenders had this lamp added as they passed through the works.

With the fourth tender, No. 3114, entering traffic behind No. 21C4 *Cunard White Star* in October 1941, Bulleid replaced the footsteps and handrails on the rear of the tender with twin tubular ladders of $1\frac{1}{2}$ in diameter steel tube. Although these ladders were used on all the Bulleid tenders, the actual size and shape varied and was different in the British Railways period compared to the Southern Railway design. On the 5,000 gallon tenders, the ladders, one each side of the tender, were set inside the buffers and ran from above the buffer beam to the top of the rear tender rave and were provided with three tubular rungs.

After the war, the high rear rave of the 5,000 gallon tenders, approximately 2 ft tall, was cut down to a mere 4 in. This necessitated the provision of new ladders, of the same design as those used on the Q1 class, and again constructed of tubular steel with three rungs, but these were now closer together since the ladder was shorter. At the top, the stiles of the ladder curved over into two semi-circular loops to provide handrails. The bottom of the ladder was welded to the running plate above the buffer beam, and in 1956 British Railways commenced replacing these ladders with its own design. With the provision of the twin ladders, the single two-step ladder running down from the buffer beam at the rear of the tender was removed. It was replaced by a pair of tubular steel

The high rave at the rear of the tenders was cut down and tender No. 3118 running with No. 21C8 *Orient Line* is shown with the tubular steel ladders, only one of which is visible. At the top, the stiles of the ladders curved over to provide handrails, and at the bottom the ladder was welded to the top of the buffer beam. Footblocks have now been added to the buffers, and the central ladder below the buffer beam has been replaced by a ladder suspended from the buffer beam and the buffer itself

ladders, one either side, suspended beneath the buffer by one stile and attached to the face of the buffer beam by the other.

The buffers of the first tenders, of standard Southern Railway design, had no foot blocks but these were added later with the modification to the ladders. In the mid-1950s British Railways repositioned these short ladders to just below the tender tank, behind the buffer beam, matching those of all the other Bulleid Pacifics. The cab ladder, with three steps, of a similar design to the first rear ladders, was of $\frac{1}{2}$ in steel bar, and hung down from the front plate of the tender. At the cab end of the tender were two dome-shaped water fillers, fitted in addition to the large circular water filler, which was set centrally on the rear of the tender top behind the vacuum reservoirs. These additional front fillers were provided to assist in replenishing the tank without the necessity for the fireman to climb to the top of the tender. However, crews found it difficult to immediately shut off the water when the tank was full, frequently resulting in a cascade of water into the cab causing wet feet and clothing and making front filling unpopular and seldom used. Heavy brake application would also cause water surges and cascades into the cab. The one useful purpose, however, was to check the water level in the tank, as Bulleid did not fit water gauges. The front water fillers were removed in the early 1950s.

The use of a tender cab was new for the Southern although these had been used for both LMS and LNER Pacifics. The tops of the tenders were connected to the cab roof with canvas sheeting and the front of the first two tenders, i.e. inside the cab, incorporated many new ideas for the Southern crews. Bulleid used the tender bulkhead to provide lockers for the crew similar to those on the later 'Lord Nelson' tenders, with initially two lockers on the driver's side, but latterly one for the fireman and two for the driver. Set on the tender front were two brackets labelled 'Helmet' for the crew's wartime steel helmets. On either side of the tender, behind the water fillers, were the black-out sheets, designed to be pulled forwards over the cab entrances. The bottom half of the tender front was set forward about 1 ft in front of the lockers, forming a shelf, and set above this was the shovelling plate and coal door to the bunker. The larger entrance to the coal bunker was positioned centrally, adjacent to the crew's lockers. The hand brake, on the fireman's side, was in the form of a separate pillar, the handle rotating horizontally.

These tenders were not completely satisfactory and commencing with tender No. 3113 the cab end was modified, most noticeable externally being the fitting of black-out slides in place of the canvas sheets. The bulkhead was re-arranged with a fire iron tunnel on the driver's side just inside the side raves, and to compensate for loss of coal space the bulkhead was brought forward about 1 ft so the lockers were flush with the lower front shovelling plate area. A locker for the fireman was now provided and to permit rotation of the brake handle, the fireman's locker was shorter. Post-war, in the autumn of 1945, the black-out slides were added to tender No. 3113, although tender No. 3112 never received these slides. Inside, both tenders were modified to the new standard of lockers, fire iron tunnel, etc.

Adhesion was a problem with the 'Merchant Navy' class and in an attempt to improve the situation for tender-first running, a pair of sandboxes and pipes were fitted to the front of the tender below the fall plate. They were manually activated, gravity-fed, and the delivery pipes, oddly, faced the rear of the tender and were added only after all the first series tenders had been completed. The second series was built with these sandboxes but all were removed after the locomotives had been rebuilt by British Railways. Set inside the coal bunker, just under the overhanging roof of the tender cab, was a 1 in diameter perforated water pipe controlled by the fireman for spraying the coal

On tender No. 3113 attached to No. 21C3 *Royal Mail* the blackout canvas sheeting has been replaced by sliding metal sheets, and the driver's side now has a fire iron tunnel inside the curved raves. The front water filler is visible inside the side rave. Both engine and tender are in photographic grey livery

Author's collection

in the bunker to lay the dust. The final modification to the original 5,000 gallon tenders was the fitting of TIA, dealt with for all the tenders on pp. 113–16.

It was found that the first series of tenders, with their thin plate and welded construction, were not as strong as earlier Southern tenders of riveted construction and in 1944–5 strengthening had to be carried out, as well as repairs to split welds. Starting in 1956, the 5,000 gallon tenders had their raves cut down (modified) by British Railways but only eight were treated; the other two, Nos 3115 and 3117, needed further major work and the whole tender tank was scrapped and replaced by British Railways's own design. In 1948, tender No. 3115 had been modified, when it was altered with locomotive No. 35005 *Canadian Pacific* for use with a mechanical stoker.

SECOND SERIES TENDERS

Nos 3121–30 fitted to locomotives Nos 21C11–20
5 tons coal, 5,100 gallons water
Tare weight: 22 tons 1 cwt
Fully laden weight: 50 tons 2 cwt
6 wheels on equal wheelbase, 6 ft 6 in + 6 ft 6 in

The frames, wheels and wheelbase were very similar to the later first series. Holes were drilled in the frames for the long link spring hangers, but by this time the later pattern of springs and hangers were used. The holes remained unused in the frames. The pipes for steam heat on the right-hand side and vacuum on the left-hand side were readily visible since the lower edge of the tender sides was absent. The cab ladder was the same as on the first series, but the two-runged rear tender ladder of tubular steel was fitted one side to the face of the rear buffer beam, supported at the bottom rung to the guard irons and the other side under the tender tank.

The raves of the tender ran without any change in height from front to rear and curved

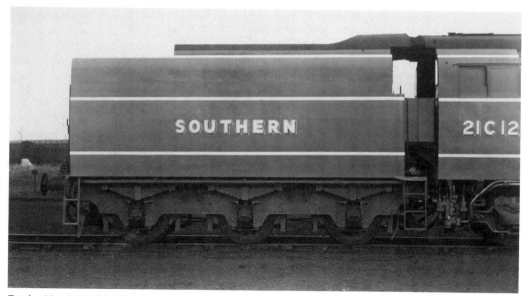

Tender No. 3122 of 5,100 gallon capacity fitted to the second series of engines, shows the different spring hanger brackets, although holes have been drilled for the long hangers used on the first series. The steam heat pipe is now visible. The tender sanding pipe is below the front step, and the brake blocks and rigging can also be seen. The rear step is now hung from the buffer beam and the tender frame, with a lower support on the guard iron. The Southern sunshine lettering and numerals, and the steel sheeting fitted to the cab windows should be noted

Author's collection

The cab end of a 5,100 gallon tender shows the arrangement of this series. The oval front water fillers are behind the glass spectacles in the space between the side rave and coal bunker. Three lockers are now provided for the crew. No water gauge was fitted, but a tap on the left-hand side gave a crude indication of the tender tank water level

Author's collection

An overhead view of tender No. 3121, of 5,100 gallon capacity, attached to No. 35011 *General Steam Navigation* at Salisbury in 1948, showing the arrangement of the vacuum cylinders, the inset coal bunker, water filler and rear ladder on these tenders. The lower attachment point of the ladders to the guard iron can be seen, and the side raves are used for fire iron storage

G. Heiron

inwards at the top. At the front, the coal bunker raves curved up and round to form the tender cab roof and behind the coal bunker were the usual three vacuum reservoir cylinders, offset to the left. At the rear of the tender, the two tubular steel three-rung ladders stopped short, just below the raves, and had no hand loops at the top as on the original wartime ladders of the first series. The front water fillers, now oval and with flat tops, were provided for tenders Nos 3121–7 attached to locomotives Nos 21C11–17; the last three tenders had the fillers plated over before entering service, with the others soon following. Behind the vacuum reservoir cylinders was the Bulleid style water filler, which opened to a full circle as the hinges were set behind the filler hole on the tank top.

The space between the coal bunker, now narrower and longer, and the raves was fitted with a hinged glass spectacle at the front providing rear vision for tender-first running and space for the fire irons. Stands were provided so the irons did not rest on the filler tops.

THIRD SERIES TENDERS

Nos 3341–50, fitted to locomotives Nos 35021–30
5 tons coal, 6,000 gallons water
Tare weight: 21 tons 10 cwt
Fully laden weight: 53 tons 6 cwt
6 wheels, wheelbase 7 ft + 7 ft 4 in

The first two locomotives of the third series, Nos 35021 and 35022, were completed at Eastleigh in the autumn of 1948, before Brighton Works was ready with the tenders. Consequently, spare 'West Country' class 4,500 gallon and 'Battle of Britain' class 5,500 gallon tenders were borrowed to enable the engines to enter service. Later locomotives, Nos 35024, 35026 and 35027 also entered service with 'West Country' or 'Battle of Britain' class tenders. The tenders had wheels and springing, vacuum pipes, brackets and lower cab and lower rear ladders and Bulleid-style water fillers similar to the second series. The axlebox covers on this series were all lettered S/E\R. Raves were of similar design to the 5,100 gallon tenders, and the coal bunker, appearing small in relation to the size of the tender tank, also had incurving sides joined at the front to conform to the cab roof shape.

There were no front water fillers, but space for the fire irons was provided as with the second series tenders. The rear of the tender was the same as the second series, although the 6,000 gallon tenders had a coupling light when built. The two rear tubular steel ladders, each three-runged, only had loops at the top on the inner stile of each ladder. On the tender tank top were the TIA water treatment tank and the three uncovered vacuum reservoir cylinders, normally lying flat behind the coal bunker and usually off-centre to the left. A circular link behind the water filler provided a lifting point, the other two links being within the coal bunker.

These two photographs show front and rear views of the 6,000 gallon tenders. The front of the tender is temporarily fitted with buffers for the journey from Brighton to Eastleigh, and the cab end arrangement was similar to the 5,100 gallon tenders. The ladders on the rear of the tenders had loops on the inner stile only, and just visible is the TIA tank on the right-hand side

P. Short

Tender No. 3345 illustrates the vacuum cylinder arrangement of some of the 6,000 gallon series. The TIA tank is on the right adjacent to the ladder, and the filling pipe runs down beside the inner stile of this ladder to the buffer beam. The notice below the coupling light is to inform of the fitting of the TIA equipment

J. Kent

MECHANICAL STOKER TENDER, NO. 3115

In October 1947, Bulleid obtained a reconditioned Berkley Mechanical Stoker in Canada, and in Eastleigh Works No. s21C5 *Canadian Pacific* was eventually fitted with it in March 1948. In order to fit it into the tender, possibly some coal space, and certainly some water

Tender No. 3115 fitted to No. 35005 *Canadian Pacific*, shown here at Clapham Junction on 13 August 1948 during the trials with the mechanical stoker, had two SR-style four-rung ladders fitted. A raised top was fitted to the tender tank to compensate for loss of tank space due to the stoker equipment. Note the opened water filler on the tank top

H.C. Casserley

space, especially in the tender well area had to be sacrificed. To reduce this loss of water capacity, the tender tank top was raised approximately 14 in and two SR-style four-rung ladders were fitted, the tops of which were visible over the raves as were the vacuum reservoir cylinders. The front water fillers and blackout slide were removed.

The mechanical stoker, driven by an auxiliary steam engine, had a three-section helical conveyor screw to move coal from the tender to the firebox and required coal of a uniform size. A coal crusher mounted at the forward end of the tender conveyor screw helped, but the coal had to be smaller than usual and this in turn brought about increased dust, contained to a certain extent by the canvas cover fitted over the coal space. The mechanical stoker experiments finished in April 1951 but the tender was not converted back to the standard first series, becoming one of those rebodied in May 1959 with a 5,250 gallon tank.

COAL- OR SELF-WEIGHING TENDER, NO. 3343

In 1952, it was decided that each British Railways region would have a coal-weighing tender to assist in tests of water and fuel consumption. The coal-weighing decision was definitely a LMR(BR) influence, but whereas the LMR had four, the ER had four and the

A rear view of tender No. 3343, the self-weighing tender, taken at Wilton South shows the two large 'Lord Nelson'-type vacuum cylinders on the left and the TIA tank on the right. The filling pipe for the TIA can again be seen. The weighing equipment for the coal bunker is housed in the padlocked locker in front of the vacuum cylinders. The tender cab roof has been added, and the new flexible coal-watering pipe is visible

G. Shelley

WR had two, the SR only possessed one coal-weighing tender. The LMR and ER tenders survived until the tenders were scrapped, but with the steel yard-arms removed. On the Southern Region tender No. 3343, a standard 6,000 gallon third series tender, was selected in May 1952 and modified by removing most of the top of the original tender. The inset coal bunker had vertical upper sides and a curved top to the rear of the bunker and, beside it, leaving a gap for visibility when running tender-first and for placing the fire irons, was a small rave about 8 in high. To the rear of the bunker was the weighing equipment, supplied by the Transport and Engineering Co., Lancaster, England, housed in a rectangular and padlocked metal box to enable measurements to be obtained of the weight of the coal used. A steel yard-arm giving the weight of the bunker was suspended by two camshafts, one each side, with the major bar giving the weight in 10 cwt divisions from 0–8 tons, and the minor bar weighing from 0–10 cwt in 7 lb divisions. The bunker was rigidly secured when the locomotive was moving. Weighing was carried out when the locomotive was lit up, before leaving the shed, at the start and finish of the journey attached to carriages and when the locomotive was back at the shed. Ash and smokebox char were also weighed on arrival at the shed.

The rear of the tender had the normal lights and ladders of a third series tender; the TIA tank was on the rear right-hand side but the vacuum cylinders, displaced by the bunker-weighing controls, were replaced by two larger cylinders of the 'Lord Nelson' type, 3 ft long and 2 ft diameter, and set transversely to the left. Originally the front of

This view of the self-weighing tender in lined Brunswick green with the small BR emblem was taken at Eastleigh on 12 July 1952. The tender sand pipe can be seen behind the tender cab ladder, and in front of the ladder the drive for the Flaman speed recorder can be seen entering the cab. The tender has no cab roof
L.Elsey

the tender had no side or top curvature to give protection for the crew when running tender-first, but a cab was fitted almost immediately. On 20 December 1961, the tender was removed from No. 35024, and after dismantling of the self-weighing equipment, the tender was rebodied. This tender, more than others, suffered badly from splitting welds in the tank at the front.

TEMPORARY TENDERS

LMS Type

In the 1948 Locomotive Interchanges, the 'Merchant Navy' class was to represent the Southern Region for the Express Passenger type of locomotive. The four engines chosen were Nos 35017, 18, 19 and 20, with No 35018 remaining on the Southern Region. The Southern Region had no water-troughs and none of the Southern Railway tenders had water pick-up scoops. In order to compete equally on other Regions with longer non-stop runs, it was decided to temporarily fit three of these four locomotives with LMS tenders fitted with water scoops. No. 35018 ran with its Bulleid tender. The standard LMS 4,000 gallon, six-wheel tenders were used, which unfortunately were in unlined black livery and lettered 'British Railways' in white, clashing with the malachite green and yellow of the engines.

Temporary LMS tender No. 10219 attached to No. 35019 *French Line C.G.T.* at Paddington on 20 April 1948 for the Locomotive Interchanges

No. 35021 *New Zealand Line* ran with a 5,500 gallon 'Battle of Britain' class tender while awaiting completion of the 6,000 gallon 'Merchant Navy' class tenders. Photographed on 2 November 1948 at Eastleigh, both engine and tender are in ex-works condition, with the engine's nameplates covered. Note the lettering and numerals on the tender and engine

W. Jackson

Lightweight Pacific Type

Two types of tender were fitted to the lightweight Bulleid Pacifics – the 'West Country' and 'Battle of Britain' classes; the standard 8 ft 6 in wide, 4,500 gallon and the larger 9 ft wide, 5,500 gallon type. Some of these tenders were put to temporary use by five locomotives of the third 'Merchant Navy' series while awaiting completion of their own 6,000 gallon tenders.

Locomotive number	Tender number	Water capacity (gallons)	Date fitted	Date received 6,000 gallon tender and tender number	
35021	3333	5,500	9.48	11.48	3342
35022	3335	5,500	10.48	1.49	3345
35024	3333	5,500	11.48	2.49	3346
35026	3260	4,500	12.48	7.49	3350
35027	3288	4,500	12.48	4.49	3349

These locomotives and tenders were painted in unlined malachite green with various types of lettering.

TIA WATER TREATMENT

It is appropriate that mention is made of water treatment in the section on tenders. Prior to 1946, water treatment, aimed at preventing boiler corrosion, reducing scale and sludge deposits, extending boiler washout times and reducing priming was virtually unknown. East of Exeter, much of the feed water was from chalk-based sources, containing calcium and magnesium bicarbonate, which was treated at the large motive power depots by a sodium carbonate, calcium hydroxide and sodium aluminate softening process, with the precipitation of the harmful salts in the form of a sludge. West of Exeter, bypass filters, using briquettes, containing sodium carbonate and tanin, treated the raw water on its way to the storage tanks, and because of the low natural hardness of this water, sludge formation was minimal. In the 1940s haphazard attempts had been made to treat the boiler water itself by adding briquettes to the boiler after washout, and occasionally to the tender tank. Chemical checks on feed and boiler water were rare, resulting in unreliable treatment of the water supply. However, by 1943–4 corrosion had been noted on the water side of the inner firebox plates of the 'Merchant Navy' boilers, where scale formation was high, and temporary repairs were made by welding additional diaphragm patches around the syphon holes.

In 1946, the advice of T.H. Turner, a water treatment chemist was sought, and he suggested that the French TIA (Traitement Intégral Armand) system should be used to reduce the corrosion, scale formation and pitting. After the corrosion investigation, all the fireboxes from the boilers of the first series of locomotives were renewed and similar work was carried out on the second series boilers in 1950–3; in the latter case, TIA was not generally fitted until renewal of the fireboxes had taken place. The French Railways had extensive experience of TIA with steel fireboxes, and Bulleid introduced the system into the 'Merchant Navy' class in 1947, the third series of locomotives being fitted when built.

Bulleid may well have used the system from the inception of the class in 1941 had not the Second World War intervened. Each locomotive was fitted with a steam-heated holding tank for the TIA water treatment compound – about 3 ft long, 1 ft 6 in wide and 1 ft high – set on the rear of the tender behind the coal bunker. The water treatment liquid contained sodium carbonate, tanin, antifoam and sometimes sodium phosphate (Calgon). It was fed at a controlled rate into the water tank, and caused precipitation of

On tender No. 3346 of 6,000 gallon capacity, attached to the newly rebuilt No. 35018 *British India Line*, the siting of the TIA tank and its filling pipe is clearly shown behind the vacuum cylinders on the rear of the tender. There are no handrails on the smoke deflectors in this February 1956 photograph

the calcium and magnesium salts in the boiler, forming a sludge with the tanin. The sludge was periodically removed by a manual blowdown valve situated on the front of the firebox, whose operation was initially noted on a suitable recorder on the footplate. The tanin reduced the boiler corrosion by decreasing the oxygen content of the water and the antifoam agents – organic polyamides and polyoxides – assisted in the inhibition of priming in the boiler by the reduction in surface tension of bubbles in the boiler water. The composition of the TIA chemicals was adjusted to the degree of hardness of the feed water, and the boiler essentially acted as a softening vessel, with the removal of the chemical products by blowing down. Boiler washout periods were dramatically extended in some cases from seven to fifty-six days, coinciding with the inspection period for firebox stays and plates.

By 1956, the TIA system was being replaced by the BR briquette tube feeder, which was simpler, more compact and cheaper and involved the use of briquettes rather than the TIA liquid. The briquettes were of similar chemical composition to the external water treatment reagents used in the 1940s, and contained antifoam to reduce priming. The briquette tube feeder was a cylindrical steel tube 3 ft 6 in long and 10 in diameter, with a

For the BR water treatment system the only visible sign was the circular top to the briquette holder. This is seen here on modified tender No. 3122 attached to No. 35012 *United States Lines*, positioned to the right of the water filler on the rear of the tender tank. A yellow triangle below the cab side engine number, a replacement of the earlier yellow circle, indicated that the BR briquette water treatment system was in use

M. Mensing

circular lid on a 1 ft square top and fitted to the top of the tender tank adjacent to the water filler. The main section of the tube projected into the water space, and six pairs of removable plugs were set into the tube at 4 in intervals, readily seen in the sectional view of the tender of No. 35029 *Ellerman Lines* at the National Railway Museum, York.

The briquettes were added to the filler on an internal stand, the base of which had four holes to expedite water circulation. Plug adjustment and briquette grade were stipulated by the water treatment section of the Chief Mechanical and Electrical Engineer, and were obviously dependent on the hardness of the source water. Charging of the tube feeder with fresh briquettes was carried out every three or four days, and boiler water was sampled every other day from the gauge glass drain cock, after blowing down and refilling the boiler. After chemical analysis by the water treatment controller, decisions could be made regarding changes required in the water treatment. Instructions were issued to drivers concerning the procedure for manual blowdown of the boiler, both on the road and on shed.

MODIFIED TENDERS

Thoughts of modifying and improving both classes of the Bulleid Pacifics had been circulating for some time prior to eventual rebuilding. Drawings in 1951 show ideas for the 'West Country' class ranging from a two-cylinder 'Britannia' type of locomotive to the ultimate design selected. Six locomotives, three 'Merchant Navy' class and three 'West Country' class were chosen as guinea pigs for modification, prior to the official report on the proposed rebuilding – although the final type of design had not been resolved. Among the improvements were some involving the tender, with the most visible being the cutting down of the side and rear raves of the tender body. Other small improvements resulting from the modification or cutting down included a sloping cover to the fire iron trough, which now became a tunnel for the fire irons, with a brass-framed spectacle glass at the cab end. In addition, the rear of the coal bunker was raised in a curve and the vacuum cylinders were now covered. Eventually all tenders had standard British Railways ladders with square section loops on the outer stile only, replacing the Southern Railway semi-circular loops on the inner stile. Catches to the lid and on the tender top which could be released by the foot were added to the Bulleid designed water filler in the 1960s. All tender axleboxes were eventually fitted with a modified axlebox cover, lettered S/E\R with an oil lubrication nipple below the lettering.

The first tender to be cut down in February 1952 was a third series 6,000 gallon tender No. 3342, attached to locomotive No. 35021, which today runs behind No. 35028. The other two 'Merchant Navy' tenders modified were the second series 5,100 gallon tender No. 3122 attached to locomotive No. 35012, and tender, No. 3124 attached to locomotive No. 35013. Another 6,000 gallon tender, No. 3347, running with locomotive No. 35020, was modified in June 1953, and the coal-weighing tender No. 3343 had a special cut-down in 1952. The early cut-down tenders were paired with unrebuilt engines, but when the locomotives were rebuilt, the modified locomotives had, with one exception, No. 35020, which was rebuilt in May 1956, a cut-down tender. This locomotive was fitted with the original 6,000 gallon tender No. 3345 from 25 May until 11 July 1956. This tender was used because it was easier to support the cables from the engine to the dyna-mometer car, and it was much more convenient to use the facilities for carrying weighed 1 cwt sacks of coal for test purposes using a high-sided tender.

On the modified tenders, the lockers, hand brake, door to the coal space and

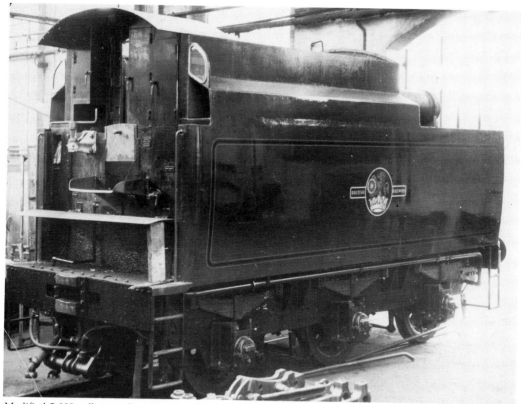

Modified 5,000 gallon tender, showing the fire iron tunnel with rear spectacle for tender-first running, and straight-sided coal bunker. The long spring hangers have been removed and the vacuum pipe is now visible below the tender tank. The aperture for the water gauge can be seen to the left of the brake handle

Author's collection

An overhead view of the modified 5,000 gallon tender No. 3119, taken at Exeter Central in June 1957, showing the vacuum cylinders, Bulleid water filler and TIA tank on the right of the vacuum cylinders

R.C. Riley

shovelling plate remained unchanged, but the tender sandboxes were removed. On the fireman's side at the cab end of the tender was a neat brass-framed water gauge, activated by a pivoted arm and ball in the tender water tank. On the centre line above the recessed door to the coal space was a light to assist the fireman in bringing the coal forward. The vacuum reservoirs were now covered, and improvements were made to the water strainer in the tank well to prevent ingress of coal particles into the feed water. Shut off valves were provided to enable the sieves to be drained without the necessity of draining the tank, as had been the case with the original tenders.

First Series: 5,000 gallon modified tenders

It is appropriate that the first tender of this series to be modified was the original tender No. 3111 attached to locomotive No. 35001. Work commenced in June 1956 with the removal of the raves, revealing the coal bunker standing with straight sides and front and a top curve to the rear. In this series, if not previously attended to during earlier work on the tender, the long spring hangers were removed, the rear lower tender steps were moved from under the buffer to below the corner of the tender tank, and the rear ladders had British Railways square loops on the outer stile. These tenders received the Bulleid design of water filler, later improved when the foot catches were added. Tender No. 3111 was fitted with TIA water treatment and with the TIA tank on the right-hand corner of the tender, the three vacuum cylinders being piled up into a pyramid. Most unusually for a modified tender, these cylinders were not covered but were banded together as in Southern Railway days. When the British Railways water treatment system, which took up much less room, came into use the vacuum cylinders, now covered, were repositioned behind the coal bunker and offset to the left.

Second Series: 5,100 gallon modified tenders

The 5,100 gallon cut-down tenders were unique among the Bulleid modified tenders in that the vacuum cylinders were completely enclosed, with two distinct sizes of these cylinder covers. On the later British Railways rebodied tenders, the vacuum cylinders were similarly enclosed. With the loss of raves on cutting down, the coal bunker showed an incurved top to the sides, a front curve up to the tender cab – this was missing on

This side view of tender No. 3121 of 5,100 gallon capacity shows the large cover to the vacuum cylinders of this series, and the ladder arrangements with a square section on top of the outer stile of the rear ladders. The coupling light is visible and to its right are the remains of the clips holding the TIA tank filling pipe. Note the holes in the rear of the side rave and the vacuum cylinder cover – do they have any purpose?
F.R. Sherlock

some tenders – and a newly added curve on the rear. The cab end was unaltered, except for the removal of the forward water fillers and sandboxes, and the addition of the water gauge on the fireman's side. The early tenders had Southern Railway rear ladders, altered later to the British Railways type.

It was the arrangement and covering of the vacuum cylinders and the TIA treatment tank that resulted in the variations in these tenders. When the first tenders, No. 3122 in July 1952, No. 3124 in December 1952 and No. 3121 in August 1957, attached to locomotives Nos 35012, 13 and 11 respectively, were modified the TIA box was placed longitudinally on the left-hand side with the cylinders lying to the right-hand side. A large cover, the width of the coal bunker, enclosed the cylinders and from a rectangular hole in the lower left-hand side about one third of the TIA box protruded towards the rear of the tender, enabling it to be filled with treatment fluid.

In the 1960s, the small vacuum cover variation appeared, and a small casing, the same as that on the British Railways rebodied 5,250 gallon tenders, was used. The end of the cover was filled in, completely enclosing the two large 3 ft long and 2 ft diameter vacuum cylinders, similar to those on the coal-weighing tender. The briquette holder for the British Railways water treatment was positioned beside the water filler on the right-hand side of the rear of the tender top.

Third Series: 6,000 gallon modified tenders

As already noted, the first modified 'Merchant Navy' tender was a 6,000 gallon tender, No. 3342. The removal of the raves showed that the top of the sides of the coal bunker curved inwards and the front curved into the cab roof as on the 5,100 gallon tenders. Below the tank, the tender remained unaltered, and at the cab end the only change was the addition of the water gauge and the fire irons tunnel. The TIA box was sited to the rear of the tender tank top on the right-hand side; later the change to British Railways water treatment was easy and its filler was generally placed in the same area. The early

No. 35020 *Bibby Line*, fitted with a 6,000 gallon modified tender No. 3344, is photographed at Clapham on 23 May 1959. The partially covered vacuum cylinders, the fire iron tunnel and the curves to the coal bunker can be seen. Just visible to the right of the tender water filler is the BR water treatment briquette holder. Below the cab side engine number is the yellow circle, first used to indicate that BR water treatment is in use

J. Kent

119

Tender No. 3118, a rebodied tender of 5,250 gallon capacity, coupled to No. 35008 *Orient Line* at Nine Elms on 1 July 1967, a week away from the end of Southern steam. The single rear ladder had a combination of SR and BR top sections, and between the two rectangular water fillers on the tank top was the BR water treatment briquette holder

G.B. Wise

tenders of this series still retained the TIA water treatment and Southern Railway ladders, but later all were converted to the British Railways type of water treatment and ladders.

BRITISH RAILWAYS REBODIED TENDERS

Trouble was experienced with corrosion on some of the earlier first series tenders, all of which required new wash plates and additional strengthening in 1944–5. Additional plating and further strengthening was carried out on some tenders during the period from 1945 to 1947. In British Railways days, to overcome similar trouble with the 'Merchant Navy', 'West Country' and 'Battle of Britain' tenders, an entirely new tender tank body was designed and built at Ashford Works, with a nominal capacity of 5,250 gallons of water. Ten tanks were produced, and six were fitted to 'Merchant Navy' tender frames between 1958 and 1963, one of which was modified to 6,000 gallon capacity. Three tanks were used for the 'West Country' and 'Battle of Britain' tenders. The remaining tank body was never used as a tender and remained at Ashford as a stationary storage tank.

Although of increased capacity, these tanks could be used on 'Merchant Navy' first series tender frames, and the first 'Merchant Navy' tender to be rebodied was No. 3115 attached to locomotive No. 35005 in May 1959. The new tenders still retained the 5 tons coal capacity but the tank sides were higher than the other Bulleid tenders. The fire iron tunnel was sunk into the top of the tender, this now presenting a continuous line from front to rear. The two vacuum cylinder reservoirs, each 2 ft in diameter, were completely covered, the cover being similar to that of the small second series. In each corner at the

120

rear of the tender top were two rectangular water filler holes, with the long axis lying across the tender and hinged to open to the front. Set between the filler holes was the circular British Railways water treatment cover.

Ladders and handrails on these tenders differed from those on the other 'Merchant Navy' tenders. The handrails at the cab end each had a small grab handle at the bottom, surmounted by a longer handrail. At the rear corners of the tender were two vertical handrails running from the bottom of the tank to approximately half-way up, with a third handrail running horizontally on the right-hand side. The single rear four-rung ladder, offset to the left, had raised grab handles to both stiles; the one nearest the centre in the British Railways rectangular style and that on the left being semi-circular in shape similar to the Southern Railway type. Apart from the handrails, the cab end of the tender followed the normal modified pattern. The water gauge and the coal space light were present, as was a grab handle on some but not all of the tenders, situated on the side of the centre locker.

Plans were drawn up in 1963, but never put into practice for a further modification of this series of tender. In service it was found that the positioning of the two rectangular water fillers served no useful purpose, and it was decided to replace them with a single central rectangular filler, and two side ladders with rectangular and semi-circular grab handles would replace the single central ladder.

One other 'Merchant Navy' tender was also rebodied. This was the 6,000 gallon tender No. 3343, which ran as a normal tender behind locomotive No. 35025 from November 1948 to May 1952, and was then rebuilt as the coal- or self-weighing tender. When the body was condemned in December 1961, it was decided to rebuild the tender tank but, owing to the longer frames of the 6,000 gallon tender, the new body had to be lengthened by approximately 2 ft. The rear ladder arrangement differed from other rebodied tenders since two ladders were restored with Southern Railway design semi-circular tops.

EXTERNAL VARIATIONS

Early days

The first 'Merchant Navy' Pacific No. 21C1 *Channel Packet* must surely have provoked cries of amazement on its inaugural public appearance in 1941. Devoid of the normal locomotive superstructure, its air-smoothed casing rose from the cab to the front of the smokebox ending in a widow's peak. There were no smoke deflectors or visible chimney, simply a rectangular slot above the oval smokebox door. The top of the casing was flat, with a circular chimney flush with the casing, and in front of the chimney a small rectangular slot connected with that above the smokebox. To the rear of the chimney was a circular pivoted cover, unique to No. 21C1, which Bulleid had provided to be used to cover the chimney aperture when the engine was not in steam, but it is doubtful if it was ever used. The three safety valves were positioned flush on the casing top and set slightly forward of the circular whistle aperture, midway between the cab and the smokebox front.

The external appearance of the second locomotive, No. 21C2 *Union Castle*, was modified by enlarging the aperture above the smokebox door, giving a greatly increased

No. 21C2 *Union Castle* at Merstham on 4 July 1941, with a larger cut-out above the smokebox door than that on No. 21C1 (see opposite page) and the chimney visible. The cast front number plate is mounted vertically above the buffer beam

Author's collection

area, by almost following the upper curve of the casing to the widow's peak, the electric route indicator lamp being moved to the peak itself. The larger cut-out exposed the top plate of the irregularly shaped smokebox, which sloped back towards and beyond the chimney. On the upper casing the chimney and front slot were combined to give a square aperture with radiused corners. This modification improved smoke clearance and was incorporated in the remaining eight locomotives of the first series during their construction. From a high view the chimney was revealed as a stovepipe fitted with a lip. With the completion of the first series by July 1942, the smoke clearance problem still remained. Bulleid himself had commented on smoke clearance in the programme for the naming ceremony of No. 21C1 – 'this opening (above the smoke box) forms the mouth of a funnel, tapering to a narrow slot in front of the chimney, discharging a stream of air upwards at high velocity, acting as a screen to the exhaust'. In practice this did not work

No. 21C1 *Channel Packet* in March 1941 showing front number plate, 'Southern' horseshoe-shaped smokebox plate, electric route lamps and disc holders in their original positions. Footblocks and front step on driver's side buffer only. There is a narrow rectangular air-slot above the smokebox door, with the electric route lamp above it. The contours of the air-smoothed casing curve down under the cylinders and join the base of the buffer beam

Author's collection

123

and smoke drifted around the cab, frequently obscuring the crew's vision. Bulleid was aware that locomotives with long boiler barrels and short chimneys suffered from steam and smoke drifting down along the barrel and obscuring the lookout on the leeward side, and admitted that the driver's vision could be impaired in the 'Merchant Navy' class. Numerous reasons have been given for the failure of smoke clearance in the Bulleid Pacifics, but the initial attempt on No. 21C1, similar to a design for LNER A3 Pacific No. 2747, *Coronach*, built in 1928, was possibly unsuccessful due to low pressure areas along the casing sides, which retained the exhaust rather than clearing it.

The problem was tackled in at least two ways. No. 21C6 *Peninsular & Oriental S.N. Co.*, No. 21C8 *Orient Line* and No. 21C9 *Shaw Savill* were initially modified in the autumn of 1942, by increasing the area of the rectangular air-flow slot above the smokebox door. No. 21C10 *Blue Star* was then used as a mobile test bed from December 1942, with modification to the chimney height and rectangular air-flow slot above the smokebox door. This proved unsuccessful, since the exhaust did not rise clear and gathered like smog around the cab windows, even when alterations were made to the chimney lip. Recourse was made early in 1943 to a 1/10 scale model using the wind tunnel at University College, Southampton. The model had a removeable front end, enabling different proposals to be tried, although as in all wind tunnel experiments it is not possible to completely parallel the multitude of air flows found in natural conditions on

Left: No. 21C6 *Peninsular & Oriental S.N. Co.* showing the air space above the smokebox fitted to Nos 21C3–10 when built, the modified position of the front number, route lamps and irons and the footsteps set into the sloping front. On the smokebox the 'Southern' horseshoe is now a roundel, with date and place of construction, and a cross added to each side of the construction date. There is a catch for the smokebox door on the left of the photograph. The top route lamp is on the widow's peak and the stovepipe chimney is visible
Author's collection

Right: No. 21C10 *Blue Star* in May 1943, with the casing above the smokebox brought forward in the shape of a cowl, and small individual smoke deflectors fitted, which stood proud of the main casing at their rear
A. Cook

The new style of smoke deflector and top cowl can be seen on No. 21C10 *Blue Star* in May 1946. The smokebox door catch fitted on the fireman's side of the door is readily visible, and the engine is fitted with limpet board for the casing

Author's collection

the railway track. There is evidence that at least two other models of smaller dimensions were used in these trials. One of these models, still with the widow's peak, had vertical slots within the casing on either side of the smokebox. The other model was similar to No. 21C10, with completely incurved casing of sides and top of the smokebox casing. Neither had smoke deflector plates, but both had fairings behind the chimney. A compromise was finally reached with these experiments, and No. 21C10 was modified with a separate top cowl extending forward and across the top plate of the smokebox. Short individual smoke deflectors were fitted, standing proud of the main casing at their rear, but at the front joined to the main casing, with a similar inward curvature. Cine film taken from the driver's front window showed improved smoke clearance, but forward vision was now diminished by the additional width of the smoke deflectors. These were redesigned to give a flatter configuration on other members of the first series when they were modified between 1943 and 1944. This new front end arrangement gave a greater upward air-flow around the chimney, and an air-flow along the sides, reducing the troublesome low pressure areas.

The second series of locomotives, Nos 21C11–20 built in 1944 and 1945, showed a front end design similar to that of the modified first series, with the inverted trough front cowl and separate short vertical smoke deflectors. These extended back only as far as the rear edge of the outside cylinders, and in depth came about 6 in below the central yellow line. When built there was a fairing around the chimney. In 1947 both the length and depth of the smoke deflectors were increased by about 2 ft and 5 in respectively, giving improved smoke clearance and a more aesthetically pleasing front end. The deflectors on the first series were modified at the same time, and the third series when built followed the design of the deflectors fitted to the second series. Some anomolies in deflector length appeared in locomotives involved in the 1948 Interchange Trials, although only one 'Merchant Navy' was fitted with extended deflectors – No. 35020 *Bibby Line* – a locomotive which was spare and did not in fact take part in the trials. The

Extended deflectors were fitted to No. 21C20 *Bibby Line*, one of the Locomotive Interchange engines. In this May 1948 photograph, with LMS tender No. 10373 attached to the engine, the front sandbox was reached through a slide in the deflector. A Flaman speed recorder has been fitted, and the drive of the unit passes from the rear driving wheel to the base of the cab

Author's collection

deflectors on No. 35020 extended rearwards almost to the centre driving wheel, covering the front sandbox filler, which was lengthened with the sliding filling panel placed in the smoke deflector itself. The long deflectors were kept until the engine was rebuilt.

Chimney and fairings

In 1946, experiments were carried out with some of the first series following the introduction of fairings behind the chimney on the second series of locomotives. It is known that at least three locomotives (Nos 21C1, 2 and 4) were modified but results could not have been conclusive since the final ten engines (Nos 35021–30) were built with projecting chimneys and no fairings.

Introduction of the fairing involved building up the rear top of the smokebox so there was a slope from smokebox front up to the top of the casing. A fairing was fitted behind the chimney giving a level surface from the top of the chimney to the top of the casing. This arrangement was akin to that of Gresley's LNER P2 class No. 2001 *Cock o' the North*, although the Bulleid Pacifics differed significantly in also having the inverted front trough. However, in the early 1950s the fairing became standard for all Pacific chimneys. Anomalies did exist with the single blastpipe chimney fitted to No. 35019 *French Line C.G.T.* in June 1951 and No. 35022 *Holland America Line* in February 1953, which were stovepipe chimneys without lips.

Additionally No. 35019 was fitted with small steam jets adjacent to the chimney, and the last engine to be rebuilt, No. 35028 *Clan Line*, was noted in March 1959 with a protruding chimney and no fairing. When rebuilt, the new chimney fitted to the engines was the same size as the earlier lipped chimney but was of cast-iron construction with a petticoat below, based on the design for the 'Lord Nelson' class, No. 30852 *Sir Walter Raleigh*.

The stovepipe chimney with the fairing behind is shown here on No. 35006 *Peninsular & Oriental S.N. Co.* at Wilton in the 1954 period. The safety valves are in their original position in a well, and the sliding cover to the whistle valve is visible, which replaced the earlier lifting type of cover

G. Shelley

Air-smoothed casing

On the first two engines the air-smoothed casing was constructed of 16 swg steel sheeting, the sections being riveted and bolted together, but none, apart from the sand fillers, was designed to open and shut easily. The complete casing could in theory be removed as an inverted 'U' for access to the boiler fittings, an operation occasionally noted at Eastleigh Works. With the numerous bolts holding each section together, it was probably easier to remove and stack each part as required – certainly this would take up less space than if the complete casing was removed. The air-smoothed casing on No. 21C1 *Channel Packet* was raised over the driving wheels and curved downwards behind the cylinders and in front of the firebox. The outside cylinder casing was rounded at the bottom, and the casing on No. 21C1 continued forward to join the bottom of the buffer beam, and was slightly deeper over the front cylinders than over the ashpan. When No. 21C1 received the modified front end in December 1943 to assist in smoke clearance, the casing remained essentially the same. Eventually, by 1947, the rounded section in front of the cylinder was removed and the locomotive resembled others of the first series.

The casing of the other engines of the first series, Nos 21C2–10 was similar to that of No. 21C1, although the cylinder cladding curved under as a separate portion and the

A fire under the air-smoothed casing of No. 21C5 *Canadian Pacific* resulted in the removal of the casing. The photograph of the fireman's side shows the splashers for the driving wheels, lubrication pipe runs, the water feed to the clack valves behind the chimney, the safety valves and the horizontally mounted whistle in front of the steam dome. Note too the boiler and steampipe lagging, the sandboxes for the middle and front driving wheels and the cover to the rear cast truck. The additional window added to the top of the cab is visible above the front of the window frame.The driver's side again shows pipe runs, with the pipes for the vacuum ejector and the blower running along the middle of the boiler, and the steam reverser and linkage over the rear driving wheel. The valve for the steam manifold is seen on the top of the boiler adjacent to the steam dome

Author's collection

casing itself continued forward to join the buffer beam half-way down. The side casings of Nos 21C3–10 were constructed of limpet board – a corrugated asbestos board – which was lighter than sheet steel, but was obviously more brittle. On these locomotives a horizontal T-shaped bar ran along the casing midline to act as an additional support for the limpet board.

The second ten of the class, Nos 21C11–20, followed the lines of Nos 21C3–10, except that in this series the base of the casing was a little higher; that on the tender, cab and firebox being level with the top of the buffer beams on the engine and tender. The curves of Nos 21C1–10 over the driving wheels had gone, the firebox end being a diagonal. Behind the cylinders the casing was vertical with the cut-out over the driving wheels being slightly higher, and in front the casing ran from the top of the buffer beam to the cylinders. When built, the casing on No. 21C11 had a reversion in style to that of No. 21C1, with the lower cylinder cladding carried forward and enveloping the bottom of the buffer beam. The remainder of the lower casing of No. 21C11 was the same as that of Nos 21C12–20. No. 21C11 retained this style long enough to be painted green, but during 1947 the lower cylinder cladding was removed to match Nos 21C12–20.

The casing contours of the third series, Nos 35021–30, followed those of Nos 21C12–20, although the smoke deflector plates were larger, extending rearwards to a position approximately half-way along the slide bar. In 1952, it was decided that to improve maintenance and accessibility, some elegance of line would have to be sacrificed, and the casing in front of the cylinders and the buffer beam was removed. This was applied to all locomotives.

The cab of No. 21C1 was built to the full Southern Railway loading gauge of 9 ft, but the width of the boiler casing made the front windows appear as rather narrow slits. On the side of the cab, small sun shields were fixed above the front windows, and these may

No. 21C11 *General Steam Navigation* was built with a bulbar curve to the casing in front of the cylinders and is photographed here at Eastleigh in black livery

Author's collection

The differences in casing contours are seen in this photograph of No. 35008 *Orient Line* and No. 35013 *Blue Funnel*. The former engine was one of those fitted with limpet board for the air-smoothed casing, in an attempt to reduce the excessive weight of the locomotive. The casing in front of the cylinders has not yet been removed from these locomotives. No. 35008 is fitted with the modified cab, giving improved forward vision, while that fitted to No. 35013 is of the original type. The rain gutter is just above the cab windows on both locomotives
L. Elsey

have helped on occasions to trap exhaust smoke and steam in front of them. The lower side section of the cab swept down in a curve, matching somewhat the curves in the lower casing, and the lower portion of the rear of the cab curved inwards beyond the top half. Side visibility was provided by two square, sliding windows, which during the war contained sheet steel rather than glass. The window frames, both the inner sliding ones and the outer fixed frame set within the cab side, were metal, as were those of No. 21C2. The window frames of Nos 21C3–20 were wooden, with Nos 35021–30 having brass window frames. There was no rain gutter for Nos 21C1 and 21C2, but from No. 21C3 it was set high up on the cab above the windows and in line with the ladder angle (gutter) on the boiler casing. Later, in BR days, the guttering was lowered to a position just above the windows as on the later engines.

With the second series the casing became a little more angular (other than No. 21C11's short-lived cylinder casing) and the cab too lost the lower curve and was vertical. The major improvement from the point of view of crew comfort was at the rear of the cab, where the side sheets were turned in about 12 in. This helped to prevent draughts, and to aid tender-first running a glazed, metal-framed window was set in the upper part matching that set in the tender. The cab handrails were similar to those of the first ten engines, being a single long rail from the central yellow stripe to just above the cab steps.

The third series, Nos 35021–30, followed the second series in casing layout.

Cab windows and wedge-shaped cabs

Forward visibility had always been a problem with the Bulleid Pacifics and earlier attempts at improved smoke clearance in 1943 had only been partly successful. The

It was not always easy to fill the sandboxes sited high on the casing, and the sliding covers to the fillers were frequently left open. No. 35006 *Peninsular & Oriental S.N. Co.* shows the open sand fillers while heading towards Exmouth Junction shed after arriving with a down train at Exeter Central on 25 July 1959. Sanding was to the middle and rear driving wheel only. The locomotive was also fitted with a modified cab, which improved forward visibility

C. Haydon

forward visibility was limited by the small front window, glare and reflection from the footplate and the air-smoothed locomotive casing, so in August 1947 an attempt was made to improve cab visibility. The upper front corners of the cab were sliced off and larger front windows placed at an angle, and the mid-line of the cab was shaped into a shoulder. No. 21C8 *Orient Line* was the first engine modified to a similar style to that appearing on the 'Battle of Britain' Pacific, No. 21C164 *Fighter Command*, though the remainder of the cab and the two side windows were unaltered.

It was soon found with No. 21C8 that the crew could not reach out easily to clean the new front windows from the two side windows. Consequently, three small rectangular upright windows were fitted, which could all be moved to provide room to reach round and wipe the front windows, and the front outermost side window was fitted with a glass windshield. Between 1948 and 1953 all of the other nineteen engines of the first two series were modified with new wedge cabs and side panels, with three side windows. No. 35008 was altered to this three side window system in July 1949. Commencing with No. 21C2 a small window was fitted above the main cab window on the fireman's side, possibly to illuminate the cab and the hydrostatic lubricator, since with wartime blackout restrictions illumination from the shuttered side windows would be limited, even in daylight. This additional window was fitted to most of the first twenty engines, although the hydrostatic lubricator was only fitted to the first ten locomotives. The window was plated over from 1947, since post-war there was glass again in the side windows.

With the alteration of the first series cabs, the opportunity was taken to modify the front lower portion of the cab to a vertical format by removing the lower curve and, more importantly for the crew, to introduce the complete turned-in rear of the cab sheeting, with a window for tender-first running. The second series received the standard wedge cabs, with Nos 35017, 18, 19 and 20 being the first modified in time for the Interchange Trials of 1948. The third series, Nos 35021–30, were built with the modified cabs and three side windows. When the class was rebuilt, the standard cabs were retained with the lower sides cut away. However, for most engines, the cab handrails were modified, with the single long handrail being altered to a long rail set over a short grab handle. A foothole was cut into the lower cab sheeting to enable the crew to reach the running plate from the footplate.

Sanding and sandboxes

As built, Nos 21C1–5 had steam sanding only to the front of the centre driving wheels, which proved inadequate. The remainder of the first ten engines had sanding added to the leading pair of driving wheels and between 1943 and 1946 sanding was fitted to the third pair of driving wheels. In addition, two manually-operated sandboxes supplied sand to the tender; oddly, the sand pipes pointed to the rear. The locomotive sandboxes were situated behind the casing, and the filling openings were rectangular with rounded corners and horizontal sliding covers set almost on the mid-line of the casing.

The second series of locomotives, Nos 21C11–20, and the third series, Nos 35021–30, had sanding to all driving wheels and to the tender. The idea of having sandboxes, kept warm and dry by boiler heat, was American in origin; in America, however, the boxes could be filled by overhead piped dry sand whereas in the British sheds the sand had to be carried up a ladder in buckets to fill the boxes. Inevitably sand was spilt, and in filling the front sandboxes contamination of slide bars occurred. In September 1948, No. 35012 had the front sandboxes blanked off and in addition in 1949 and 1950 a number of locomotives including Nos 35001, 2, 5, 9, 14, 15, 17, 18 and 19, had a cover fitted over the outside of the slide bars to protect them from sand abrasion. This was not the complete answer, and from 1951 the front sand pipes were removed, the filling holes blocked off and the unnecessary covers removed, though not always simultaneously. When No. 35020 had extra-long smoke deflectors fitted in 1948 these covered the front sand-filling holes, and access to the sand filler pipe was provided via slides in the long deflectors; however, these too were later plated over.

After rebuilding, the sanding to the front driving wheels was restored but the sand pipe to the rear driving wheel was turned forward to provide sand for tender-first running. The centre and rear driving wheel sandboxes and filler pipes were now more accessible, being set at running plate level, and the front sandbox was fitted just above the running plate by the smokebox. Sandboxes were still on the tender but were not used and were removed commencing in 1962.

Inspection hatches

Although the casing could be removed, it was soon found that some items underneath required ready access. Commencing with No. 21C3 *Royal Mail* two upward-opening hatches were provided; one on the driver's side of the locomotive in the top casing above the rear arm of the name plate gave access to the steam manifold valve, while on the fireman's side, the whistle valve was now reached via a hatch situated almost directly over the centre driving wheel. The hatches continued in use for some years and were fitted to the second series of engines. By 1947 the securing catch was altered to a lever control with locomotives being altered as they came into works. The last series, Nos 35021–30, were fitted with the lever control when built. It appeared that the upward-lifting hatch gave trouble at times because the BR design introduced in 1952 slid sideways and was provided with two grab handles. All thirty engines received this modification before rebuilding commenced in 1956.

Whistle

The whistle on No. 21C1 *Channel Packet*, with a tone of middle C, was situated horizontally under the top casing on the fireman's side approximately over the central driving wheel. It was invisible from the ground but from above an aperture about 10 in diameter could be seen on the side of the top casing, between the safety valves and steam dome. On No. 21C3 *Royal Mail*, a hatch to the whistle valve was provided and it is believed at the same time the whistle was repositioned. With this resiting of the whistle, a new rectangular opening was made in the top of the casing between the dome cover and the safety valves which occupied the width of the top portion of the casing with the whistle positioned horizontally along the mid-line of the opening. This re-arrangement was made to all engines.

Boilers

Bulleid decided that the boiler pressure for his Pacifics should be 280 lb sq in. The three Ross pop safety valves were located in front of the dome on the front ring of the boiler, forming a triangle with the apex pointing towards the firebox. With the thermic syphons possibly causing turbulence, there was a risk of lifting water through the valves if they were sited in the more usual firebox position. Three holes about 8 in diameter were all that was visible in the top casing between the front and middle driving wheels.

Although the boilers for the last twenty engines and the five spares, all of which were built at Eastleigh, differed in the position of the underside taper from the original ten boilers, all still had their safety valves in front of the dome. The valves were, however, recessed into the boiler shell.

In the early 1950s three modifications occurred affecting the safety valves. The first was a well for the valves, the second was the resiting of the safety valves to a position behind the dome and the third was the reduction of boiler pressure from 280 lb sq in to 250 lb sq in. This last modification was initially considered in 1946 to promote economies in boiler repairs, since the full boiler pressure was rarely used in the steam chest. The position of the well for the safety valves immediately in front of the whistle recess improved accessibility and was the first but least documented change. The bottom of the well could be removed to gain access to the base of the safety valves and although not all engines were so dealt with Nos 35010, 15, 16, 19, 24, 26 were, and Nos 35001, 6, 11, 14, 19 had an additional bar fitted across the well.

Although there were good initial reasons for positioning the safety valves towards the front of the boiler, one disadvantage, perhaps not foreseen, was that heavy braking caused surging of the boiler water so that the valves lifted below their rated pressure. The valves were resited, not on the firebox top, but at the rear of the boiler between the firebox and dome. Three valves were retained, now set in a shallow trough in line across the boiler and projecting from the bottom of the well, each being at right angles to the boiler surface. The first locomotive to carry such a modified boiler was No. 35024 in November 1952, the next No. 35008 a year later. The boilers of twenty-four engines were modified, Nos 35001–8, 10, 14–17, 19–24 and 26–30, with the modification being completed by January 1957. The remaining six locomotives, Nos 35009, 11–13, 18 and 25, were rebuilt prior to this alteration being carried out, and on the rebuilt engines the valves were more prominent. The resiting was completed with the rebuilding of No. 35011 in July 1959.

Wheels

The wheels were a Bulleid patent – a variation on the American 'Boxpok' wheel – designed in conjunction with Messrs Thomas Firth and John Brown and given the designation BFB. The advantages over conventional wheels were threefold. Broken spokes were eliminated, tyres were fixed, not with a Gibson retaining ring and set bolts, but were shrunk into a lip, a system which became standard on British Railways, giving a uniform and continuous support to the tyre, and finally the weight of the wheel was reduced. This was something Bulleid needed for the engines, with a 10–20 per cent reduction claimed over the conventional spoked wheels.

The wheel centres were cast steel, with bridging pieces radiating from a corrugated centre plate, and on the driving wheels a series of pear-shaped and circular holes and slits. To balance the crank axles, lead was added, as were invisible plates on the rear, their presence indicated only by blocked up holes. The small wheels on the bogies, pony trucks and tender only had circular holes. No. 21C18 *British India Line* was experimentally fitted with fabricated driving wheels, but these were not successful and were

The middle driving wheel of No. 35027 *Port Line* photographed at Blunsdon in October 1984. As the wheel is from a rebuilt locomotive an additional balance weight has been added, and the modified four-stud fitting for the rods can be seen

Author's collection

134

Fabricated driving wheels were initially fitted to No. 21C18 *British India Line*, photographed at Southampton. Sun shields are mounted over the front window of the cab and the rain gutter is immediately above the side windows. Glass has now replaced the wartime steel in the side windows. A cast rear truck is fitted to this engine

Author's collection

replaced by the standard cast type. On rebuilding, the engines had both internal and external balance weights, with those on the centre driving wheels being larger than on the leading and trailing wheels. The balance weights on some engines, such as No. 35024 *East Asiatic Company*, were offset, and not with the straight axis at 180 degrees in relation to the crankpin.

Pockets

In all new designs and rebuilding some problems occur, and in the rebuilt Bulleid Pacifics the normal blind guides to the outside valve spindles gave trouble, although twenty engines appeared in this guise. It will be recalled that the unconventional Bulleid valve gear was replaced with Walschaerts' valve gear, with the retention of outside admission for the outside cylinders and blind guides to the valves. To overcome this problem, the valve spindles were extended which necessitated piercing the front sloping sections of the running plate. Initially, open-ended pockets were employed and fitted to No. 35019 *French Line C.G.T.* and No. 35024 *East Asiatic Company* in May and April 1959 respectively. Ash and grit caused problems and closed-end pockets were introduced, which were of three types, each getting progressively larger. The first type, seen on No. 35022 *Holland America Line*, being round truncated cone valve spindle pockets.

135

No. 35006 *Peninsular & Oriental S.N. Co.* at Templecombe, with the final design for the front pockets for the valve spindle guides. The casing for the guides is on both sides of the smoke deflectors, and provides an additional step. The AWS battery box is mounted between the front frames behind the lower route disc, with the detector protected by a steel plate mounted behind the coupling. The drive for the Smiths speedometer can just be seen on the rear driving wheel. On the smokebox is a grab handle to assist in the closure of the door
D. Mackinnon

These were situated on the inside of the smoke deflectors, at the level of the footsteps, inside the deflector plates.

By August 1959, the second type had been devised, consisting of a rectangular hollow box in the same position as the round pocket, but with an extra footstep fitted above and retaining the original outside footstep. Nos 35001, 3, 4, 5, 6, 8, 11, 12, 18, 19, 21, 28 and 29 had this modification. For the third and what became the standard pocket, the fitment was not only deeper but wider, and for the first time was fitted both inside and outside the smoke deflectors. The smoke deflector was fitted around the pocket and the top of the pocket supported an inside step with the outside step being repositioned about 4 in higher on top of the pocket. All engines received standard pockets, except for No. 35018, this engine retaining the small rectangular pockets until withdrawal from service.

Speed recorders

Soon after the war No. 21C2 *Union Castle* was fitted with a Flaman speed recorder capable of giving both a visual indication and paper record of the speed, and then early in 1948, No. s21C5 *Canadian Pacific*, soon to be renumbered as No. 35005, was also fitted with this equipment. Later that year all Bulleid Pacifics involved in the 1948 Interchange Trials, Nos 35017, 18, 19, and 20, were so equipped. The shaft drive of the speed recorders, running from the rear driving wheel on the fireman's side was held by an inverted triangular bracket attached to the casing above the offside rear driving wheel. The drive to the speedometer was via this horizontal shaft to the base of the cab where it was connected to the speedometer and recording gear. On completion of the trials, the brackets and the speed recorders remained on some engines – No. 35018 *British India Line* was still fitted in July 1952 and No. 35017 *Belgian Marine* a year later – but all evidence of the recorders was removed on rebuilding.

In the late 1950s, it was decided that selected main-line locomotives should be fitted with a Smiths speedometer. The flexible drive led from the rear near side driving wheel into the driver's side of the cab, where the large speedometer dial gave a clear indication of speed, but with no recording facility. All the rebuilt engines were fitted with speedometers, calibrated to a maximum speed of 100 mph.

ATC/AWS

In 1958, BR announced that automatic train control (ATC) would be fitted to locomotives. This electromagnetic system was based on the Hudd system on the London, Tilbury and Southend section of the London Midland Region, and was redesignated automatic warning system (AWS) by 1960. On the locomotive there was a receiver under the front buffer beam, with a steel protection plate to prevent damage by the screw coupling. Power supply for the system was a Nife accumulator, fitted on the original and rebuilt Bulleid Pacifics in a battery box located over the front buffer beams between the frames. In the cab on the driver's side were the bell, horn, reminder disc and cancelling button. All the 'Merchant Navy' class were fitted with AWS, the first being rebuilt engine No. 35001 *Channel Packet* in August 1959. The first section of Southern Region line to be fitted with AWS was that from Salisbury to Exeter Central, completed in March 1960, and forming the initial part of a five-year plan to cover the routes from Waterloo to Exeter Central and to Bournemouth West.

Minor front end modifications

When built, No. 21C1 *Channel Packet* had its cast number plate set on the sloping front above the buffer beam, with the lower lamp brackets and electric route lamps set on the vertical front surface just below the buffer beam. The number plate was moved to the lower vertical sheeting by August 1941, with the repositioning of the lamp brackets and electric route lamps to the upper sloping section previously occupied by the number plate. Footholes were cut in the sloping front section, being positioned inside the route indicator lamps, and the redesign featured on all subsequent engines. The middle lamp brackets and electric route lamps were sited on the forward section of the casing almost in line with the lower smokebox hinge.

When the Southern route discs were used these protruded beyond the outside casing, obscuring forward vision and in some circumstances the discs were removed by passage of trains on adjacent tracks. In April 1946, the lamp irons on No. 21C1 were moved to the smokebox door, and the other members of the class followed suit later. Another front end modification was the fitting of a grab handle to the fireman's side of the smokebox door on Nos 21C11–15 when already in traffic, and to Nos 21C16–35030 before entering traffic. Although of the first series only No. 21C5 *Canadian Pacific* and No. 21C7 *Aberdeen Commonwealth* had a smokebox door grab handle, when rebuilt the handle was fitted to all the locomotives. Perhaps the catch fitted to the right-hand side of the door on Nos 21C3–10 when new was in some way designed to act as a grab handle for opening the smokebox door – certainly this function was provided by the repositioned lamp brackets.

Rear trucks

Two types of rear truck were fitted to the engines, with the cast type fitted originally to Nos 21C1–20 and a fabricated truck being fitted to the final series, Nos 35021–30. The reason for this change in construction was to produce a structure that was lighter in weight than the original and parallels the use of fabricated frame stretchers rather than the cast type. The cast truck was covered with a sheet of leather or rexene, possibly to reduce the influx of ash and dust from the ashpans onto the bearing surfaces. From about 1946 these outer covers were removed, and the fabricated trucks fitted to the final series of locomotives were never covered.

In the period 1949–67, while in works the two types of truck were interchanged between locomotives, with some members of the first two series running with the fabricated trucks and some of those of the final series running with the cast type. In the 1960s, the division for the two types of truck on the rebuilt engines was as follows:

Cast trucks, as fitted originally when built;
Nos 35001, 5–10, 12–14, 16, 18, 20 – with, in addition, those which were fitted initially with fabricated trucks;
Nos 35021, 22, 24–5, 27–9.

Fabricated trucks, as fitted originally when built;
Nos 35023, 26, 30 – with, in addition, those which were fitted initially with cast trucks;
Nos 35002–4, 11, 15, 17, 19.

LIVERIES

When O.V.S. Bulleid was appointed as Chief Mechanical Engineer of the Southern Railway in 1937, there were already suggestions that Maunsell's green livery should be brightened. Eventually, in mid-1939, after various combinations had been tried, malachite green, edged black and lined in yellow was chosen. No. 21C1 *Channel Packet* was turned out in malachite green, but in a matt finish, as it was thought that this would not highlight blemishes in the air-smoothed casing. There were three horizontal yellow lines, with the top line cut across the top washout plug above the cab windows and along the tender rave. The middle line incorporated the bottom of the cab window, and the bottom line was 3 in above the wheel cut-out. The rear of the tender was unlined green and the wheels were green with black axle centres and tyres. The top of the casing down to the ladder angle or guttering on the locomotive was matt black and the top of the cab and tender raves black, with a band of green between this and the top yellow line. The front of the locomotive, top of the tender and below the casing were all black, as were the bottom of the cylinders and the casing forward of the buffer beams. The ground to the smokebox and tender ownership plates, the front and cab side number plates and the nameplates were red, which was also the colour of the buffer collars and beams.

After completion of Nos 21C1 and 21C2, it was found necessary to reduce the locomotives' weight, and two of these procedures affected the livery. The first was the use of limpet board on the casing sides to replace the previous 16 swg steel sheet, and the second was the abandonment of the cast tender plates lettered 'Southern' and the

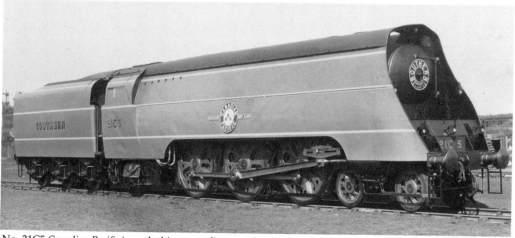

No. 21C5 *Canadian Pacific* in malachite green livery at Eastleigh in December 1941. The middle yellow line was repositioned to conceal the strengthening rib for the limpet board used for the casing, and the base of the cylinders was painted black. Gilt lettering and numerals were used on this and other malachite green locomotives. Note the cover over the rear truck, the sanding to the middle driving wheel only and the use of sheet steel in the cab side windows. Compared with Nos 21C1 and 2, the nameplate and bottom yellow line were lower
B.I. Fletcher collection

three cast number plates, necessitating the use of painted letters and numbers. The strengthening batten used to support the limpet board was painted yellow to become the middle line of the livery, and was about 2 in below the line of the first two locomotives. One other alteration to the livery, and probably the only addition in weight to the locomotive, was the increase in the smokebox door ownership plate to a full circle. The enginemen regarded the horseshoe-shaped smokebox door plate of Nos 21C1 and 21C2 as being an 'upside-down horseshoe' and as such unlucky, so the new plates were based on superstition. Two minor differences were made to the livery of No. 21C3 *Royal Mail* after the official photographs in works grey and before it entered traffic in malachite green. The painted front numerals were reduced in height from 9 in to 6 in and the 'C', both on the cab side and front of the engine, was considered to be a number and not a letter, hence it had no internal black lines.

By July 1941, the Southern Railway decided that all locomotives except the 130 express passenger locomotives of the 'Lord Nelson', 'King Arthur' and 'Schools' classes should be painted unlined black and to compensate for the loss of green the sunshine lettering was introduced. This lettering used yellow (old gold) rather than gilt, green blocking on black locomotives with yellow (sunshine) highlights, still with the internal black lines, although hand-painted gilt lettering, black blocking and yellow highlights was used for Nos 21C4–6 only. The numbers were a little simpler and were in yellow with green blocking and yellow highlights but no internal lines; the side letters were 9 in high and the numerals 9 in high with 6 in high front numbers. Early in 1942 war conditions forced the Southern Railway to paint even the express passenger locomotives unlined black. Although Nos 21C1–6 were painted green ex-works, No. 21C5 *Canadian Pacific* became the first of the class to be painted black when it was named in March 1942, but No. 21C2 *Union Castle* retained its malachite green livery until June 1944, being the last of the class to be painted black. During the remainder of the war, the only minor alteration to the livery was that on repainting, the letter 'C' in the numbers, previously larger to match the number plates of Nos 21C1–2, was now the same size as the numerals themselves.

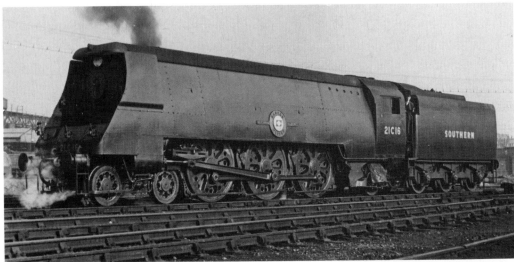

No. 21C16 *Elders Fyffes* in black livery with no lining in 1946 at Nine Elms. Sunshine lettering was used for the engine numbers and 'Southern' on the tender, with a red ground to the roundel on the smokebox and the nameplate. The letters and numbers in the engine number were all of the same size. Short smoke deflectors were fitted

Author's collection

When Nos 21C11–20 of the second series were built, all were initially painted unlined black. In February 1945, No. 21C12 *United States Lines* returned to Eastleigh Works for repairs to a broken chain, and with its naming ceremony planned for early April the locomotive was repainted. For the naming ceremony, the locomotive's casing, cab and tender were malachite green, with a varnished top coat and with three horizontal yellow lines; the rear of the tender unlined green, the wheels green with black axle centres and tyres and the coal bunker green up to the same level as the casing and then black above. The smoke deflectors were finished in malachite green, with two horizontal yellow lines and black above the ladder angle. The cowl was varnished black, not green. The cylinder casing, a continuation of that of the locomotive, was green. By August 1947 all the other engines of the first and second series had been similarly painted.

British Railways was formed on 1 January 1948, with six regions replacing the four companies. From the middle of January 1948, engines began emerging from the works still in the previous livery with the addition of, for the Southern Region, a temporary 's' prefix and the wording 'British Railways' on the tender in the previous company's style of lettering. No transfers were available, so the sunshine lettering was written by hand. The only 'Merchant Navy' to carry the temporary 's' prefix was No. s21C5 *Canadian Pacific* between 20 March and 8 April 1948, although No. 21C19 *French Line C.G.T.* received the prefix in works in March 1948 but was renumbered before leaving. By late March 1948, the full renumbering scheme had been announced, with the Bulleid style of notation being discarded and the 'Merchant Navy' class numbered as 35001–20; the first locomotive to be renumbered in this scheme being No. 35005 *Canadian Pacific*. When renumbered, the engines were to carry an LMS-style cast-iron smokebox number plate, which on the Bulleid Pacifics entailed the removal of the circular 'Southern' plate.

After April 1948, while all engines had to be renumbered before leaving the works, if a locomotive did not require repainting it returned to traffic still lettered 'Southern'. No. 21C2 *Union Castle* did enter works in August 1949 but was not renumbered,

The temporary 's' prefix introduced in 1948 for the Southern locomotives, was only carried by No. s21C5 *Canadian Pacific*, seen here in malachite green livery on 20 March 1948. The Flaman speedometer drive can be seen running from the rear driving wheel, and the engine was also fitted with the Berkley mechanical stoker at this time. This locomotive was soon to lose the smokebox roundel and become renumbered in the BR classification as No. 35005

Author's collection

probably due to the presence of the cast number plates, until a second visit to works, becoming No. 35002 in January 1950. At Eastleigh an experimental bold Gill Sans lettering was tried which was plain yellow with a black outline and, to accompany this, plain yellow numbers were used. During June 1948 the standard medium Gill Sans commenced, but in December 1948, BR heeded what the critics had been saying for some time, that no lettering of 'British Railways' was necessary. So, for a period awaiting the arrival of the new emblem transfers, the tenders were left blank. With the fitting of the LMS tenders for the Interchange Trials, these were not permitted to be repainted to match the engines' livery, but were unlined black with white lettering.

The third series, Nos 35021–30, were painted in malachite green but, due to the late delivery of the tenders, all were not lined. Those fitted with the 6,000 gallon tenders when built were lined in standard Southern style, with the lining positions as on the second series except that the taller coal bunker was completely black. Engines No. 35024 *East Asiatic Company* and No. 35026 *Lamport & Holt Line* were painted BR standard blue, never having received the full lined malachite green livery.

To comply with general BR painting instructions, Eastleigh commenced painting 'Merchant Navy' cylinders black in 1949. To prevent a rather odd appearance, the casing between the cylinders and the buffer beam to the depth of the cut-out over the driving wheels was also black, giving a black splash skirt only on the front of the locomotive.

During 1948, BR had been carrying out experiments with various liveries, and early in 1949 the standard colours were announced, one of which, that for the most powerful express passenger locomotives, was blue with black and white lining. In February 1949, No. 35024 *East Asiatic Company* entered Eastleigh Works to receive its 6,000 gallon tender and was the first of the class to be painted in this livery. The initial attempt was blue with 2 in horizontal crimson lines, the blue replacing malachite green, and the red the horizontal yellow lines! The blue was the standard blue – a mid to dark shade – with the locomotive casing, including the cylinders, cab and tender sides and rear and wheels in this colour, with black axle centres and tyres. The buffer beam and ground to the nameplate were red, and the top and front of the casing and all items below it were

On 8 July 1950, No. 35012 *United States Lines* leaves Southampton Central. A smokebox number plate has been fitted and the number is on the cab side, but the tender side is blank

W. Gilburt

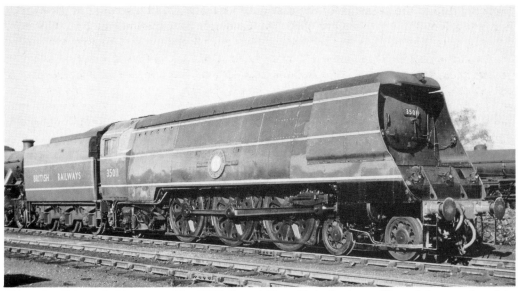

Although still in malachite green, No. 35011 *General Steam Navigation* has a BR smokebox number plate and is lettered 'British Railways' in Gill Sans lettering on the tender, when photographed in October 1950 at Eastleigh. The cylinders and front skirt between the buffer beam and cylinders were painted black. Lightening holes can be seen in the front of the frames above the buffers, and the engine is fitted with the modified cab

L. Elsey

At Brighton on 18 February 1949, No. 34024 *East Asiatic Company*, with covered nameplates, displays the new blue livery with three red stripes, and the large BR emblem, which was hand-painted, on the tender. The 6,000 gallon tender is fitted with TIA, and the sand pipe to the front tender wheel is visible. Cab side numbers were yellow

W. Jackson

black. A British Railways smokebox number plate was fitted, and the cab number was in Gill Sans figures, 10 in high in yellow, edged in black. Centrally placed on the tender, between the middle and lower red lines, was a hand-painted large size British Railways lion-over-wheel emblem.

The engine left Eastleigh Works on 12 February and ran to Brighton on 18 February for inspection, entering traffic on 22 February and reaching Exeter Central, before returning for amendments at Eastleigh on 2 March 1949. The red lines were not approved and the official black and white lining was substituted with only two lines on the sides, at the top and bottom. While No. 35024 *East Asiatic Company* was in the blue and red livery, the nameplates were affixed and uncovered as usual for inspections. The trip to Brighton saw them covered but, somehow, at Exeter Central they were on view! On entering traffic after the repainting with black and white lines, the nameplates were covered pending the naming ceremony to be carried out on 5 May 1949. However, prior to this, the locomotive re-entered Eastleigh Works in late April and the wheels and the complete splash skirt from the front of the locomotive to the rear of the tender was painted black and approved after inspection. This amended livery was to become the standard for the class, although until July 1949, when No. 35026 *Lamport & Holt Line* appeared in blue, malachite green was still in vogue, possibly to use up stocks of the paint.

British Railways found, as had been predicted, that the blue paint did not wear well, so that livery was abandoned in mid-1951. Nos 35011, 14 and 23 were never painted blue, going straight from malachite green to the new colour of Brunswick green. All blue

The standard blue livery is shown on No. 35024 *East Asiatic Company* at Axminster in 1950, with smokebox door number plate and BR emblem on the tender, now in line with the cab side numbers. The two horizontal lines are black with white lining, and the complete splash skirt below the lower line is black. The 'Devon Belle' battens are on the top of the smoke deflectors

B. Wright

The final BR colour scheme is displayed by No. 35014 *Nederland Line* in Brunswick green with black and orange lining, and a black splash skirt to engine and tender. A strengthening strut has been added to the lower inner section of the smoke deflector

Author's collection

With the modification of the tenders, rectangular panels of lining on the cab and the modified tender were used. No. 35012 *United States Lines* shows the new livery in this July 1952 photograph. The experimental lining on the locomotive is the same style as the panels. This trial was of brief duration. The small BR emblem is on the tender, and the black splash skirt is limited to the area in front of the cab and on the cylinders themselves. The buffer beam is red, and the smokebox front and the top of the casing black. The front sanding has been blanked off

Author's collection

locomotives on repainting were finished in Brunswick green, lined black and orange with the green replacing the blue, and the black and orange replacing the black and white lining, with no green visible between these lines. This remained the standard livery until the class was rebuilt, although changes to the lining were made on those engines acquiring modified tenders prior to rebuilding.

In early 1952, came thoughts of possible modification to all the Bulleid Pacific locomotives to increase reliability, and experiments commenced with the 'Merchant Navy' Pacifics, the most obvious change being the cutting down of the tender side raves. A rethink of lining was necessary, and the solution was to treat the rear half of the locomotive and cab as a conventional locomotive and the front half as a Bulleid Pacific. The tender and cab lining were rectangular panels of orange and black with the Brunswick green visible between each colour. On all these engines the British Railways lion-over-wheel emblem on the tender was reduced to the smaller size of 15½ in high, the coal bunker sides became green, while the rear of the bunker, including the vacuum cylinder cover, was black.

In February 1956, No. 35018 *British India Line* emerged from Eastleigh Works as the first rebuilt engine, with its livery based on that of a British Railways 'Britannia' class Pacific. It was now a conventional locomotive without air-smoothed casing, and its livery changed accordingly, although it was still Brunswick green, lined black and orange. The boiler and dome, cab front and sides, tender sides and rear, including the coal bunker, and the running plate valance were green, with the smokebox and chimney, smoke deflectors, cylinders and the frames of the locomotive and tender, including the wheels and springs, and the top of the running plate painted black. The

The livery of the rebuilt locomotives was more conventional. No. 35017 *Belgian Marine* is seen in ex-works condition in Brunswick green, with the five boiler bands in orange and black. Smokebox and cylinders are black, with lining applied to the cylinders. The new BR crest on the tender was not in line with the cab side numbers

L. Elsey

146

The nameplates were cast at Eastleigh in three sections. The wooden pattern is shown here, with the lettering for *Bibby Line* the central circular section of the pattern

B.I. Fletcher

The left-hand nameplate of No. 21C1 *Channel Packet*. Note the hexagonal-pentagonal cap for the coupling rod

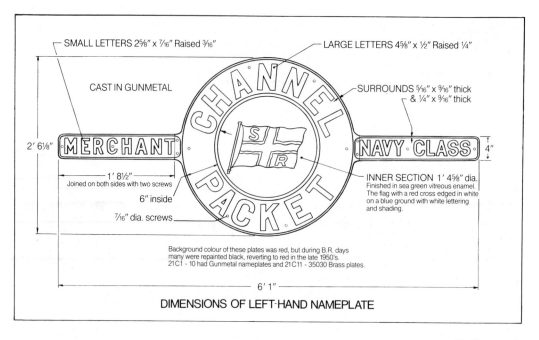

SMALL LETTERS 2⅝" x ⁷⁄₁₆" Raised ³⁄₁₆"

LARGE LETTERS 4⅝" x ½" Raised ¼"

CAST IN GUNMETAL

SURROUNDS ⁵⁄₁₆" x ⁹⁄₁₆" thick
& ¼" x ⁹⁄₁₆" thick

2' 6⅛"

MERCHANT

NAVY·CLASS

4"

1' 8½"
Joined on both sides with two screws

6" inside

⁷⁄₁₆" dia. screws

INNER SECTION 1' 4⅝" dia.
Finished in sea green vitreous enamel.
The flag with a red cross edged in white
on a blue ground with white lettering
and shading.

Background colour of these plates was red, but during B.R. days
many were repainted black, reverting to red in the late 1950's.
21C1 - 10 had Gunmetal nameplates and 21C11 - 35030 Brass plates.

6' 1"

DIMENSIONS OF LEFT-HAND NAMEPLATE

D. Gomersall

five boiler bands spaced from the front of the firebox to the rear of the smokebox were lined orange and black. The cylinders had two vertical orange and black bands at each end, although No. 35023 *Holland–Afrika Line* was noted with red and not orange cylinder lining in March 1965. On the running plate there was a single ¼ in orange line along the top and bottom of the plate. The cab and the cut-down tender lining were rectangular, with the green visible between the lining, and the tender still carried the small British Railways emblem.

A new BR crest was introduced in 1956, consisting of a red demi-lion holding a silver locomotive wheel issuing from a heraldic gold crown, but it did not come into use on the Southern Region until Spring 1957. The Bulleid Pacifics, even with cut-down tenders, had the large size emblem, 21¾ in high, which was smaller than the 28 in of the old emblem. The crest was, in fact, the heraldic badge of the British Transport Commission, and was applied to all rebuilt engines.

Although the original idea of a patriotic 'Victory' or 'Battle' class seemed appropriate for Bulleid's Pacifics, Britain and the Allies in 1941 had few victories to celebrate. Eventually the idea of names of shipping lines using Southampton was accepted and the title 'Merchant Navy' class was given to the locomotives. No. 21C1 *Channel Packet* was named at a ceremony held at Eastleigh Works on 10 March 1941, performed by the Minister of Transport, the Rt Hon J.T.C. Moore–Brabazon, in the company of the Southern Railway Chairman Mr R. Holland-Martin, General Manager Mr E.J. Missenden and Mr O.V.S. Bulleid. After the ceremony, the speeches and the ride in the cab for the minister, a commemorative plaque was placed on the driver's side of the cab; the cab plaque for No. 21C1 was unique and was not repeated in any of the other engines. The programme for this naming ceremony listed names for the first ten locomotives and stated that a replica of the house flag would be incorporated in the nameplate.

The nameplates were cast at Eastleigh and Mead, McLean of London contracted to produce the vitreous enamel plaques. For each locomotive in Southern Railway days

Driver T. Clark returns to the footplate after a quick oil round at Southampton Central on 3 March 1963 with the 10.30 a.m. Waterloo to Bournemouth train. The lining to the cab and the continuous single orange line to the running plate can be seen. Above the cab number is the 8P power classification of the 'Merchant Navy' class, and the fitting of the BR water treatment is indicated by the yellow triangle

G.M. Cashmore

three plaques were ordered, two for use on the locomotive, and the third for incorporation in the top of a coffee table, made at Eastleigh, as a gift to the person naming the locomotive. There was at least one member of the class for which only two plaques were produced – one of which was incorporated into the coffee table. The left-hand plaque was hand-painted, the central enamel flag being regularly touched up when the engine was in works. The metal portions of the plate were cast in the brass foundry at Eastleigh using a wooden pattern, with the circular plate and the two wings common to all nameplates. For the 'Merchant Navy' class, although the wings had standard-sized letters, there was variation in letter size for the actual shipping line names, since the circular nameplate was of a standard size. The Southern Railway was very proud in producing left and right nameplates, in order that the flag flew backwards as the locomotive moved forwards – it would be unkind to draw attention to tender-first running!

The raised letters and rim of the nameplate were bright, while the ground was red in Southern and early British Railways days, until BR decided in 1952 that the nameplate ground should be black. However, in the late 1950s this was altered to red, but Eastleigh

Works appeared not to have been officially informed, because rebuilt Pacifics were still turned out with black nameplate grounds as late as 1961! When the locomotives were rebuilt, a supporting frame was made to accommodate the curvature of the boiler sides in order that the nameplate face remained vertical.

Lettering size

Wings
'Merchant Navy' class: $2\frac{5}{8}$ in high

Locomotive name
3 in high: 35006, 11, 12, 15, 16, 17, 18, 21, 22, 23, 24, 25, 26, 27, 28, 29, 30
$3\frac{5}{8}$ in high: 35007
$4\frac{5}{8}$ in high: 35001, 2, 3, 4, 5, 8, 9, 10, 14, 20
Unusual: 35013, name 3 in, latin notation 2 in high
         35019, top lettering as script 4 in and 2 in high, initials $4\frac{5}{8}$ in high

DRIVING AND FIRING

Much has been written about driving and firing the 'Merchant Navy' class, but it is appropriate that in this book some comments from the drivers are included. Peter Christmas joined the Southern Railway in July 1943 as an engine cleaner at Salisbury – 'the only day I ever cleaned an engine!' Duties those days for an engine cleaner also included acting as a call boy, 'calling up crews from midnight until 6.00 a.m., a hazardous occupation at times since you never knew what might be thrown down from the bedroom window, especially if you knocked at the wrong one. You may wonder why the crews were not aware of their duties from their previous day's work, but it was wartime, and numerous roster alterations and "specials" involved last minute organizing.'

'My first duties as a cleaner/fireman involved putting up and securing the anti-glare sheets between the engine and the tender to comply with the blackout regulations. On the "Merchant Navy" class there was a sliding shutter between the engine and tender

No. 21C3 *Royal Mail* receives attention at Salisbury shed in 1942, with the bottom yellow stripe of the malachite livery just visible. This engine was the first Pacific to participate in regular passenger working

H.W. Attwell

No. 21C6 *Peninsular & Oriental S.N. Co.* is in black livery in this wartime photograph taken at Salisbury, probably in 1944. The early type of blackout sheets between the tender and engine have been replaced with metal slides, just visible inside the tender rave. Sanding was now to all the driving wheels, and the sandbox sliding covers are clearly visible on the casing. The clasp brakes and brake rigging can be seen, and the additional bar on the casing for the limpet board

K. Robertson collection

which cut off much of the stray light from the firebox, but on many of the older classes the anti-glare sheets really were needed. Since Salisbury was a fairly large depot, I was soon rostered to the locomotive preparation and disposal turns, and even the running turns to Chilmark and Dean Hill ammunition depots.

'Having prepared the engine for the 6.50 a.m. stopping train to Waterloo, I was informed by the main-line driver that his regular fireman had not arrived, and that I would be taking his place on the cab of No. 21C8 *Orient Line*. The load was eleven coaches, with the return trip being made on the 12.50 p.m. down West of England train. It was no use being overawed as the job had to be done, with the first problem being to master the steam-operated firedoors. I was soon to find out that if the coordination was not right as the treadle was depressed to open the doors, that there was a severe jarring of the hands and wrists. In addition there was the ignominy of the shovelful of coal being deposited over the cab floor, rather than into the back corners where I had been told to fire! The technique for firing the Pacifics was to fire to the corners and then to build up the fire under the door, which made it easier to bounce the shovel onto the corners of the grate. Although the maximum boiler pressure was 280 lb sq in, the maximum pressure I was able to maintain was 220 to 240 lb sq in, but with the coaching of Driver Pearce and the station stops the boiler pressure did not fall too low. The displacement lubricator was set to three drops per minute, supplying the front end of the locomotive. By Basingstoke I was beginning to gain confidence, although by Woking the proliferation of trains and the combination of coloured light and semaphore signals was in complete contrast to the usual traffic in the Salisbury area! Waterloo was even more confusing and the terminal platform was approached with some relief.

'Coaling and turning were carried out at Nine Elms and then back to Waterloo to couple up to the return train. When we were given the right of way, I was soon to find that the fire was disappearing faster than I could keep up, since the coal at Nine Elms was the hard variety, and we used the soft Welsh coal at Salisbury. We made Woking in thirty-one minutes, but the road from here onwards was a slight uphill gradient, but Worting Junction was reached on time with 220 lb sq in pressure in the boiler. The arrival at Salisbury was greeted with relief, but at least I had survived my first main-line firing turn – and could almost say I enjoyed it. In fact, the following day I was congratulated by the Mayor of Salisbury who also happened to be Foreman Saunders from the running shed.

'It was not until after the end of the war that I first worked to Exeter, when with No. 21C7 *Aberdeen Commonwealth* we had a load of fourteen bogies. The road west of Salisbury consisted of a succession of undulations, with the momentum gathered on the downhill sections aiding the following uphill run. This was an altogether different form of locomotive work to the almost straightforward running between Salisbury and Waterloo. One memorable run was with No. 35020 *Bibby Line* in its rebuilt state, shortly after the locomotive had completed the trials with the Western Region dynamometer car. To follow on from these trials the engine was diagrammed to work a series of normal service trains to include such runs as the "Bournemouth Belle," "Royal Wessex" and the

Although not the trial recounted here, No. 21C2 *Union Castle* worked a sixteen-coach test train to Bournemouth on 17 October 1945, running non-stop in each direction. The names of the driver and fireman are not recorded, but Inspector Danny Knight, impeccably dressed, was on the footplate with the crew

H.W. Attwell

153

"Atlantic Coast Express". I was booked as fireman to Driver Whitehorn of Salisbury on the down "Atlantic Coast Express," which was being worked in several divisions at this time. After taking water our departure was eight minutes late, and we were allowed a time of seventy-six minutes for the seventy-six miles to Sidmouth Junction. The load was thirteen bogies, and to keep us on our toes we had Inspector Smith of Exmouth Junction on the footplate with us. Semley, seventeen miles from Salisbury and on a level with the top of the cathedral spire – 404 ft above sea level – was reached in twenty-one minutes. A buckled rail at Gillingham produced a speed check of 50 mph, but the thirty-nine miles to Yeovil Junction were passed in thirty-eight minutes. Sutton Bingham produced a further mile of speed checks, this time of 15 mph, but with use of a full regulator to Crewkerne and half regulator downhill towards Chard lost time was regained, aided by the almost eleven miles of downhill running.

'One of the problems with the class had been the early failures of the steel fireboxes due to poor water treatment, which was overcome by Bulleid with the introduction of the TIA treatment, and later superseded by the simpler BR water treatment. It was necessary to remove the solids produced by the water treatment from the boiler. This was simply carried out by the use of the blowdown valve operated at fixed points on the track, which removed the solids from the boiler along with some of the boiler water. On the Salisbury to Exeter run we operated the blowdown valve just beyond Axminster for thirty seconds, leaving us with about half a glass of water in the boiler. Honiton bank required full regulator, with the severest part of the climb being that on Ivy Green with a gradient of 1 in 70 for seven miles, easing off half-way through Honiton tunnel. Although the rebuilds were fitted with speedometers and records of speeds were easier

No. 35020 *Bibby Line* at Sidmouth Junction with the 3.00 p.m. Waterloo to Plymouth train on 3 August 1964
P.W. Gray

to note than with the original engines, the stories of 100 mph running down the gradient to Axminster were not upheld on this day. We did however reach Exeter Central on time at 2.05 p.m., having run the eighty-eight miles in eighty-nine minutes, and in spite of the comments No. 35020 *Bibby Line* seemed to run as freely as her unrebuilt sisters.

'The tales of the class being stopped to obtain the assistance of the local fire brigade to deal with the oil-soaked lagging fires were certainly true. On one occasion I was working with Driver Pistell on the down 11.00 a.m. "Atlantic Coast Express", when after a speed check at Berrylands we were stopped at Weybridge to be told that the engine was on fire. On this occasion it was a false alarm, but it was one which had cost us several minutes and the possibility of a late time ticket. The time for the twenty-seven miles from Woking to Worting Junction was twenty-six minutes, but with the thought of a late time ticket we completed the distance in twenty-one minutes. Running problems with the injectors were few, but I well remember one that beset Driver Earle and Fireman Lawrence when working the down "Atlantic Coast Express". The injectors could be used singly or as a pair and on this occasion the rear injector would not shut off, since the steam cock on the injector had become uncoupled. With the thought of the boiler water level rising to dangerous levels they decided to try and attract the signalman's attention by using the whistle to convey to him the fact that a note was being dropped off tied to a lump of coal with the request for a fitter to be on hand at Salisbury. The train arrived at Salisbury in seventy-five minutes for eighty-four miles, still with some water in the tender, and after repairs was able to continue to Exeter.

'The class was designated as mixed traffic by their designer, and one duty they used to perform was to work the milk tanks from Templecombe to Clapham. If cheese was not

The 3.54 p.m. milk train empties to the West Country pass Clapham Junction hauled by No. 35003 *Royal Mail*, a freight turn for the class. The route was via East Putney and then on to the main line at Wimbledon
Author's collection

being produced at Bailey Gate on the Somerset and Dorset, the milk tanks were made up to a load of 23 with a van making up the load to 723 tons. The signalman at Templecombe had instructions not to let the train leave unless it could be guaranteed a clear road to Semley. Sand was frequently required to provide additional adhesion, and there was always an attempt to get the train moving well through Buckhorn Weston in order to negotiate the wet Gillingham tunnel, approached at a gradient of 1 in 90. When the east end of the tunnel was reached the engine had to keep up the momentum to climb Semley bank, where there were catchpoints at the top; but once at Semley the train would more or less push you to Salisbury!

'I was passed as a driver in February 1958, and one of the first turns after this was to work the 6.00 p.m. Waterloo to Exeter train, where we were relieved at Salisbury. The engine for this run was No. 35013 *Blue Funnel*, and we were loaded to eleven coaches. I was always instructed to leave Waterloo with a full tender of water and a boiler not overfilled to avoid priming, a problem which was rather detrimental to the valves and pistons. Although the "ACE" timings to Woking were twenty-eight minutes for the twenty-four miles, this time could be bettered and we passed the station in twenty-seven minutes. With stops at Basingstoke and Andover this train gave the inexperienced driver two attempts to draw up alongside the water column before this was put into practice at Salisbury. Salisbury was always approached at 10 mph, after the disaster with the 1906 boat train. The signal always seemed to be on and it was important not to overshoot the starting signal as only six minutes were allowed to take water. Eventually the "ACE" was given a booked time from Salisbury to Exeter of ninety-four minutes for eighty-eight miles, and eighty minutes for the eighty-four miles from Waterloo to

The last down 'Atlantic Coast Express' ran on 4 September 1964, and is seen leaving Salisbury behind No. 35022 *Holland America Line* at 12.24 p.m. for points west

D. Mackinnon

Salisbury. The most impressive part was the seventy-five minute down and seventy-four minute up schedule for the taxing switchback of the 1 in 80–100 gradient of the Salisbury–Sidmouth Junction section, a real test relished by the crews of the rebuilt Pacifics.

'The Southern Region now has notices explaining to the public that trains may be late in the autumn due to leaves on the running rails. But this is not a new problem, and was one which frequently taxed the Pacific drivers, especially those on the unrebuilt engines. It was normally the fireman who controlled the sanding on the engines, but the sand had to be used sparingly as there was only about sixteen minutes' sanding available from a full sandbox. The rebuilt locomotives were less prone to slipping, possibly because there was better weight distribution or the slipping could be more readily controlled as the sandboxes were easier to get at and thus more frequently filled! Firing on the first ten engines provided additional income for the Coal Board when there were problems or failures with the hydraulic reverser, and one was forced to drive in full gear.

'Driving, and especially firing, was hard work with unsocial hours, but the pleasures were in the completion of a job well done on a locomotive that was in both the original and rebuilt forms among the best in the country. Steam could have carried on for some time, but I do not think that it would survive in this day and age with the conditions we put up with.'

Russ Coffin was one of the drivers whose first view of the new 'Merchant Navy' class was in the form of a coloured postcard, sent to him while on service in the war. He initially tried to join the Southern as a cleaner on leaving school in 1937, but was called up in 1938, and it was not until his demobilization in 1946 that the chance came again to join the railway. This time the welcome was with open arms, as strong young men were in great demand by the locomotive department, being paid about £5 per week for their labours. He didn't arrive immediately on the footplate of a 'Merchant Navy', but the engines featured prominently at his depot of Nine Elms.

'With men leaving the railway regularly for better paid jobs, promotion was fairly rapid from the shunting links, and I soon found myself in No. 9 link. This was mainly concerned with preparation and disposal work, Waterloo relief work and for the firemen seemed to be an exercise in muscle development. The variety of engines at Nine Elms allowed me to make comparison of the footplate controls of many of the Southern engines, and it was also interesting to see that none of the Exmouth Junction Pacifics I fired or drove ever gave us mechanical trouble – perhaps they had a better labour situation than we did in London.

'From the fireman's viewpoint, in spite of the comment that the Pacific cab was like a "firelit cavern full of untidy piping", the piping was the result of the grouping of the controls for the driver on one side of the cab and those for the fireman on his side of the cab. The general layout of controls was admirable, especially as the purpose of each fitting was indicated by an adjacent brass plate. The cab floor was particularly spacious, while the steam and water valves for the injectors were controlled by hand wheels under the fireman's tip-up seat with the overflows being sighted through two small cut-outs in the cab floor, illuminated at night by electric light. The live steam injectors, of Davies and Metcalfe Monitor pattern, were good and easy to operate, and it was safer to view their operation through the floor cut-outs than leaning over the cab side. One of the problems with the Bulleid cabs was that the steampipes radiated a lot of heat. The design of the cabs was such that the roof ventilator was not very effective, and when stationary the cab quickly became like a sauna. However, in spite of only being constructed of light sheet metal on an angle iron frame, there were none of the ear-jarring rattles that

No. 21C1 *Channel Packet* was initially employed on freight turns, and is shown here in a wartime photograph

seemed to plague many of the other Southern engines after a few thousand miles of running.

'The firehole was positioned at just about the right height above the floor, and with the tender shovelling plate set to match, the fireman didn't have to bend down too much or even to move his feet when firing. I liked the Ajax firehole door, which was much superior to those on other regions, but not all firemen used the steam operation for working the firedoors. Its use required a certain knack, and although it seemed to have been well used by the crews at Salisbury and Exmouth Junction, it was not appreciated by crews on the Eastern section. The "Merchant Navy" firebox, about 7 ft square, looked as big as a small room at first, and though initially not fitted with a rocking grate, disposal was easier with the hopper ashpans. I was not the only fireman to have problems with the drop grates when fitted, and the idea of having two degrees of rocking – the gentle one for fire cleaning when running – was not always satisfactory in practice. The Detroit sight feed lubricator fitted to the first ten locomotives seemed to have been positioned for the unwary fireman to knock his head on, and we were grateful when its function was taken over by a normal displacement lubricator! I was one of the fireman who was never at home with the Detroit lubricator, which fed the valves and cylinders, and often had problems in regulating the oil supply. The provision of electric lighting was long overdue, and I had noticed that in Germany even the smallest shunting engine had electric lighting with the small turbo generator being mounted on the top of the boiler. The Stones turbo generator fitted to the "Merchant Navy" engines was mounted under the driver's side of the cab, and if it would not start the end cover was swung back and the rotor given a gentle push with a pencil – which was rapidly removed! The BR standard engines were strangely not supplied with electric lighting, apparently because the cost would be an additional £200 per engine. We were condemned to the paraffin flare lamp, but one would have thought that the savings in paraffin would have offset the cost of the electric lights.

'Both the driver and fireman had poor lookouts from the cabs, which although improved with changes in the cab windows, was not as good as on more conventional engines, until the class was rebuilt. To be fair to the designer, the forward lookout from other large Pacifics such as the LMS "Duchess" class appeared to me little better than on the Bulleid Pacifics. However, many of the Southern signals were well sited, and it

The enclosed motion left little oiling round for the driver, but here attention is given to the front slide bar on No. 35017 *Belgian Marine*

Author's collection

The poor forward vision from the cab was improved with the fitting of the modified cabs. No. 35028 *Clan Line*, as yet un-named, hurries through Eastleigh on 9 April 1949, with the smoke rising clear of the modified cab

W. Gilburt

was only in extreme weather conditions that their viewing proved difficult. It appeared that the multiple-jet blastpipe gave a soft exhaust, which was never ejected clear of the engine. My limited experiences with No. 35019 *French Line C.G.T.*, fitted with a single blastpipe, showed that this system gave better clearance but it was not adopted and the engine reverted to the multiple-jet exhaust. The oval-shaped smokebox door was fastened by the usual dart and crossbar arrangement, with the latter fitted vertically instead of the more usual horizontal position. For some reason the crossbar – slightly bowed in shape – could be turned either way round, with the bow facing the tubeplate – which was correct – or facing the front, which was wrong. If the door was tightened in the incorrect position, steaming was impaired as the door would not be airtight and there would be no smokebox vacuum. When taking over an engine I would always glance at the door, and if a lot of thread was showing on the dart, knew at once that the crossbar was the wrong way round, and would have to be repositioned. Cleaning out the smokebox, never a pleasant job, especially on a windy day, was no worse than any other type of locomotive, although the length of the smokebox required the use of a long-handled shovel. One advantage of the multiple-jet blastpipe was that there was never any great accumulation of smokebox ash, since the blastpipe ejected much of it up the chimney! Some of the rebuilt engines had a self-cleaning smokebox, but this apparatus seemed to baffle the steaming, even if it did get rid of the ash.

Cleaning out the smokebox was never a very pleasant task, and is carried out here on No. 35023 *Holland–Afrika Line*. The photograph was taken at Weymouth shed on 30 June 1967, with just nine more days of Southern steam left. This locomotive hauled the last up Channel Islands boat train on the penultimate day of Southern steam, 8 July 1967

S. McCaughie

160

'The hopper-type ashpans were not always as convenient as might be supposed. The doors to the hoppers had to be levered open, frequently with the coal pick, at the same time as the wind direction was observed. The ash could be dislodged from the hoppers with a rake or pricker, but if this tool was missing the more unscrupulous firemen would give the hoppers a good walloping with the coal pick to dislodge the ash! This maltreatment didn't do the ashpans much good, but there always seemed to be a dearth of the proper tools for the job. Those of us in the top link with regular engines sometimes had special small rakes made up by the shed blacksmith, but unless these were kept locked up, they were soon lost to other sheds or never returned after use by disposal crews.

'Filling the sandboxes was another job that had to be undertaken, and it was one that I am sure the designer never attempted himself. A tedious and laborious job on any engine, which had not been modified at all in the past hundred years. At Nine Elms the sand was dried in a furnace which consumed vast quantities of coal, and was sited alongside No. 1 shed road. Sand had to be carried in either a 2 gallon bucket or in a special sand container across anything up to twenty-five roads, and by the time the engine was reached one's arms felt as if they were leaving their sockets. If sanding a conventional engine the bucket then had to be lifted above your head and placed on the running plate. You then followed suit by climbing the buffer beam, edging round the smoke deflectors and then lifting up the bucket to fill the sandbox. Try wearing well-studded boots on wet and greasy plating to appreciate the perils, although if luck was with you a funnel might be found to assist the flow of sand into the box. Spillage was inevitable, the conscientious firemen sweeping this off, while the less diligent would leave it to blow over the motion.

'The attempts to prevent the sand reaching the slide bars by blanking off the front filling hole of some of the engines and by fitting metal dust covers to others of the class was not wholly successful. Fitting dust covers to the slide bars gave problems with lubrication to the bars and this was discontinued, but eventually the front sandbox and the piping were blanked off, until the locomotives were rebuilt. Although the Bulleid Pacifics have been criticized for needing a ladder or trestle to obtain access to the sandboxes, in my opinion it was an easier task to fill the sandboxes with this means of access than clambering over the slippery footplating on the other engines. If Bulleid's ideas of refilling sandboxes by means of overhead pipes had come to fruition, we would still have had to clamber up ladders to locate the sand pipe nozzles into the sandboxes, and to open and close the covers to the sandboxes!

'The tender cab was an unheard-of luxury, although with the cab being almost totally enclosed it could become a little warm. The provision of lockers for both driver and fireman, and for the storage of food, tools, oil bottles and lamps, was far superior to the old-fashioned boxes found on other Southern tenders. The shovelling plate was at the correct height, and a vertical sliding plate could be lowered to shut off the coal supply and keep out the dust, and the damping down of the dust was helped by the provision of a coal-watering pipe on the tender controlled by a valve on the footplate. Although the tender was self-trimming, it was occasionally necessary to attack the pile of coal with the coal pick, with access being provided via a door mounted above the shovelling plate. None of the firemen used the front water filling points except for checking the volume of water in the tender tank – why Bulleid didn't fit a water gauge is a mystery. The provision of a trough for fire irons alongside the coal bunker was a good idea, although the use of mechanical coaling plants and small coal necessitated the regular clearing out of the troughs by one of the shed labourers. When the tenders were modified and the troughs plated over to provide a tunnel for the fire irons, this unnecessary chore ceased.

The smaller water capacity of the tenders of 5,000 gallons was just sufficient for the Waterloo to Bournemouth run with half a dozen stops if the engine was newly ex-works. Many of the footplate crews wished that the ideas of putting in water troughs had been more actively considered, to give peace of mind if unforeseen delays were encountered.

'As the boilers were such good steam producers, firing on the "Merchant Navy" class was not a difficult job. It didn't appear to matter whether one belonged to the "little and often" or the "nob 'em up and bash 'em" brigade. Bulleid was adamant that he had not designed the engines with coal economies in mind, and, in spite of the variable quality of coal in the 1940s, steam could be produced from coal that would have dampened many other engines. With good hard coal liberties could be taken, and a light fire would suffice to start with. Welsh coal was a different story, and a good body of well-burnt coal was needed to start with. A haycock-shaped fire gave good results with Welsh coal, but a gently sloping fire was best for the hard coal, which had a very long flame and needed a lot of top air to avoid excessive smoke. I once relieved an Exmouth Junction fireman at Salisbury who had an enormous fire in the grate, almost up to the base of the syphons; my seat was occupied until we reached Wimbledon, seventy-five miles from Salisbury, and then I only placed a light shovelling around the 'box to ensure that there was enough steam to reach Nine Elms after the arrival at Waterloo. In 1954, I fired on No. 35014 *Nederland Line*, fitted with the self-weighing tender, on the "Bournemouth Belle" loaded to 450 tons. Coal burnt on the down trip was 37 lb per mile, and on the up

Although the rebuilt locomotives provided easier access to items such as the sandboxes and the lubricators, they also involved more of the traditional oiling round for the driver. No. 35022 *Holland America Line* receives attention at Exmouth Junction in 1964, and provides an interesting comparison with the rebuilt 'Battle of Britain' class Pacific, No. 34052 *Lord Dowding*

D. Mackinnon

trip where the gradient was more severe we burnt 44 lb per mile, using the "little and often" technique. These figures were bettered by one of the other firemen who used the "nob 'em up and bash 'em" technique.

'For the driver the preparation of the engines in their original form was very easy. There was only the outside engine to oil plus the slide bars, piston glands and a few other oil boxes with tail trimmings in them. On the footplate were two large missionary boxes, containing the oil feeds via vented and broken syphon pipes to the coupled wheel axleboxes and horn guides, the inside piston rod gland and some of the external parts of the valve gear. I cannot recall an instance of a hot box on the engine driving wheels, which says a lot for the enclosed system of lubrication of the motion. Another of Bulleid's strange ideas was to place the Wakefield mechanical lubricators for the valves and pistons under a hinged flap below the smokebox door. Although the lubricators were fitted with fine mesh filters, smokebox ash still made an entry, and drivers maintained that fastening the lids down tightly created an airlock, preventing oil from flowing to the pumps. The lids were thus left loose, providing an entry for smokebox ash, although the system was modified by providing breather pipes, sealing the lids down, and feeding the oil from a central reservoir tank, fitted with a heavy brass cap which screwed onto the filler hole. This solved part of the problem, but it was now impossible to tell whether each individual lubricator was functioning correctly. The pumps fed oil to the valve rocking shafts, the latter being one of the major initial problem areas in the valve gear. Lack of lubrication for the connecting link of the rocking shaft, which worked in exhaust steam, rapidly produced problems with the pin joints. The valves and pistons suffered very little from carbonization, possibly due to the effective atomizer and the anti-carbonizers in the oil. The linkage driving the oil pumps always looked inadequate, and frequently developed slack, which as the valve gear was notched up and travel was reduced, resulted in a decreased oil supply to the valves and cylinders.

'The enclosure of the middle engine and valve gear in the sump with automatic lubrication, made no call on the driver's preparation time or agility, for which many elderly and portly men were grateful. The pressure in the sump was measured on two oil pressure gauges on the footplate, where the values should have been about 20 lb sq in – though there were never many worries if the figures were less than this! Nothing could be done on the road if the pressure was low, and frequently the cause was found to be blocked filters in the sump itself. Many stories surround the sump of the Pacifics, but suffice to say that on the one occasion that I saw inside the sump all the working motion was shining as if it was made from stainless steel. No doubt condensation was a problem if the engines were standing and not in routine use, and there were times when the shed staff had to drain the water from the sump, caused by condensation. We certainly had fires on the engines with the oil-soaked lagging catching alight, but the funny thing is that fires on the current diesel and diesel multiple units never provoked the same condemnation as the Bulleid fires.

'Climbing into the cab, the driver's controls were conveniently placed on his side of the cab. The regulator of the pull-out pattern, rather like that of the Gresley Pacifics, was not all that sensitive and did need a gentle touch. The steam reverser was not unique to these engines, as many classes of SR locomotives were fitted with them, either of the Drummond pattern or of the Stirling design. The former pattern, fitted to the first ten "Merchant Navy" locomotives, was always slow and erratic, which is strange since when fitted to LSWR engines it always gave a better performance. The last twenty locomotives were fitted with a modified steam reverser, which, although not perfect, was a little easier to use and keep in a set position than the earlier model. The Southern

163

The rebuilt engines were reputed not to run as freely as the original members of the class. Rebuilt No. 35028 *Clan Line* shows a turn of speed with the Okehampton to Surbiton car carrier, photographed near Talaton on 15 August 1964

P W. Gray

was not the only company to use steam reversing, but we appeared to have the least satisfactory design to use. As the locomotive was not a shunting engine there was no real need to fit a rapid-acting reverser, although Bulleid is reputed to have stated that there was no room to fit a normal screw reverser with the wide firebox on the class, without the provision of a complex linkage. The steam reverser was, in spite of all its failings, simple to use. The operating handle was pushed forwards or backwards, according to the direction of travel required, and then raised to unlock the hydraulic cylinder, and by depressing a small cam-operated steam valve, steam was admitted to the power cylinder. Raising the lever to its maximum position depressed a larger cam-operated steam valve for rapid movement such as when reversing the engine. Lowering the operating handle cut off the steam and closed the valve on the hydraulic cylinder, setting the valve gear at the desired position.

'It was really quite easy to notch up the valve gear slowly or a little at a time, or even to make small adjustments to the setting by using the first or small steam valve. Some of the drivers I fired to always tried to use the large valve, with the likelihood of the engine flying into back gear while travelling at speed. This is well described by R.G. Jarvis , who relates that when travelling on the footplate of a "West Country" class Pacific, "the driver decided at 75 mph that he would pull the reversing gear up a bit tighter. Before the driver realized what had occurred, the engine had gone into full reverse with a terrible vibrating and shaking. Fortunately nothing came to bits." This was the exception rather than the rule, and the steam reverser generally performed as well as could be expected. Being situated between the frames, with the control valve under the boiler casing forward of the cab, it was not all that accessible. A scale on the reverser quadrant

164

in the cab was marked with the various degrees of cut-off, with a pointer coupled to the reversing gear itself indicating the position set. The accuracy of the scale was doubted by a number of footplate crews, but in fairness the accuracy of a number of screw- or lever-operated reversing gears gave no true indication of the amount of cut-off. The driver usually worked on the principle of so many turns of the screw or notches on the lever quadrant, with the per cent cut-off never entering the matter at all as far as driving was concerned.

'The brake was controlled by a Davies and Metcalfe solid jet vacuum ejector, with a steam brake for the engine itself and vacuum brake for the tender. The ejector was a bulky piece of equipment, and on the M-type ejector the vacuum limit valve or pepper-pot, as it was called, was situated on a casting that stuck out to the left across the driver's lookout window. Being the subject of much complaint, and in view of the already poor vision from the cab, it was eventually moved a little to the right which improved matters. The later locomotives were fitted with the D-type of ejector, which was more compact, and together with the "V" front to the cab gave a less restricted front view. The steam brake was powerful, but inclined to be all or nothing, a failing it had in common with other types of steam brake. Even the best ones are not all that sensitive, which may explain why no pressure gauge has ever been provided for the driver to see just what presure he is putting in the cylinders. When backing onto the train, control was applied by the more sensitive vacuum brakes on the tender. A small displacement lubricator was provided for the steam brake in the cab, as well as the usual gauges for the vacuum brake pipe and reservoir indicators. The steam sanding and the blower were controlled by Klinger-pattern valves, which were lever operated and rapid in action, with the sanding having controls on both the driver's and fireman's side of the cab. With the controls for the cylinder drain cocks placed conveniently next to the reversing gear, the driver, sitting on a reasonably comfortable seat, could operate all the controls with ease.

'How did all this fit in with the actual driving? Certainly a technique was required that differed from the conventional, as the engine was fitted with a combination of small diameter cylinders, short stroke, large piston valves and big steampipes which together with an insensitive regulator could make for a certain touchiness when starting. My own method was to open and close the regulator in a definite rhythm with the exhaust beats, until the engine was on the move, when the cut-off could be reduced to about 45 per cent and the regulator opened wider. As speed increased, the cut-off could then be shortened until the running cut-off was reached, but it was essential to watch the steam pressure gauge, which, if it started to fluctuate indicated that the cut-off was too short. The knowledgeable driver would also realize that as speed increased, the valve rocking shafts were subject to torsional stress, with the tendency of the valves to increase their travel and thus increase the cut-off. It was thus desirable to watch this point from the angle of fuel and water consumption. When firing to a variety of drivers, often with the same engine, train and schedule, it was possible to burn a ton more coal on the round trip to Bournemouth and back with driver A compared to driver B; the latter understanding what was going on at the front end in comparison with the former who did not know or particularly care! The Rugby tests demonstrated that the cut-off could change unpredictably, with no action on the part of the driver, and that the actual cut-off bore no relationship to the setting of the reversing gear. This latter characteristic was a phenomena of the locomotives, well known to the footplate crews!

'Some critics have stated that the engines were over-boilered, but a driver wants steam to run the train and the fireman wants to produce the steam as easily as possible. The engines would probably have steamed on anything, but with the good production of steam came the problem of its removal from the safety valves. Initially the valves were sited forward on the boiler barrel, but when braking there would be a frequent surging of water in the boiler and discharge of water and steam from the valves, often to the consternation of the public. We used to avoid this by keeping the water level down and reducing the pressure prior to making a stop at certain stations – Winchester on the down trains was such a station. One of the problems with the discharge of water and steam was that the water would leave a deposit on the seat of the valve, causing it to blow off below the setting of 280 lb sq in. This pressure was more in the nature of a reserve than a pressure we frequently used, and a value of between 240 and 250 lb sq in was usually the norm. The reduction in working pressure to 250 lb sq in which was started in 1952 did not markedly affect performance, but was, I am sure, a factor in prolonging firebox life.

'The reputation of the Pacifics as consumers of vast quantities of coal may well be true, but as footplate men we were never given any incentive to save on coal consumption, and frequently observed the vast waste of coal that took place in the locomotive sheds. The story related by one old driver that "the company buys the coal to burn, so I'll help 'em get rid of it" was certainly true! Oil consumption on the Pacifics was higher than on a conventional locomotive, but with the design of the valve gear enclosed in the sump there was little that could be done. Likewise the water consumption was high, but with a careful driver there were very few occasions when there were problems with low water levels in the tender tank. Although I never experienced any serious mechanical failure on the road, and the reliability of the engines increased as the years went by, any failure of the valve gear usually meant being hauled off the train. The figures produced by the Southern to reinforce the data for rebuilding the class, showed that the "Merchant

Bulleid power, with No. 35007 *Aberdeen Commonwealth* and No. 35008 *Orient Line* hauling a Southern Region 'Farewell to Steam' special from Weymouth to Waterloo, passing Upwey Wishing Well Halt on 2 July 1967. The former engine acted as pilot as far as Bournemouth Central

R.A. Lumber

Navy" class spent an average of sixty-two days out of service for running repairs and examinatons in 1952, with the more conventional "Lord Nelson" class spending forty-nine days out of service. Comparable costs of repairs per engine mile were 14 pence as against 11 pence for the "Lord Nelson" class, and 7 pence per mile for the LNER A1 class! With the rebuilding, the savings in coal and water were 10 per cent and 8 per cent, which, together with the savings in maintenance, reinforced the economic reasons for the rebuilding of the class.

'The rebuilt engines were certainly more conventional to look at, but never seemed to run as freely as the original members of the class. The riding was not as good, but the forward visibility was vastly improved. The conventional screw reverser was not universally liked, as it required a lot more effort to use than the original steam-operated type. The disposal of the engine was eased by the installation of a rocking and tip-up grate, but the inadvertent disposal of live coal into the hoppers could cause them to distort. The conventional Walschaerts valve gear now required regular oiling, and the inside motion was not always easy to reach. The provision of a garlic or aniseed big end heat detector was new to Southern practice, with the hot big end being unknown in the original locomotives. The moral of all this is that the old adage of "simplicity, reliability, accessibility" still reigns supreme, and that in the rough and tumble of operating locomotives under the British system this policy as shown by the rebuilt engines may well be the best one! Perhaps the state of the class can be summed up by the late Don Bradley, who states that "they [the 'Merchant Navy' rebuilds] were the finest express locomotives to work in the country".'

With scenes such as this, it was certainly worthwhile being an engineman. At Exeter Central, young admirers watch the arrival of the 'Devon Belle' from Waterloo, hauled by No. 35004 *Cunard White Star* in the late 1940s
Western Times

A FITTER'S NIGHTMARE?

There are numerous tales of the difficulties encountered by the fitters when the first locomotives of the 'Merchant Navy' class were introduced; many relate to the investigation of defects in the sump of the engines. Rather than retell all the problems which were encountered, the story of one young apprentice's experiences with the locomotives shows how the Nine Elms fitters coped with the Pacifics.

Ted Benn started his locomotive work not on the Southern, but as a temporary fitter's lad at the old Great Eastern works at Stratford in North London. By 1941 he was old enough to become an apprentice fitter on the Southern, based at Nine Elms, where towards the end of the year, No. 21C1 *Channel Packet* was stabled at six road in the new shed.

'It is difficult, even now, to describe the feelings of the shed staff on seeing No. 21C1, complete with many innovations foreign to the steam locomotives as we knew them. No

No. 21C1 *Channel Packet* was named at Eastleigh on 10 March 1941, with the ceremony being performed by the Minister of Transport, Rt Hon J.T.C. Moore–Brabazon. Many of the windows in the dining hall behind the locomotive have been boarded up in this wartime scene. On the dais, Bulleid is the third from the right

workshop manual, no operator's handbook, and the only advice was the garbled tales of problems which had arisen at Salisbury shed with fractured rocker shaft keyways and smokebox steampipes and the reversing gear. In addition, there were the stories that the time taken on repairs to the locomotives was often four times that taken for the "King Arthur" class, and, in the war, time was at a premium.

'The first work on a "Merchant Navy" at Nine Elms involved the locomotive's brakes, since it was noticed that the trailing brake blocks on the engine were hanging off the wheels by about 4 in. The brakes were duly adjusted to the usual standards and the engine lost 20 minutes with the brakes dragging on the return Waterloo–Salisbury trip! Gradually more of the class worked into Nine Elms on regular turns, but even so one always had a feeling of pride on seeing them on shed. We now had locomotives different from anything else in the world, and as the men became acquainted with them, locomotive performances were discussed. The early days of prostrate firemen, unable to feed the beasts, became a thing of the past, as the importance of the back corners of the firebox became appreciated.

'The lack of work being booked on them was disconcerting, and the odd sandpipe blocked up or a self-adjusting tender brake that didn't take up, was about all, apart from the checking of the oil level in the sump and its regular topping up with 3 or 4 gallons of oil. After some months, lack of oil pressure in the sump lubricating system became common, but it was found that if the two felt oil filters were thoroughly washed in paraffin the problem was cured. In fact there was sufficient splash lubrication taking place to ensure that no harm was done.

'The first broken Klinger gauge glass caused a few hectic minutes. The glass itself was flat, about ¾ in thick, and could be loosely described as being clamped against joints in a box by a series of set screws at the back. After cleaning all the joint faces, the unit was rebuilt, and the set screws nipped up. When replaced on the back head and the cocks opened, the joints leaked as they warmed up; remedial action was taken by very carefully tightening up the set screws – uneven tightening resulted in a cracked glass! The Klinger-pattern gauge was new to the Southern, and prior to its introduction the drivers had been responsible for the gauge glasses. After a few gauge glass panics it became the practice for most "running work" fitters to have a spare assembly made up ready for such emergencies. It was not unknown for a fitter and mate to travel to Waterloo, changing the unit on the way – not a popular job.

'In the early days the class did not stay long at Nine Elms; coal, water and a sump check, then straight onto the going out road. After the fire had been cleaned on arrival at the depot the firebox was filled up while still under the coal hopper, so that the tender could be topped up after the fire had been built up. The method of packing up the firebox around the back corners with the hard Yorkshire coal at Nine Elms resulted in the emission of copious amounts of thick smoke for the remainder of the stay on shed! The firehole door was left open for the trip to Waterloo, and, with the blower on, the green fire would have been burnt through when Waterloo was reached. This frequently resulted in the fitters attending to the gauge glasses arriving at the terminus with burnt boiler suits, the heat of the fire being initially unnoticed!

'One of the modifications carried out on the locomotives was the reduction in boiler pressure and the resiting of the Ross safety valves, with stories both of damaged platform roofs at Winchester and the railway being sued for cleaning costs for ladies dresses when the valves lifted at 280 lb sq in. At Nine Elms, the visiting "Merchant Navy" class were stabled near the new shed, where roads 1–10 were equipped with sheet asbestos-covered smoke shutes. Platform roofs were not the only areas damaged when the safety valves lifted.

'The first member of the class to become derailed was a victim on the curved approach to the coal stage. The centre pair of driving wheels were derailed and the breakdown crew tried the standard procedure of running them on again with ramps. After three or four attempts, with the rail breaking each time, it was decided that the frame rigidity of the engine would not allow the locomotive to give to the curve. The relatively small regulator pilot valve, and large main valve port area at small openings resulted in a very undocile engine under these conditions, and once on the move the steam brake was not as sensitive as that on a vacuum braked locomotive. This minor derailment was concluded with the 45 ton breakdown crane being brought up from Feltham where it was kept for safety during the blitz and the derailment gang, working under the lifted locomotive, laying a new length of rail to enable the rerailing to be concluded.

'At the end of 1943, I applied to be transferred to Eastleigh to complete my apprenticeship, and by 1944 work had commenced on the second series of the class. Although the work was interesting the spirit of Nine Elms was not present, and I returned to London in 1946. By this time there was an allocation of the class to the shed, where the light and intermediate repairs were undertaken. Lack of booked work on the class was still apparent, even though the engines were by now undertaking much of the heavy passenger work on the Southern. Normal replacement of brake blocks, hoses,

In the erecting shop at Eastleigh Works, No. 21C1 *Channel Packet* is hoisted by two of the overhead travelling cranes, each of 60 tons capacity. The photograph was probably taken in August 1947, when the locomotive was in the works for a boiler change

steam valves and gauge glasses was carried out but the problems of hot bearings, axlebox or coupling and connecting rod bushes were very rare.

'The lack of major bearing repairs was fortunate. The gantry cranes on roads one and ten were unable to lift the locomotives, and secondly the screwed hexagonal–pentagonal retaining caps on the crankpins, designed by Reg Curl at Eastleigh, were located by a block of offset pentagonal shape inserted into the outside of the crankpin. If these had been fitted tightly, the extractor stud thread provided was not man enough to remove them. On one occasion the added application of a 35 ton breakdown jack under the ring spanner only sufficed in lifting the wheel off the rail, and the final removal was achieved by some very careful cutting with the oxy-acetylene torch.

'Another problem, unforeseen by Bulleid when the engines were designed, was the turbo generator failure brought about by the standard shed method of illumination, the flare lamp. If one of these lamps was positioned underneath a cable conduit, the wire insulation melted – it was rubber in those days – and a short circuit resulted. The shed electrician was never very happy when this happened.

'The flare lamp was a true running shed feature, but it possessed a number of annoying properties. It always filled the air with black smuts, and if fitted with a wire hook there was nowhere to hang it, or if perched in the right place to provide illumination it fell over at the crucial moment, tipping hot mineral oil over you. However, it did function well on the odd occasion, but had the habit of getting too hot and then either blowing the filler cap off and catching fire or blowing the wick out of the spout if the cap was a good fit. Of course the oil-soaked lagging of the locomotives was also ignited by the odd flare lamp failure! The acetylene lamps issued did not have all the disadvantages of the flare lamps, but unfortunately provided a very directional light beam and needed a fresh charge of calcium carbide and water at the most crucial moment!

'Oil was, of course, the *bête noire* of the Pacifics. The cork gaskets of the sump assembly allowed oil to creep and the whole underside of the locomotive was coated with sump oil, with every nut securing the sump having an oily drip on the end of it. Working on stopped engines with valve and piston examinations resulted in oil-soaked boiler suits by the end of the first day. These exams involved more work than on the normal run of the locomotives, more stripping had to be done to disconnect the valves from the rocker shafts, and of course it was dirtier work. It was, however, quite straightforward, with one fitter and his mate on the outside cylinders and the second fitter and his mate working on the inside cylinders.

'The only real problem was the removal of the inside piston, which was a taper fit onto the piston rod – to which it became firmly attached. Our method, very unofficial and brutal, was to insert three thin wedges between the piston and the cylinder walls, with strips of emery cloth covering them. The engine was then moved back with pinch bars, the piston head remaining stationary at the mouth of the cylinder bore from where it could hopefully be removed. The lazy fitters have been known to give the examination of the inside piston a miss, but the size of the piston rings had to be seen at the next exam. The build up of carbonized oil was never a problem with the Pacifics, with their mechanical lubricators, although some of the "Arthurs" and "Nelsons", with the Detroit lubricators under the control of the fireman, did present carbonization problems. The siting of the mechanical lubricators under the smokebox was not ideal, since it allowed the ingress of fine ash and dust into the oil reservoirs and under the non-return valve, resulting in inefficient cylinder lubrication as indicated by the squealing and groaning of the pistons. Surprisingly little damage ever appeared to be done with this reduced lubrication!

The siting of the mechanical lubricators under the smokebox door was not ideal, and problems have arisen in this September 1950 view of No. 35014 *Nederland Line* at Bournemouth Central. Covers have been fitted to the slide bars to prevent the ingress of sand during filling of the sandboxes

Author's collection

Much of the major repair work to the class was carried out at Eastleigh, where No. 35006 *Peninsular & Oriental S.N. Co.* is under general repair in August 1953

Author's collection

'The loss of sump oil was always a big problem, and if the engines were left standing for any time the build up of water in the sump could be considerable, assisted by the occasional weepy rivet in the boiler barrel. The topping up of sump oil was carried out by two ex-fitters' mates who had volunteered to work alternate twelve-hour shifts, checking and filling the sumps from 4 gallon drums. Records were kept of the individual oil consumption of each engine.

'The steam reversers, like all hydraulically locked designs, required refilling with oil occasionally, and of course they were not positioned in the most accessible location. In addition there was a knack in filling them to prevent airlocks forming, and thus making them even more difficult to set. Oil was frequently dripping off the casing edges where the reverser was sited, owing to the presence higher up under the casing of a large bundle of $\frac{3}{8}$ in oil pipes, fed from the trimming boxes on the footplate. The chafing together of the pipes with the vibration of the engine induced cracks which allowed a continuous drip of oil to fall on the wheels and the outside motion. Although the steam reversers were open to criticism, there was only one real problem that I was presented with at Nine Elms. A fitter who refilled a reverser on a Salisbury engine forgot to retighten two air-bleed taps. The engine left the shed, arrived at Loco Junction signal-box where it was put into back gear to proceed to Waterloo. This completely emptied the locking cylinder, and resulted in the gear being unable to be fixed in any position. The crew worked a parcels to Salisbury in "full gear" for the whole journey, losing eighteen minutes. Some of the lost time was covered by the guard's notes on permanent way slacks, but the discourse between the crew and the fitter concerned the following night is not worthy of publication.

'The only complete failure of one of the class that I was involved with, was with No. 21C9 *Shaw Savill* on an up train at Clapham Junction. Together with my mate we had travelled to the Junction on a light engine to find No. 21C9 standing forlornly at the end of the platform. The Salisbury driver said that the engine "didn't know whether to come or go in back gear or fore gear after stopping at Clapham". It was apparently a

Which one would you prefer? The drivers said the original locomotives, such as No. 35003 *Royal Mail*, and the fitters probably the rebuilds such as No. 35002 *Union Castle*. Both are on shed at Nine Elms in the 1958–9 period

M. Arscott

173

valve problem, and I found myself as one of the few people who had to enter the sump on a Pacific while not on a pit. In this situation it was a case of under the footplate between the engine and tender, crawl under the ashpan until you come to the back of the sump. Removal of the back inspection plate showed that one of the small discs at the rear of the forked big end had become detached and was laying across the teeth of the chain-drive sprocket. What was occurring was that the chain was now being lifted once every revolution, so that eventually the valve timing was so far out that the engine was unable to move! No. 21C9 was eventually dragged back to Nine Elms by our light engine, and further investigation revealed that the driving wheels would have to be dropped, a job carried out at Stewarts Lane drop pit, as there was no means of lifting the engine at Nine Elms.

'From a fitter's viewpoint, the unrebuilt "Merchant Navy" class provided a challenge to keep them in top form. Unlike the following BR standard classes they were not provided with any form of maintenance instruction manual; their design features certainly tested the ingenuity of the fitters at times but it was not always the tale of horrors that have been promulgated in the past. Valve and piston examinations were a little more awkward, and piston and valve rings were the only replacements routinely required. Nine Elms certainly did not require the wagon loads of spares that some tales report.'

APPENDIX A

'Merchant Navy' Locomotives and Tenders

Locomotive number and name	Date to service	Tender number and (date in service)	Locomotive Rebuilt	Locomotive Withdrawn	Tender Scrapped
21C1 *Channel Packet*	6.41	3111, 3112 (5.41), 3111 (5.41), 3349 (3.65)	8.59	11.64	5.65
21C2 *Union Castle*	6.41	3112, 3115 (3.52), 3112 (3.52)	5.58	2.64	12.64
21C3 *Royal Mail*	9.41	3113, 3117 (2.44)	8.59	7.67	12.67
21C4 *Cunard White Star*	10.41	3114, 3113 (1.44), 3121 (10.65)	7.58	10.65	2.66
21C5 *Canadian Pacific*	12.41	3115, 3348 (10.65)	5.59	10.65	Note 1
21C6 *Peninsular & Oriental S.N. Co.*	12.41	3116 throughout	10.59	8.64	Note 2
21C7 *Aberdeen Commonwealth*	6.42	3117, 3114 (5.44), 3127 (9.66)	5.58	7.67	4.68
21C8 *Orient Line*	6.42	3118, 3343 (2.62), 3118 (10.64)	5.57	7.67	10.68
21C9 *Shaw Savill*	6.42	3119 throughout	3.57	9.64	Note 3
21C10 *Blue Star*	7.42	3120, 3122 (12.64)	1.57	9.66	Note 4
21C11 *General Steam Navigation*	12.44	3121, 3129 (10.65)	7.59	2.66	Note 5
21C12 *United States Lines*	1.45	3122, 3343 (7.52), 3122 (7.52), 3120 (12.64)	2.57	4.67	11.67
21C13 *Blue Funnel**	2.45	3123, 3124 (8.50)	5.56	7.67	4.68
21C14 *Nederland Line*	2.45	3124, 3123 (6.50), 3343 (10.52), 3126 (7.56), 3345 (3.65), 3115 (9.65)	7.56	3.67	9.67
21C15 *Rotterdam Lloyd*	3.45	3126, 3343 (7.56), 3123 (6.58)	6.58	2.64	12.64
21C16 *Elders Fyffes*	3.45	3125 throughout	4.57	8.65	12.65
21C17	4.45	3127, 10123 (LMS 4.48), 3127 (6.48), 3114 (9.66)	3.57	7.66	9.66

176

Belgian Marine 21C18	5.45	3129, 3343 (7.52), 3346 (10.52), 3118 (12.61), 3343 (10.64)	2.56	8.64	Note 6
British India Line 21C19	6.45	3128, 10219 (LMS 4.48), 3128 (5.48)	5.59	9.65	1.66
French Line C.G.T. 21C20	6.45	3130, 10373 (LMS 5.48), 3130 (6.48), 3347 (6.52), 3345 (5.56), 3344 (7.56)	4.56	2.65	3.65
Bibby Line 35021	9.48	3333 (BB), 3342 (11.48), 3126 (10.65)	6.59	8.65	10.65
New Zealand Line 35022	10.48	3335 (BB), 3345 (1.49), 3347 (6.56)	6.56	5.66	Note 7
Holland America Line 35023	11.48	3341 throughout	2.57	7.67	4.68
Holland–Afrika Line 35024	11.48	3333 (BB), 3346 (2.49), 3123 (11.52) 3343 (5.58), 3346 (12.61)	4.59	1.65	5.65
East Asiatic Company 35025	11.48	3343, 3350 (6.52)	12.56	9.64	Note 8
Brocklebank Line 35026	12.48	3260 (WC), 3350 (7.49), 3130 (6.52), 3349 (3.65), 3111 (4.65)	1.57	3.67	9.67
Lamport & Holt Line 35027	12.48	3288 (WC), 3349 (4.49), 3130 (3.65)	5.57	9.66	Note 9
Port Line 35028	12.48	3344, 3345 (7.56), 3126 (3.65), 3342 (10.65)	10.59	7.67	Note 10
Clan Line 35029	2.49	3347, 3129 (7.52), 3113 (10.65)	9.59	9.66	Note 11
Ellerman Lines 35030	4.49	3348, 3345 (10.65)	4.58	7.67	11.68
Elder-Dempster Lines					

NOTES

1. No. 35005, *Canadian Pacific* preserved, attached to tender No. 3119.
2. No. 35006, *Peninsular & Oriental S.N. Co.* preserved, but without a tender.
3. No. 35009, *Shaw Savill* preserved, but without a tender.
4. No. 35010, *Blue Star* preserved, but without a tender.
5. No. 35011, *General Steam Navigation* preserved, but without a tender.
6. No. 35018, *British India Line* preserved, attached to tender No. 3350.
7. No. 35022, *Holland America Line* preserved, but without a tender.
8. No. 35025, *Brocklebank Line* preserved, but without a tender.
9. No. 35027, *Port Line* preserved, attached to tender No. 3116.
10. No. 35028, *Clan Line* preserved, attached to tender No. 3342.
11. No. 35029, *Ellerman Lines* sectionalized at NRM, York, with tender No. 3113.
* No. 21C13 was named *Blue Funnel*, although the nameplates carried the name *Blue Funnel Line*. The nameplates were later altered to *Blue Funnel Certum Pete Finem*.

APPENDIX B

'Merchant Navy' Tenders

Tender number	Date entered service	Locomotive number (and date)	Modified	Re-bodied	Withdrawn	Tender Attached to	Scrapped
3111	2.41	21C1, 35001, 35026 (4.65)	6.56	2.63	3.67	35026	9.67
3112	5.41	21C1 (5.41), 21C2 (6.41), 35002	5.58	4.60	2.64	35002	12.64
3113	9.41	21C3, 21C4 (1.44), 35004, 35029 (10.65)	6.58	–	9.66	35029	Note 1
3114	10.41	21C4, 21C7 (5.44), 35007, 35017 (9.66)	9.56	–	9.66	35017	9.66
3115	12.41	21C5, 35005, 35002 (3.52), 35005 (4.52), 35014 (9.65)	–	5.59	3.67	35014	9.67
3116	12.41	21C6, 35006	10.59	–	8.64	35006	Note 2
3117	6.42	21C7, 21C3 (2.44), 35003	–	8.59	7.67	35003	12.67
3118	6.42	21C8, 35008, 35018 (12.61), 35008 (10.64)	5.57	1.62	7.67	35008	10.68
3119	6.42	21C9, 35009	3.57	–	9.64	35009	Note 3
3120	7.42	21C10, 35010, 35012 (12.64)	1.57	–	4.67	35012	11.67
3121	12.44	21C11, 35011, 35004 (10.65)	8.57	–	10.65	35004	2.66
3122	1.45	21C12, 35012, 35010 (12.64)	7.52	–	9.66	35010	Note 4
3123	2.45	21C13, 35013, 35014 (6.50), 35024 (11.52), 35015 (6.58)	6.58	–	2.64	35015	12.64
3124	2.45	21C14, 35014, 35013 (8.50)	12.52	–	7.67	35013	4.68
3125	3.45	21C16, 35016	4.57	–	8.65	35016	12.65
3126	3.45	21C15, 35015, 35014 (7.56), 35028 (3.65), 35021 (10.65)	7.56	–	8.65	35021	10.65
3127	4.45	21C17, 35017, 35007 (9.66)	3.57	–	7.67	35007	4.68
3128	6.45	21C19, 35019	5.59	–	9.65	35019	1.66
3129	5.45	21C18, 35018, 35029 (7.52), 35011 (10.65)	9.59	–	2.66	35011	Note 5

Tender No.							
3130	6.45	21C20, 35020, 35026 (6.52), 35027 (3.65)	1.57	—	9.66	35027	Note 6
3341	11.48	35023	2.57	—	7.67	35023	4.68
3342	11.48	35021, 35028 (10.65)	2.52	—	7.67	35028	Note 7
3343	11.48	35025, 35012 (7.52), 35018 (7.52), 35014 (10.52), 35015 (7.56), 35024 (5.58), 35008 (2.62), 35018 (10.64)	5.52*	2.62	10.64	35018	Note 8
3344	12.48	35028, 35020 (7.56)	7.56	—	2.65	35020	3.65
3345	1.49	35022, 35020 (5.56), 35028 (7.56), 35014 (3.65), 35030 (10.65)	10.59	—	7.67	35030	11.68
3346	2.49	35024, 35018 (10.52), 35024 (12.61)	2.56	—	1.65	35024	5.65
3347	2.49	35029, 35020 (6.52), 35022 (6.56)	6.53	—	5.66	35022	Note 9
3348	4.49	35030, 35005 (10.65)	4.58	—	10.65	35005	Note 10
3349	4.49	35027, 35026 (3.65), 35001 (3.65)	5.57	—	3.65	35001	5.65
3350	7.49	35026, 35025 (6.52)	12.56	—	9.64	35025	Note 11

NOTES

1. Tender No. 3113 preserved, attached to No. 35029 *Ellerman Lines*.
2. Tender No. 3116 preserved, attached to No. 35027 *Port Line*.
3. Tender No. 3119 preserved, attached to No. 35005 *Canadian Pacific*.
4. Tender No. 3122 preserved, attached to No. 34101 *Hartland*.
5. Tender No. 3129 sold by Woodham's to Briton Ferry Steelworks, and frames and wheels used as ingot carrier.
6. Tender No. 3130 preserved, attached to No. 34067 *Tangmere*.
7. Tender No. 3342 preserved, attached to No. 35028 *Clan Line*.
8. Tender No. 3343 preserved, attached to No. 34105 *Swanage*.
9. Tender No. 3347 sold by Woodham's to Briton Ferry Steelworks, and frames and wheels used as ingot carrier.
10. Tender No. 3348 preserved, attached to No. 34039 *Boscastle*.
11. Tender No. 3350 preserved, attached to No. 35018 *British India Line*.
* - Tender No. 3343, modified to coal- or self-weighing tender in May 1952.

The above list includes known changes of tenders occurring after the engines were withdrawn from service.

APPENDIX C

Technical Drawings: 4 mm = 1 ft

1

No. 21C1 *Channel Packet*, 1941. This drawing represents the first member of the class as built, with the widow's peak, cover for the chimney, sanding to the middle driving wheel only and high middle yellow line. The 5,000 gallon tender had no rear vertical ladders, but footsteps were provided on the rear of the tender and also a two-rung ladder hung from the buffer beam for the crew to climb the tender. The swan-neck vacuum hose was a unique feature of the first three tenders and the electric route lamps were a Bulleid innovation seen on all the 'Merchant Navy' tenders. The front water fillers and hand brake are shown on the front of the tender.

Overall length: engine 46 ft $2\frac{3}{4}$ in; tender 23 ft 5 in; total 69 ft $7\frac{3}{4}$ in.

2

First series, 1944. Small smoke deflectors and an inverted hood to improve smoke clearance, together with sanding to all three coupled wheels and the central supporting bar for the limpet casing can be seen.

3

First series, 1951. Standard smoke deflectors now fitted, shown here with the batten for the 'Devon Belle' side nameplate. Sanding is to all coupled wheels, and a cover is fitted to the slide bar. The modified wedge-shaped cab has three side windows.

4

Rebuilt locomotive, 1960.

5

5,000 gallon tender, 1943. The high rear tender rave is still present, and long spring hangers were fitted. Blackout slides are on the front of the tender, with sanding to the front wheels. Two vertical ladders on the rear of the tender replace the steps of the original design, and a ladder is suspended from each buffer beam to replace the single ladder of the original tenders.

Overall length: 23 ft 5 in.

6

5,000 gallon tender, 1943, plan view. Curved side raves covered the front of the coal bunker and front water fillers were present in addition to the rear filler. Three vacuum reservoir cylinders were not covered. The air vent pipe is visible on the top right-hand side of the tender tank top.

7

5,000 gallon modified tender, 1960. Newly designed cab end of the tender. The vacuum cylinders are now covered, and the Bulleid design water filler fitted. There is a coupling light on the rear of the tender, and BR pattern rear and side ladders. An oil nipple is on each axlebox cover.

8

5,000 gallon modified tender, 1960, plan view. Note the BR water treatment, with the briquette holder adjacent to the covered vacuum reservoirs.

9

5,100 gallon tender, 1945. The side raves are separate from the coal bunker, with the vacuum pipe now visible below the tender tank. The rear ladders did not curve over the top of the tank.

10

5,100 gallon tender, 1945, plan view. Oval front water fillers fitted, and fire iron space between the side raves and the coal bunker. The three vacuum reservoirs were not covered. The air vent pipe is visible on the left-hand side of the rear of the tender tank top.

11

5,100 gallon modified tender, 1960. Note the coupling lamp fitted to the rear of the tender and BR rear ladders.

12

5,100 gallon modified tender, 1960, plan view. Two different sizes of vacuum reservoir cover were fitted, with a handrail on the rear of some of the large covers. The Bulleid pattern water filler was fitted with a catch, and adjacent to it was the BR water treatment briquette holder.

13

6,000 gallon tender, 1948. This larger tender was fitted with a rear coupling lamp when built, and SR-type rear ladders.

Overall length: 25 ft 5 in.

14

6,000 gallon tender, 1948, plan view. The three vacuum reservoir cylinders were uncovered and offset to the left. The TIA tank was adjacent to the water filler, and the tender was fitted with three lifting loops, two in the coal bunker and one in front of the water filler. In front of the rear lifting loop was the air vent pipe.

15

6,000 gallon modified tender, 1960. Fitted with BR rear ladders and a cover to the vacuum reservoir cylinders. The air vent pipe in front of the BR water treatment briquette holder was not present on all tenders.

16

6,000 gallon modified tender, 1960, plan view. Lifting loops fitted were similar to the 5,100 gallon modified tenders. The BR water treatment briquette holder was sited in the former position of the TIA tank.

17

5,250 gallon rebodied tender, 1959. Designed to fit the 5,000 gallon tender frames. A single rear ladder was offset to the left, with one stile as SR and the other as BR design.

18

5,250 gallon rebodied tender, 1959, plan view. Note the twin rectangular water fillers, with the BR water treatment briquette holder mounted between them. Lifting loops were fitted as on the 6,000 gallon modified tenders.

19

Coal-weighing tender, 1952. Based on a 6,000 gallon tender, with a coal capacity of 5 tons 17 cwt and a water capacity of 5,767 gallons. The TIA tank was mounted on the rear right-hand side of the tender, with the two vacuum reservoir cylinders set transversely on the left of the tank top.

Drawings are:

a) Left-hand view
b) Right-hand view
c) Plan view
d) Rear view
e) View of weighing mechanism
f) Cab end view

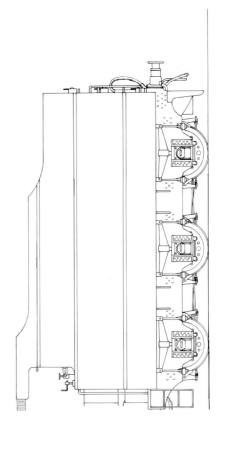

1

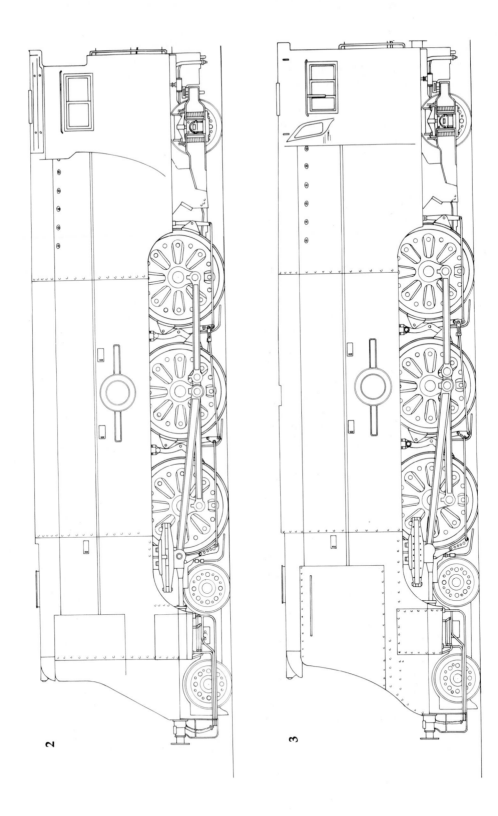

2

3

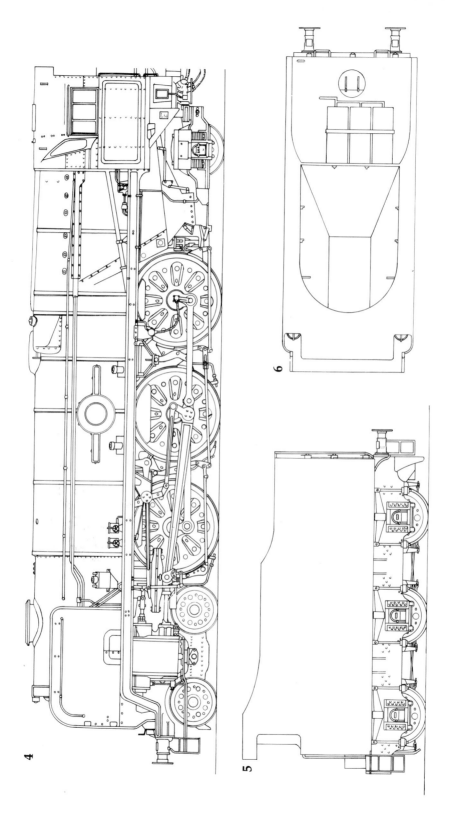

4

5

6

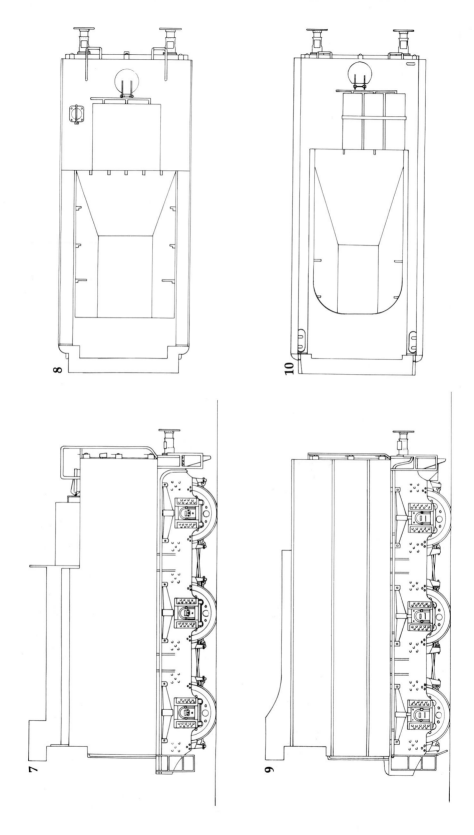

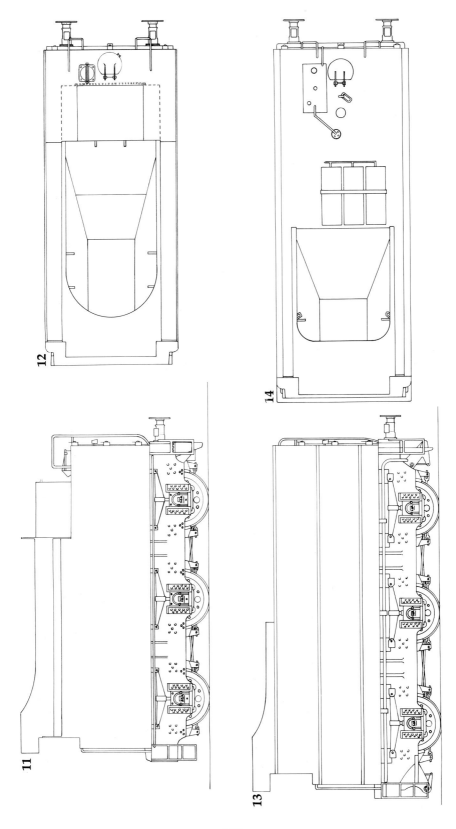

12

14

11

13

187

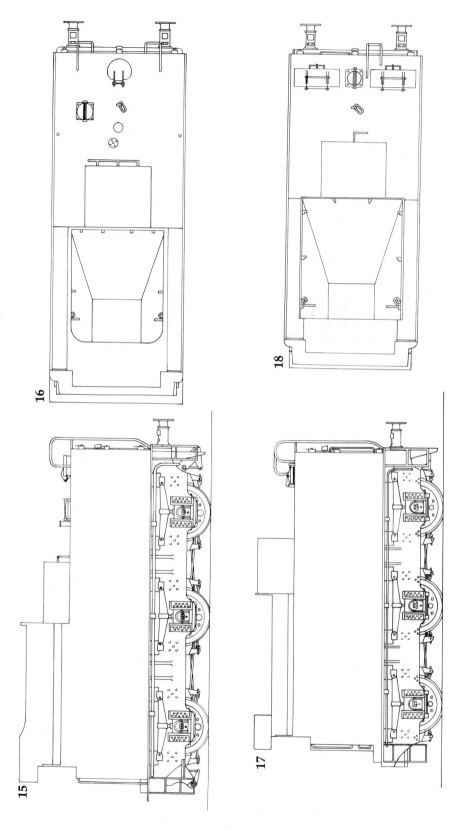

15

16

17

18

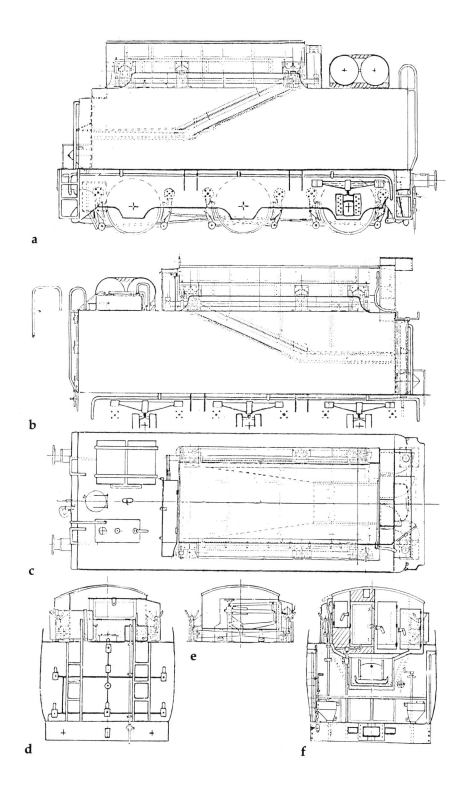

a

b

c

d

e

f

19

189

APPENDIX D

Models

One of the initial aims when writing this book was to give coverage of the models available to the reader. In the ready-to-run 00 gauge, however, there is little to commend, since name changes from 'West Country' class to 'Merchant Navy' class do not produce the correct locomotive. In N gauge, Graham Farrish Ltd has also fallen into the rebadging pit, although Langley Miniature Models Ltd has attempted to produce an N gauge model of the rebuilt class of greater resemblance to the full scale locomotive, a not inconsiderable feat in this gauge.

For those with kit building ability, Millholme Models produced an original 'Merchant Navy' in kit form, with versions of all three series of the locomotives in 00 gauge. For the rebuilt engine, kits were produced by Keyser Model Kits, and by Model Loco in 00 gauge. The latter is now the only 00 gauge kit available, sold under the Grandspot-DJH name. Articles on modelling the 'Merchant Navy' class in 00 gauge have appeared in a number of railway modelling magazines, the most notable ones being in *Model Railway Constructor*, July 1968, and *Scale Trains*, March 1984, the former covering the original and the latter article the rebuilt locomotives.

In the larger live steam gauges, there have been a number of excellent models produced, some of which have brought accolades for their builders. A model of No. 35028 *Clan Line* in $7\frac{1}{4}$ in gauge won a silver medal in class B1 at the 58th Model Engineer Exhibition in December 1988. Of course, modelling in live steam is for the true expert, but a visit to some of the model engineering tracks will give the reader the opportunity to see true engineering in miniature.

It is hoped that whatever gauge you model, there will be useful information within this volume.

BIBLIOGRAPHY

Books

Allen, C.J., *British Pacific Locomotives*. Ian Allan, 1971.

Allen, C.J., *The Locomotive Exchanges 1870–1948*. Ian Allan, 1950.

Allen, C.J., *Locomotive Practice and Performance in the Twentieth Century*. W. Heffer and Sons, 1950.

Allen, C.J. & Townroe, S.C., *The Bulleid Pacifics*. Ian Allan, 1976.

Austin, S., *From the Footplate – the Atlantic Coast Express*. Ian Allan, 1989.

Austin, S., *Great Preserved Locomotives. 'Merchant Navy' No. 35028 Clan Line*. Ian Allan, 1986.

Beavor, E.S., *Steam was my Calling*. Ian Allan, 1974.

Bird, J.H., *Southern Steam Surrender*. Kingfisher, 1987.

Bradley, D.L., *Locomotives of the Southern Railway*, parts 1 and 2. The Railway Correspondence and Travel Society, 1975.

British Transport Commission, British Railways, *Report on the failure of the crank axles*. 1954.

Locomotive Performance and Efficiency Test Bulletins:
No. 10 Merchant Navy Class. 1955.
No. 20 Modified Merchant Navy Class. 1960.

Bulleid, H.A.V., *Bulleid of the Southern*. Ian Allan, 1977.

Bulleid, H.A.V., *Master Builders of Steam*. Ian Allan, 1963.

Burridge, F., *Nameplates of the Big Four*. OPC, 1975.

Chapelon, A., *La Locomotive à Vapeur*. J.B. Ballière et fils, 1952.

Cox, E.S., *British Railways Standard Steam Locomotives*. Ian Allan, 1966.

Cox, E.S., *Locomotive Panorama, Vol. 2*. Ian Allan, 1966.

Cox, E.S., *Speaking of Steam*. Ian Allan, 1971.

Creer, S. & Morrison B., *The Power of the Bulleid Pacifics*, OPC, 1983.

Day-Lewis, S., *Bulleid, Last Giant of Steam*. George Allen & Unwin, 1964.

Dendy-Marshall, C.F., Revised by R.W. Kidner *The History of the Southern Railway*. Ian Allan, 1963.

Elsey, L., *On Southern Metals*, OPC, 1984.

Fairclough, T., & Wells, A., *Southern Steam Locomotive Survey – Bulleid 'Merchant Navy' Pacifics*, D. Bradford Barton, 1976.

Gough, T., *The Southern West of Salisbury*. OPC, 1984.

Hardy, R.H.N., *Steam in the Blood*. Ian Allan, 1971.

Haresnape, B., *Bulleid Locomotives. A Pictorial History*. Ian Allan, 1977.

Haresnape, B., *Gresley Locomotives. A Pictorial History*. Ian Allan, 1981.

Haresnape, B., *Maunsell Locomotives. A Pictorial History*. Ian Allan, 1977.

Haresnape, B., *Railway Liveries. Southern Railway*. Ian Allan, 1982.

Haresnape, B., Revised by C. Boocock, *Railway Liveries, BR Steam 1948–1968*. Ian Allan, 1989.

Hawkins, C. & Reeve, G., *An Historic Survey of Southern Sheds*. OPC, 1979.

Holcroft, H., *Locomotive Adventure, Volumes 1 and 2*. Ian Allan, 1965.

Kidner, R.W., *The Southern Railway*. Oakwood Press, 1958.

Klapper, C.F., *Sir Herbert Walker's Southern Railway*, Ian Allan, 1973.

Nock, O.S., *British Locomotives from the Footplate*. Ian Allan, 1950.

Nock, O.S., *British Locomotives of the 20th Century*. PSL, 1984.

Nock, O.S., *Great Locomotives of the Southern Railway*. PSL,1986.

Railway Executive, Locomotive Testing Committee, *Report on Southern Region 'Merchant Navy' class locomotive No. 35005, fitted with Berkley Mechanical Stoker*. 1950.

Reed B., *Loco Profile No. 22: Merchant Navy Pacifics*. Profile Publications Ltd, 1972.

Riley, R.C., & Harris, N., *Southern Reflections*. SLP, 1988.

Rogers, H.C.B., *Bulleid Pacifics at Work*. Ian Allan, 1980.

Rogers, H.C.B., *Steam from Waterloo*. David & Charles, 1985.

Tavender, L., *HMRS Livery Register No. 3, LSWR and Southern*. Historical Model Railway Society, 1970.

Thomas, D. St.J., *A Regional History of the Railways of Great Britain, Volume 1, The West Country*. David & Charles, 1973.

Thomas, D. St.J. & Whitehouse, P., *A Century and a Half of the Southern Railway, SR 150*. David & Charles, 1988.

Townroe, S.C., *'Arthurs','Nelsons' & 'Schools' at Work*. Ian Allan, 1983.

Winkworth, D.W., *Bulleid's Pacifics*. George Allen & Unwin, 1974.

Winkworth, D.W., *Maunsell's Nelsons*. George Allen & Unwin, 1980.

Winkworth, D.W., *The Schools 4-4-0s*. George Allen & Unwin, 1982.

Winkworth, D.W., *Southern Titled Trains*. David & Charles, 1988.

Periodicals

Railway Observer
Railway World
Southern Railway Magazine
The Engineer
The Journal of the Institution of Locomotive Engineers
The Journal of the Institution of Mechanical Engineers
The Journal of the Stephenson Locomotive Society
The Railway Gazette
The Railway Magazine
Trains Illustrated

INDEX